Blackstone's

Police Q&A

Road Policing 2018

Blackstone's
Police Q&A

Road Policing 2018

Sixteenth edition

Huw Smart and John Watson

OXFORD
UNIVERSITY PRESS

OXFORD

UNIVERSITY PRESS

Great Clarendon Street, Oxford, OX2 6DP,
United Kingdom

Oxford University Press is a department of the University of Oxford.
It furthers the University's objective of excellence in research, scholarship,
and education by publishing worldwide. Oxford is a registered trade mark of
Oxford University Press in the UK and in certain other countries

Published in the United States of America by Oxford University Press
198 Madison Avenue, New York, NY 10016, United States of America

British Library Cataloguing in Publication Data

Data available

ISBN 978–0–19–880629–5

Printed and bound by
CPI Group (UK) Ltd, Croydon, CR0 4YY

Contents

Introduction

Before you get into the detail of this book, there are two myths about multiple-choice questions (MCQs) that we need to get out of the way right at the start:

1. that they are easy to answer;
2. that they are easy to write.

Take one look at a professionally designed and properly developed exam paper such as those used by the Police Promotion Examinations Board or the National Board of Medical Examiners in the US and the first myth collapses straight away. Contrary to what some people believe, MCQs are not an easy solution for examiners and not a 'multiple-guess' soft option for examinees.

That is not to say that *all* MCQs are taxing, or even testing—in the psychometric sense. If MCQs are to have any real value at all, they need to be carefully designed and follow some agreed basic rules.

And this leads us to myth number 2.

It is widely assumed by many people and educational organisations that anyone with the knowledge of a subject can write MCQs. You need only look at how few MCQ writing courses are offered by training providers in the UK to see just how far this myth is believed. Similarly, you need only to have a go at a few badly designed MCQs to realise that it is a myth nonetheless. Writing bad MCQs is easy; writing good ones is no easier than answering them!

As with many things, the design of MCQs benefits considerably from time, training and experience. Many MCQ writers fall easily and often unwittingly into the trap of making their questions too hard, too easy or too obscure, or completely different from the type of question that you will eventually encounter in your own particular exam. Others seem to use the MCQ as a way to catch people out or to show how smart they, the authors, are (or think they are).

There are several purposes for which MCQs are very useful. The first is in producing a reliable, valid and fair test of knowledge and understanding across a wide range of subject matter. Another is an aid to study, preparation and revision for such examinations and tests. The differences in objective mean that there are slight differences in the rules that the MCQ writers follow. Whereas the design of fully validated MCQs to be used in high stakes examinations which will effectively determine who passes and who fails have very strict guidelines as to construction, content and style, less stringent rules apply to MCQs that are being used for teaching and revision. For that reason, there may be types of MCQ that are appropriate in the latter setting which would not be used in the former. However, in developing the MCQs for this book, the authors have tried to follow the fundamental rules of MCQ design but they would not claim to have replicated the level of psychometric rigour that is—and has to be—adopted by the type of examining bodies referred to previously.

These MCQs are designed to reinforce your knowledge and understanding, to highlight any gaps or weaknesses in that knowledge and understanding and to help focus your revision of the relevant topics.

I hope that we have achieved that aim.

Good luck!

Blackstone's Police Q&As—Special Features

References to Blackstone's Police Manuals

Every answer is followed by a paragraph reference to Blackstone's Police Manuals. This means that once you have attempted a question and looked at an answer, the Manual can immediately be referred to for help and clarification.

Unique numbers for each question

Each question and answer has the same unique number. This should ensure that there is no confusion as to which question is linked to which answer. For example, Question 2.1 is linked to Answer 2.1.

Checklists

The checklists are designed to help you keep track of your progress when answering the multiple-choice questions. If you fill in the checklist after attempting a question, you will be able to check how many you got right on the first attempt and will know immediately which questions need to be revisited a second time. Please visit www. blackstonespoliceservice.com and click through to the Blackstone's Police Q&As 2018 page. You will then find electronic versions of the checklists to download and print out. Email any queries or comments on the book to: police.uk@oup.com.

Acknowledgements

This book has been written as an accompaniment to Blackstone's Police Manuals, and will test the knowledge you have accrued through reading that series. It is of the essence that full study of the relevant chapters in each Police Manual is completed prior to attempting the Questions and Answers. As qualified police trainers we recognise that students tend to answer questions incorrectly either because they don't read the question properly, or because one of the 'distracters' has done its work. The distracter is one of the three incorrect answers in a multiple-choice question (MCQ) and is designed to distract you from the correct answer, and in this way discriminate between candidates: the better-prepared candidate not being 'distracted'.

So particular attention should be paid to the *Answers* sections, and students should ask themselves, 'Why did I get that question wrong?' and, just as importantly, 'Why did I get that question right?'. Combining the information gained in the *Answers* sections together with re-reading the chapter in the Police Manual should lead to a greater understanding of the subject matter.

The authors wish to thank all the staff at Oxford University Press who have helped put this publication together. We would particularly like to dedicate these books to Alistair MacQueen who sadly passed away in 2008. It was his vision and support that got this project off the ground. Without his help neither Huw nor John would have been able to make these Q&As the success they are. We would also like to show appreciation to Fraser Sampson, consultant editor of Blackstone's Police Manuals, whose influence on these Q&As is appreciated.

Huw would like to thank Caroline for her constant love, support and understanding over the past year—and her ability to withstand the pressures of being the partner to a workaholic! Special thanks to Lawrence and Maddie—two perfect young adults. Last but not least, love and special affection to Haf and Nia, two beautiful young girls.

John would like to thank Sue, David, Catherine and Andrew for their continued support, and the occasional use of the computer.

1 Definitions and Principles

STUDY PREPARATION

The definitions and principles set out in road traffic legislation are critical to understanding and proving many—if not all—the relevant offences. There is little point in knowing that a particular offence can only be committed by a motor vehicle, for instance, if you don't recognise a 'motor vehicle' when you come across one.

The definitions addressed in this chapter are therefore the building blocks for the rest of the subjects that follow—so they are well worth careful study.

QUESTIONS

Question 1.1

JENKINS was stopped whilst riding a vehicle on a road. The vehicle was an old moped, which was fitted with pedals, but the engine was not working and there was no petrol in it. JENKINS was propelling the vehicle by using the pedals.

Would the vehicle being ridden by JENKINS be a mechanically propelled vehicle?

A No, it is a pedal cycle.

B Yes, provided JENKINS intended to use it as one in the future.

C Yes, provided it was constructed as one.

D Yes, provided JENKINS intended to use it as one when he was riding it on the road.

Question 1.2

HARGREAVES was driving a dumper truck on a road between two building sites. The truck collided with a cycle as HARGREAVES was negotiating a junction and the cyclist was injured. The police were called to deal with the accident. The dumper truck was intended for use solely on construction sites.

Considering the definition of a motor vehicle, under s. 185(1) of the Road Traffic Act 1988, could the dumper truck be qualified as one?

A Yes, because HARGREAVES was driving it on a road.

B Yes, if the prosecution is able to present evidence that it is suitable for use on a road.

C No, a vehicle intended for use solely on construction sites cannot be converted into a motor vehicle simply because it was being used on a road.

D No, it was only being used temporarily on a road by HARGREAVES.

Question 1.3

NICHOL owns a Mini vehicle, which was manufactured for use on the road. NICHOL has decided to take up auto-cross racing, which will take place off roads and has completely rebuilt the vehicle to use in the races. NICHOL has no intention of using the Mini on the road again.

Would NICHOL's Mini be classed as a motor vehicle at this time, under s. 185(1) of the Road Traffic Act 1988?

A No, because NICHOL does not intend to use it on the road.

B Yes, because it has retained its original character of a vehicle intended to be used on a road.

C No, because NICHOL has changed its character so that it is no longer suitable for use on the road.

D Yes, because it was the manufacturer's intention that the vehicle would be used on the road.

Question 1.4

MERSON was thinking of buying a hover board to use as personal transportation to and from work. Most of MERSON's journey was through a large park, but parts of it were on public roads.

Which of the following statements is correct, as to where MERSON could use this transportation device lawfully?

A The device could be used lawfully in the park, but not on the road or the pavement.

B The device could not be used lawfully in any of these locations.

C The device could be used lawfully in the park or the pavement, but not on the road.

D The device could be used lawfully in the park, but not the pavement; it could be used lawfully on the road if it was registered as a road-legal vehicle.

Question 1.5

SEXTON's car had broken down on the driveway and was left there for a number of months and during this time the insurance expired. SEXTON sold the car to STEPHENS and agreed to help tow it to STEPHENS's house. STEPHENS towed the car, while SEXTON sat in it and steered.

Should SEXTON's car have been insured while it was being towed?

A No, although it remained a motor vehicle, it was exempt for the purposes of insurance while it was being towed.

B Yes, it was still a motor vehicle and was not exempt from the requirement for insurance while it was being towed.

C No, it was not a motor vehicle while it was being towed; it was classed as a trailer, which is exempt from the requirement for insurance.

D Yes, it was classed as a mechanically propelled vehicle while it was being towed and was not exempt from the requirement for insurance.

Question 1.6

LOPEZ was giving his daughter LUCY driving lessons in his own private car. The first time he took her out on a road, LOPEZ allowed LUCY to take control of the foot pedals, while he leant over and took control of the steering wheel for the first 20 minutes or so. LOPEZ also kept his hand on the handbrake in case LUCY was unable to stop in enough time. He did this until LUCY gained enough confidence to drive on her own.

Would LOPEZ's actions be sufficient to satisfy a court that he was a 'driver' in these circumstances?

A No, only one person may be the driver of a vehicle at any one time.

B Yes, a court could decide LOPEZ was a 'driver' in these circumstances.

C Yes, a supervisor will always be a 'driver' while they are in a position to assume control of the vehicle if necessary.

D No, a supervisor will only be a 'driver' if they are supervising in a vehicle fitted with dual controls.

Question 1.7

MICHAELS was driving his car on a road when his mobile phone rang. He did not have a hands-free kit; therefore he stopped at the side of the road. MICHAELS answered the phone while his car was stationary, with the engine still running. He remained in this position for ten minutes, before completing the call and driving off.

In these circumstances, would MICHAELS have been the driver of the motor vehicle, while it was stationary?

A No, as the vehicle was stationary, he was no longer a driver.
B Yes, he will be a driver until the end of his journey.
C No, the vehicle was stationary only for a short period of time.
D Yes, it's irrelevant how long the vehicle was stationary for.

Question 1.8

REID was sitting in a car on a road with a steep gradient—the vehicle was pointing downhill. It had been snowing heavily and there was ice on the road. REID turned on the engine and released the handbrake and was about to set off slowly; however, the vehicle started sliding down the hill. REID had no control over the vehicle and was trying to apply the brakes, or turn the vehicle into the skid, but it continued sliding sideways down the hill and collided with a wall.

Could REID be held to have been 'driving' in these circumstances?

A No, at no time was REID in full control of the propulsion of the vehicle.
B Yes, even though REID did not have full control of the propulsion of the vehicle, the engine was running and this amounts to driving.
C No, a person may not be 'driving' when they are only attempting to control the movement of the vehicle.
D Yes, whether or not the engine is running is irrelevant when deciding if a person is driving; it's whether they have some control of the propulsion of the vehicle that counts.

Question 1.9

KELLY was drunk and decided to drive home. He opened his car door and sat in the driver's seat. However, when KELLY tried to start the car, he could not do so because he was using his house keys. Eventually KELLY managed to find the correct key, but the car would not start, as the battery was flat.

1. Definitions and Principles

In these circumstances, which would be the first point at which KELLY has 'attempted' to drive his car?

A He did not attempt to drive the car at any time.

B When he tried to start the car with the correct key.

C When he first sat in the driver's seat.

D When he tried to start the car with the house key.

Question 1.10

WATKINS borrowed his friend's car one evening and went out drinking. On his way home, he went to a takeaway restaurant. WATKINS was overheard by CARTER, boasting about driving home. It was obvious that WATKINS was drunk and CARTER telephoned the police. WATKINS was leaving the premises when the police arrived.

In relation to the proof required to establish whether a person is 'in charge' of a vehicle, which of the following is true?

A WATKINS must show that there was no likelihood of him resuming control of the vehicle while he was drunk.

B The prosecution must show that WATKINS intended to drive the vehicle in the future.

C WATKINS must show that he had no intention of resuming control of the vehicle while he was drunk.

D The prosecution must show that there was a likelihood of WATKINS driving the vehicle in the future.

Question 1.11

SHAWCROSS was driving a motor vehicle and was involved in an accident, having injured a pedestrian in the car park of a large out-of-town shopping area. The police were called and it transpired that SHAWCROSS was a disqualified driver. The location had the traditional appearance of a car park, with parking bays either side of a carriageway for vehicles to pass to various shops in the vicinity and road markings and directional signs to assist motorists. The accident occurred in one such carriageway.

Given that under s. 103 of the Road Traffic Act 1988 a person is guilty of an offence if, while disqualified, they drive a motor vehicle on a road, which of the following statements is correct as to whether this location could qualify as a 'road'?

A A car park would not generally be a road, but the road markings and directional signs will establish the location as a road.

B A car park will not generally be a road, but it may be declared as one in exceptional circumstances.

C A car park will not generally be a road, but if the court finds that the carriageway is a road in these circumstances, it will transform the rest of the location into a road.

D A car park is provided for parking vehicles and could not be a road in any circumstances.

Question 1.12

HILL owned a farm near the coast that could be reached by driving along a grassy track from a country road. The country road was maintained by the local authority, but the track was owned and maintained by HILL; the track had no gate and ran past his farmhouse to a secluded beach. Local people drove down it regularly in the winter; however, in the summer HILL would turn people away to prevent a large volume of traffic crossing his land, at a time when he was busiest on the farm.

Could the track owned by HILL qualify as a 'road' as defined in s. 192(1) of the Road Traffic Act 1988?

A No, the track is maintained by HILL and it would be a private road.

B No, because HILL turns people away in the summer, it makes the track a private road.

C Yes, the track is a road to which the public has access; therefore it is a 'road' under the Act.

D No, it would be obvious to the public that it is a private track; therefore it is not a 'road' under the Act.

Question 1.13

VIVIER arranged a Scout fête, and was given permission to use a field belonging to GILES, a local farmer. On the day of the fête, entry was restricted to members of the local Scout groups, and drivers of vehicles were charged £1 each for entry.

In relation to road traffic offences, would GILES's field qualify as a 'public' place in these circumstances?

A No, as entry to the field was restricted to certain people.

B Yes, as members of the public were allowed access.

C Yes, people were using the field with GILES's permission.

D No, as the people using the field were charged for entry.

Question 1.14

TANNER was stopped by Constable CHEN one evening as she drove her vehicle in an access road leading to a block of flats. Constable CHEN suspected that TANNER had been drinking and asked her to supply a specimen of breath, which proved positive. She was later charged with driving with excess alcohol. At a later court appearance, she pleaded not guilty. TANNER relied on the defence that the access road on which she was driving belonged to a local housing department and that it was not a public place. There were signs at the entrance to the access road saying 'Private Residents Only'.

What would the prosecution need to show, in order to prove that the road was, in fact, a public place?

A The prosecution would need to provide clear evidence that the road was used by motorists other than residents.

B The prosecution would not be able to show that the access road was a public place, because of the signs that were in place.

C The prosecution would need to provide some evidence that the road was used by motorists other than residents.

D The prosecution would not be able to show that the access road was a public place, because a private place cannot become a public place in any circumstances.

Question 1.15

RICHLEY was stopped by police officers in the car park of the Red Lion public house at 9.30 pm, and asked to provide a specimen of breath for analysis, which was positive. The car park had a sign up saying 'customers only'.

Is this car park a 'public place' at this time?

A Only if the prosecution can adduce clear evidence showing who uses the car park, when and for what purpose.

B No, as only a 'special class of public', i.e. customers, are allowed to park there.

C Yes, even if the prosecution do not adduce evidence that the car park was a public place.

D No, as no invitation or permission was given to the public in general, only to persons wishing to use the public house.

Question 1.16

BAKER was driving a tractor and towing a trailer laden with hay on a road, on behalf of his employer, RICHARDSON. Constable SHAH stopped BAKER for having an insecure load, as some of the bales had fallen off the trailer and on to the road. Constable SHAH reported BAKER for the offence and later spoke to RICHARDSON, who denied responsibility as BAKER had loaded the trailer himself. RICHARDSON stated he would not have authorised the load to be carried in such a manner.

Would RICHARDSON be guilty of 'using' a vehicle in these circumstances?

A No, as he did not authorise BAKER to use the vehicle in such a way.

B No, as BAKER was not acting in the course of his employment.

C No, as BAKER was drawing a trailer, only he could 'use' it.

D Yes, he would be guilty in these circumstances alone.

Question 1.17

PRICE is the transport manager of a haulage company. He knows that most of his drivers make false entries on their tachograph sheets. PRICE has not instructed them to do this, but as it means that the drivers work longer hours on behalf of the company, he does not stop them. HILLMAN, the owner of the company, is unaware of what is happening.

Is either PRICE or HILLMAN guilty of 'causing' offences in relation to drivers' hours in these circumstances?

A Yes, PRICE only, as he has turned a blind eye to what is happening.

B No, neither person is guilty of 'causing' offences in these circumstances.

C Yes, HILLMAN only as the owner of the company.

D Yes, both people would be 'causing' offences in these circumstances.

Question 1.18

SILVER has recently re-applied for a driving licence following a period of disqualification, but has been unable to afford to buy a new car because of the high cost of insuring it. SILVER has asked to borrow STAENBERG's car for the day. STAENBERG is aware of the recent disqualification but agrees to lend SILVER the car. STAENBERG has not discussed whether or not SILVER has insurance to drive the car on the road legally.

If SILVER does not have insurance and drives it on a road, which of the following would have to be proved, if STAENBERG were to be guilty of permitting the use of the vehicle without insurance?

A That STAENBERG knew SILVER did not have insurance and that the motor vehicle would be driven on a road.

B Only that STAENBERG knew SILVER would drive the motor vehicle on a road.

C That STAENBERG knew or believed SILVER did not have insurance and that the motor vehicle would be driven on a road.

D That STAENBERG knew SILVER did not have insurance or that the motor vehicle would be driven on a road.

Question 1.19

WILSON is a driving test examiner and was sitting in the passenger seat of a vehicle being driven by CORY, who was sitting a driving test. During the test, CORY was involved in an accident with a pedestrian, having mounted the kerb while turning a corner.

In these circumstances, is WILSON guilty of aiding and abetting CORY to commit an offence under s. 3 of the Road Traffic Act 1988?

A Yes, driving test examiners are 'supervisors' for these purposes and have a duty to ensure the driver does not commit any offences.

B No, for a person to be guilty of aiding and abetting, the court would require evidence of active participation in an offence by the individual.

C No, driving test examiners are in the vehicle for a different purpose to 'supervisors' and will not generally be liable for the driver's behaviour.

D Yes, but as a 'supervisor' guilty of aiding and abetting an offence, a driving test examiner would receive a more lenient sentence by the court.

Question 1.20

MARTIN owed BELL a considerable amount of money. BELL threatened to set fire to MARTIN's car if the money was not paid immediately. MARTIN persuaded his brother to lend him the money and he drove to BELL's house. On his way, MARTIN was stopped by the police, who discovered he was a disqualified driver. MARTIN claimed he was acting under duress, and would not have driven had it not been for the threat made by BELL.

Would MARTIN be entitled to claim a defence of duress in these circumstances?

A No, the defence will apply only where death is threatened.

B No, the defence will apply only where death or serious injury are threatened.

C Yes, the defence will apply where serious damage has been threatened.

D No, the defence will not apply in a case of disqualified driving.

Question 1.21

JOHN and BARBARA were divorced and had a 12-year-old daughter who lived with BARBARA. JOHN was concerned for the welfare of his daughter as BARBARA had been displaying violent tendencies towards her. One evening, he was in the pub when he received a text message from his daughter saying that BARBARA had threatened to harm her with a knife. JOHN drove to BARBARA's house despite the fact that he had consumed six pints of beer. He then drove his daughter to his mother's house, five miles away, and attended a local police station to report the incident. The officer receiving the report realised that JOHN had been drinking and requested a sample of breath. JOHN was later found to be over the limit and was charged with driving with excess alcohol.

Would JOHN be able to claim the defence of necessity, because of the circumstances leading to his arrest?

A Yes, because his daughter had been at risk of serious harm.

B No, because it was his daughter who was at risk of serious harm and not JOHN himself.

C No, because of the distance JOHN drove after picking up his daughter.

D Yes, because his daughter was at risk of serious harm and the driving was not disproportionate to the harm threatened.

Question 1.22

BAILEY was involved in a road traffic accident which resulted in a pedestrian being knocked over on a zebra crossing. Witnesses stated that BAILEY failed to slow down on the approach to the crossing and drove straight through it, colliding with the pedestrian. When interviewed by the police, BAILEY alleged that the brakes on the car had failed at the last minute and that this was the cause of the accident. A qualified vehicle examiner later confirmed that the brakes on BAILEY's car were defective.

If BAILEY were to raise a defence of 'mechanical defect', which of the following statements is correct, in relation to what the court might consider?

A The court would not take this defence into account if BAILEY knew about the defect beforehand.

B The court would not take this defence into account because a driver has absolute responsibility for the state of their vehicle.

C The court would not take this defence into account if BAILEY knew about the defect beforehand, or could reasonably be expected to have known about it.

D The court would not take this defence into account if BAILEY had been reckless about the state of the vehicle beforehand.

Question 1.23

O'TOOLE was driving an ambulance to a serious injury road traffic accident. O'TOOLE had activated the siren and flashing lights and was approaching a junction controlled by traffic lights, which were showing red. O'TOOLE slowed down on her approach, but drove through the red light. KEYSE, a pedestrian, stepped off the pavement into the path of the vehicle and was struck by the ambulance, sustaining injuries as a result.

In relation to O'TOOLE's driving, which of the following statements is correct?

A Emergency service crews are entitled to pass through red lights, and O'TOOLE may rely on this exemption to defend her driving.

B O'TOOLE will not be liable for the injuries caused to KEYSE in these circumstances, as she warned the pedestrian of her approach.

C O'TOOLE may be guilty of driving without due care and attention, but may have a defence because of the serious nature of the accident she was attending.

D O'TOOLE will be liable for the injuries caused to KEYSE in these circumstances, even though she warned the pedestrian of her approach.

Question 1.24

Constable SAUNDERS had recently left the Roads Policing Department and was a Grade I advanced police driver. The officer was on duty in a police vehicle in the early hours of the morning, following a vehicle driving on a trunk road (speed limit 60 mph), which was driving at speeds in excess of 100 mph. The pursuit manager considered that Constable SAUNDERS was adequately trained, and authorised the pursuit to continue. However, the officer lost control of the police vehicle on a bend and collided with a wall. Constable SAUNDERS's force submitted a file to the Crown Prosecution Service (CPS), seeking advice as to whether the officer should be prosecuted for dangerous driving.

Should the CPS take Constable SAUNDERS's training into account, when determining whether or not the officer's driving was dangerous?

A No, Constable SAUNDERS is not entitled to have this training taken into account.

B Yes, depending on how recently Constable SAUNDERS was declared professionally competent to take part in pursuits.

C Yes, Constable SAUNDERS was in an authorised pursuit situation and is entitled to have this training taken into account.

D Yes, Constable SAUNDERS was on duty and is entitled to have this training taken into account.

ANSWERS

Answer 1.1

Answer **B** — A mechanically propelled vehicle is, quite simply, a vehicle that is constructed so that it can be propelled mechanically. This is regardless of what the vehicle is being used for and for that reason answer D is incorrect.

'Mechanically propelled' does not include electrically assisted pedal cycles, but it generally *does* include steam and electrically powered vehicles (see *Elieson* v *Parker* (1917) 81 JP 265). Answer C is therefore incorrect.

Finally, the prosecution bears the burden of showing that a vehicle meets the requirements of being 'mechanically propelled' (*Reader* v *Bunyard* [1987] RTR 406). Answer A is therefore incorrect.

Road Policing, para. 3.1.4

Answer 1.2

Answer **B** — A diesel dumper truck used solely for road construction work and not intended to be driven along the parts of the highway open to the public has been held not to be a motor vehicle for insurance purposes (*MacDonald* v *Carmichael* 1941 JC 27).

However, in a later case, while it was held that dumper trucks intended for use solely on construction sites will not generally be 'motor vehicles', the court did decide that if evidence can be adduced that they are suitable for use on a road, they *may* be held to be motor vehicles (*Daley* v *Hargreaves* [1961] 1 WLR 487). This does not mean that it will automatically be one, simply because it was being used on the road. Also, it has nothing to do with the owner's or manufacturer's intention (see *Nichol* v *Leach* [1972] RTR 476). Answers A and C are therefore incorrect.

It is the *use* of the vehicle that is important in this particular question, not the length of time it was driven on a road; therefore, answer D is incorrect.

Road Policing, para. 3.1.5

Answer 1.3

Answer **B** — The word 'adapted' means 'altered so as to make it fit' (*Maddox* v *Storer* [1963] 1 QB 451).

The test as to whether a vehicle is intended or adapted for use on roads is an objective one—would a reasonable person say that one of its uses would be general use on a road? (See *Burns* v *Currell* [1963] 2 QB 433.) It has nothing to do with the owner's or manufacturer's intention. Answers A and D are therefore incorrect.

A good example of this approach can be seen in *Nichol* v *Leach* [1972] RTR 476, where the owner of a Mini car rebuilt it solely for 'auto-cross' racing, never intending it to be used on a road. Nevertheless, it was held to have retained its original intended road use character and remained a 'motor vehicle'. Answer C is therefore incorrect.

Road Policing, para. 3.1.5

Answer 1.4

Answer **A** — 'Self-balancing scooters' or 'personal transportation devices' (hover boards) are illegal to ride on the road because they don't meet the requirements to be registered under either the European or British schemes for road-legal vehicles. Since the device cannot be so registered, answer D is incorrect.

A person riding such a device on a pavement would commit an offence under s. 72 of the Highway Act 1835, therefore, answer C is incorrect.

On the other hand, riding the hover board in a park, a public place, would not contravene either piece of legislation and answer B is incorrect.

Road Policing, para. 3.1.5

Answer 1.5

Answer **B** — When motor vehicles are being towed by other vehicles, they remain 'motor vehicles' (answers C and D are therefore incorrect). As a result, trailers require insurance when used on roads and in public places (*Cobb* v *Whorton* [1971] RTR 392). Answer A is therefore incorrect.

Road Policing, para. 3.1.5

Answer 1.6

Answer **B** — Section 192(1) of the Road Traffic Act 1988 states that the 'driver' is a 'person engaged in the driving of the vehicle' and this section makes provision for the 'steersman' to be a 'driver'. This was confirmed in the case of *Tyler* v *Whatmore* [1976] RTR 83, when it was held that a girl in the front passenger seat of a car who leaned across the person in the driver's seat with both of her hands on the steering wheel, steering the car, with the ignition switch and handbrake within her reach, was 'actually driving'. Answer A is therefore incorrect.

Whether a person supervising a driver from the passenger's seat is a driver will be defined by the degree of control exercised throughout by the supervisor. In *Langman v Valentine* [1952] 2 All ER 803, it was held that an instructor who retains simultaneous control of the car by keeping their hands on the brake and steering wheel may be the driver. This case predates dual control learner vehicles and demonstrates that it would be possible for more than one person to be a 'driver', even if they are not in such a vehicle. Answer D is therefore incorrect.

However, a supervisor will not always be a 'driver'; in *Evans v Walkden* [1956] 1 WLR 1019, it was held that a person was not a 'driver' when the instructor was only in a position to assume control if necessary and therefore not in control at the material time. Answer C is therefore incorrect.

Road Policing, para. 3.1.6

Answer 1.7

Answer **B** — For the purposes of road traffic offences, a person who takes out a vehicle remains the 'driver' of it, and he or she will be 'driving', until he or she has completed that journey. Therefore, even if the vehicle is stationary for some time, the person may still be the 'driver' if he or she has not completed the journey (see *Jones v Prothero* [1952] 1 All ER 434) (answer C is therefore incorrect).

A person may still be 'driving' although the vehicle is stationary, when he is buying a newspaper or when he is changing a wheel (*Pinner v Everett* [1969] 1 WLR 1266); therefore, answer A is incorrect.

In *Edkins v Knowles* [1973] QB 748, it was emphasised that the reason for stopping is relevant as it might be part of the journey, e.g. stopping at a set of traffic lights or a junction, or may mark a break in the journey; however, the court did state that the length of the break and whether the driver leaves the vehicle *is* important and the court must consider the period of time and the circumstances before making its decision. Answer D is therefore incorrect.

Road Policing, paras 3.1.6, 3.1.7

Answer 1.8

Answer **B** — There are many different cases ruling on whether or not a person is 'driving' a vehicle. In *DPP v Alderton* [2003] EWHC 2917 it was held that operating the controls of a car (accelerator, clutch and steering) which was parked on a grass verge and wheel spinning was 'driving' even though there was no movement of the vehicle. Further, a person may be 'driving' even though they are only attempting to control the movement of the vehicle. In *Rowan* v *Merseyside Chief Constable* (1985), The Times, 10 December, the defendant knelt on the driving seat, released the handbrake and thereafter attempted to re-apply it to stop the movement of the vehicle—he was held to be 'driving'. Answers A and C are therefore incorrect.

The Divisional Court has accepted a finding that a person sitting in the driver's seat of a car with the *engine running* had been 'driving' (*R (On the application of Planton)* v *DPP* [2001] EWHC Admin 450). This has been extended in *Mason* v *DPP* [2010] RTR 120, where the Divisional Court suggested that 'driving' would occur when turning on the engine. This can be compared to the situation where the person sitting in the driving seat of a stationary motor vehicle with hands on the steering wheel and the *engine off*, was held *not* to be 'driving' (*Leach* v *DPP* [1993] RTR 161). Therefore, whether or not the engine is running *is* relevant when deciding if a person is driving and answer D is incorrect.

Road Policing, paras 3.1.7, 3.1.8

Answer 1.9

Answer **D** — Acts which are merely preparatory will not amount to attempting to drive. Merely sitting in a car would not be sufficient, as this is still a preparatory act. Answer C is therefore incorrect.

It has been held that, where a defendant sits in the driver's seat of a car and tries to put his or her house keys in the ignition, that behaviour may be enough to prove a charge of 'attempting to drive' (*Kelly* v *Hogan* [1982] RTR 352). Answer A is therefore incorrect.

The fact that the vehicle is incapable of being driven will not prevent a charge involving an 'attempt' to drive (*R* v *Farrance* [1978] RTR 225). Answer B is incorrect because the question asks for the first point at which the defendant could be guilty of 'attempting' to drive.

Road Policing, para. 3.1.8

Answer 1.10

Answer **A** — The case of *DPP* v *Watkins* [1989] 2 WLR 966 outlines the principles to be applied when considering whether or not a person is 'in charge' of a vehicle.

Where the defendant is the owner of the vehicle, *or* where he or she has recently driven it, it will be for him or her to show that there was no likelihood of his or her resuming control while he or she was drunk.

Where the defendant is not the owner, or has not recently driven the vehicle, the prosecution will only need to show that the defendant was in voluntary control of the vehicle, or intended to become so in the immediate future. Answers B and D are incorrect for this reason.

Answer C is incorrect, as the defendant must show that it is *unlikely* that he will drive while unfit, not that he had no *intention* of doing so—a slight difference in wording, but nevertheless important in the context of the case.

Road Policing, para. 3.1.9

Answer 1.11

Answer **B** — The situation regarding car parks becoming roads was reviewed as a result of two cases, namely, *Cutter* v *Eagle Star Insurance Co Ltd* [1997] 1 WLR 1082 and *Clarke* v *Kato* [1998] 1 WLR 1647.

In *Cutter*, it was found that while it remained a question of fact in every case, a 'road' had the physical character of a defined or definable route or way, with ascertained or ascertainable edges, leading from one point to another with the function of serving as a means of access enabling travellers to move conveniently from one point to another along that route. The proper function of a car park was to enable stationary vehicles to stand and wait. In the ordinary use of language, a car park was not a road; they have separate and distinct characters. Where legislation referred to 'a road or other public place', the express addition of the words 'or other public place' clearly indicates that, where the word 'road' stands alone, it bears its ordinary meaning and does not extend to places such as car parks.

However, in *Clarke* it was conceded that in exceptional circumstances a car park *could* become a road (answer D is therefore incorrect), but in the event of a carriageway being found to exist within its bounds which does so qualify, the remaining area will retain its integrity as a car park. Answer C is therefore incorrect.

There is no mention in either case of road markings and directional signs establishing the location as a road and therefore answer A is incorrect.

Road Policing, para. 3.1.10

Answer 1.12

Answer **C** — A road is defined under s. 192(1) of the Road Traffic Act 1988 as:

> ... any highway and any other road to which the public has access, and includes bridges over which a road passes.

There is a great deal of case law defining whether a road actually qualifies as such for the purposes of s. 192 (and thereby attracts the many offences that stem from this definition). The courts will generally follow previous decisions.

In *Harrison* v *Hill* 1932 JC 13, it was held that a road leading off the public road to a farmhouse was a 'road' to which the public had access. The road had no gate and was maintained by the farmer, who sometimes turned people away who were using it, but at all other times it was used by people with no business at the farm at all.

This is similar to the case in question; in general, any member of the public had access to the track until HILL turned people away in the summer. Access was not restricted to a section of the public and, mostly, that access was enjoyed by the public with the agreement of the landowner and even when they tried to use the track in the summer, members of the public did not have to overcome a physical obstruction in defiance of any prohibition, either express or implied (see *Blackmore* v *Chief Constable of Devon and Cornwall* (1984) The Times, 6 December for the full effect of this argument).

Because HILL was happy to allow people access to his track when it suited him, it is most likely that the court would consider the track to be a 'road' for the purposes of the 1988 Act, and answers A, B and D are incorrect.

Road Policing, para. 3.1.10

Answer 1.13

Answer **A** — In order for a place to be a 'public place', it must be shown by the prosecution that:

- the people admitted to the place are members of the public and are admitted for that reason, and not because they belong to a certain or special class of the public; *and*
- those people are so admitted with the permission, express or implied, of the owner of the land

(*DPP* v *Vivier* [1991] RTR 205).

This case shows that the place in question must be open to *all* members of the public, without restriction (answer B is therefore incorrect). It is irrelevant whether the people are there with permission if only restricted members of the public are present. The two requirements from the *Vivier* case go hand in hand and answer C is therefore incorrect.

The fact that people had to pay to enter the land is completely irrelevant as to whether it is a public place. It is the *class of people* that are allowed entry (or not) that is important. If the fête had been open to *all* members of the public and they had all been made to pay, it would have been a public place. Answer D is therefore incorrect.

Road Policing, para. 3.1.11

Answer 1.14

Answer **A** — The circumstances in the question mirror those in the case of *R v DPP, ex parte Taussik* [2001] ACD 10. In this case, the Divisional Court took the view that the evidence provided by the police was very thin, and that they had not shown that motorists other than residents used the access road regularly. This meant that the court could not find that the road was a public place. The court held that such a road *could* become a public place (therefore answers B and D are incorrect), but it was essential that the prosecution provided *clear* evidence that the road was used by motorists other than residents and that they should present factual details of who used the road and for what purpose. Answer C is incorrect for this reason.

Road Policing, para. 3.1.11

Answer 1.15

Answer **C** — In order to prove that a place is in fact a 'public place' for the purposes of road traffic offences, it must be shown by the prosecution that:

- those people who are admitted to the place in question are members of the public and are admitted as such, not as members of some special or particular class of the public (e.g. people belonging to an exclusive club) or as a result of some special characteristic that is not shared by the public at large; *and*
- those people are so admitted with the permission, express or implied, of the owner of the land in question

(*DPP* v *Vivier* [1991] RTR 205).

Customers of this pub are members of the general public who are invited to use it by the licensee, therefore making it public and not a 'special class' of persons, e.g. members of a club, and therefore answers B and D are incorrect.

The importance of police officers providing enough evidence to show that a particular location amounted to a public place was highlighted in *R v DPP, ex parte Taussik* [2001] ACD 10. In that case the defendant was stopped as she drove out of an access road leading from a block of flats. The road was a cul-de-sac leading off a highway and was maintained by the local housing department. At the entrance to it there was a large sign saying 'Private Residents Only'. As there was no evidence from the officers themselves that they had seen motorists (other than residents) using the road, the court was unable to conclude that the road was anything other than a private one. Contrast this with *R (On the application of Lewis)* v *DPP* [2004] EWHC 3081 (Admin), where the court held it was not necessary for the prosecution to adduce evidence that a pub car park was a public place, given that it was attached to the public house and given a general invitation to use it by the licensee. Therefore answer A is incorrect.

Road Policing, para. 3.1.11

Answer 1.16

Answer **D** — Offences relating to 'using' a vehicle are generally committed by the driver and the driver's employer. For the employer to commit the offence of 'using', the person driving the vehicle must be doing so in the ordinary course of his or her employer's business (*West Yorkshire Trading Standards Service* v *Lex Vehicle Leasing Ltd* [1996] RTR 70). It must be proved that:

- the employer owned the vehicle;
- the driver was employed by the employer; *and*
- the driver was driving in the ordinary course of his or her employment

(*Jones* v *DPP* [1999] RTR 1).

It is immaterial that the employer has not specifically authorised the employee to use the vehicle in such a way (*Richardson* v *Baker* [1976] RTR 56). Answers A and B are therefore incorrect.

The owner of a trailer who is responsible for putting it on a road will not escape liability by arguing that it was being drawn and therefore 'used' by someone else (*NFC Forwarding Ltd* v *DPP* [1989] RTR 239).

Answer C is therefore incorrect.

Road Policing, para. 3.1.12.1

Answer 1.17

Answer **B** — 'Causing' will involve some degree of dominance or control, or express mandate from the 'causer'.

Causing requires both positive action and knowledge by the defendant (*Price* v *Cromack* [1975] 1 WLR 988). Therefore it is not enough that the person in charge is aware an offence is being committed; he or she must have done something to contribute to it. Neither person in the scenario could meet these criteria, as neither 'ordered' the offences to be committed (one person was unaware of what was going on).

Further, wilful blindness by employers to their employees' unlawful actions is not enough to amount to 'causing' the offence (*Redhead Freight Ltd* v *Shulman* (1989) RTR 1). Answers A, C and D are incorrect for these reasons.

Road Policing, para. 3.1.12.3

Answer 1.18

Answer **A** — Generally in order to prove a case of 'permitting' there must be proof of knowledge by the defendant of the vehicle's use *and* of the unlawful nature of that use. In other words, there must be proof that the defendant knew the vehicle was being used and that the driver was committing an offence by using it (i.e. by driving it on a road without insurance). Answers B, C and D are incorrect for this reason.

Road Policing, para. 3.1.12.4

Answer 1.19

Answer **C** — The supervisor of a learner driver *may* commit an offence under ss. 1 to 3 of the Road Traffic Act 1988, if he or she fails to supervise the other person properly (*Rubie* v *Faulkner* [1940] 1 All ER 285).

However, a driving test examiner is in the vehicle for a different purpose to a 'supervisor' and will not generally be liable for the driver's behaviour (*British School of Motoring Ltd* v *Simms* [1971] 1 All ER 317). Answers A and D are therefore incorrect.

It is possible for someone to aid and abet another to commit an offence by an omission—for example, where he or she fails to intervene; a court would not necessarily require evidence of active participation and answer B is incorrect.

There is no policy of leniency for a person guilty of aiding and abetting an offence (even if he/she is a vehicle examiner or a supervisor). Section 44 of the Magistrates' Courts Act 1980 states that a person who is convicted of aiding, abetting, counselling or procuring a summary offence is guilty of the like offence, and if the substantive offence carries endorsement, the defendant may be disqualified. Where disqualification is mandatory for the principle offender (e.g. driving with excess alcohol in the breath), a person convicted of aiding and abetting etc. is liable to discretionary disqualification. Answer D is therefore incorrect.

Road Policing, para. 3.1.13

Answer 1.20

Answer **B** — The defence(s) of duress and *necessity* will apply to cases of dangerous driving, careless and inconsiderate driving *and* driving while disqualified (*R* v *Martin* [1989] RTR 63 and *R* v *Backshall* [1998] 1 WLR 1506). Answer D is therefore incorrect. The defence of duress will only apply where the defendant was forced to commit an offence to avoid death or serious injury (*R* v *Conway* [1989] RTR 35). The defence *will not* apply in cases of criminal damage or where criminal damage has been threatened, no matter how serious. Answers A and C are therefore incorrect.

Road Policing, para. 3.1.14.1

Answer 1.21

Answer **C** — A person may claim the defence of 'necessity' when charged with a drink-driving offence. The situation was considered in the cases of *DPP* v *Tomkinson* [2001] EWHC Admin 182 and *DPP* v *Hicks* [2002] EWHC 1638 (Admin). In *Hicks*, the court found that the defence would be available only if:

- the driving was undertaken to avoid consequences that could not otherwise have been avoided;
- those consequences were inevitable and involved a risk of serious harm to the driver *or someone else for whom he or she was responsible*;
- the driver did no more than reasonably necessary to avoid harm; *and*
- the danger of so driving was not disproportionate to the harm threatened.

This ruling followed the earlier *Tomkinson* case, when the Divisional Court found that the defendant had driven a far greater distance than was necessary to avoid the relevant danger and that the defence would not be available. In the case examined in the question, unquestionably the daughter had been threatened with serious harm, which was unlawful. However, the harm threatened must also be immediate. If JOHN had been stopped by the police on the way to picking his daughter up, he may have been able to claim the defence of 'necessity', but by removing his daughter from the scene, he also removed the immediate danger from her. By continuing to drive five miles away from the danger, he did more than was 'reasonably necessary to avoid the harm', as quoted in *Hicks* mentioned previously. It could be argued that because of the distance JOHN travelled after picking up his daughter, the danger of driving while under the influence was disproportionate to the harm threatened and that he could have stopped at some point to call the police, which is why answer C is correct and answers A and D are incorrect.

The defence *may* be used where a person other than the driver is threatened, therefore answer B is incorrect.

Road Policing, para. 3.1.14.1

Answer 1.22

Answer **C** — If an unforeseen mechanical defect suddenly deprives the driver of control of the vehicle, he/she may have a defence similar to 'automatism'. The reasoning for this is that there is little distinction between a totally unexpected aberration in the bodily functions of a driver and a similar eventuality affecting the workings of a vehicle. In each case the driver has been deprived suddenly and unexpectedly of proper control of the vehicle and ought to be afforded the same 'defence' (*R* v *Spurge* [1961] 2 QB 205). Answer B is incorrect, because a driver does not have *absolute* responsibility for the state of their vehicle; if something occurs spontaneously to a vehicle which is beyond their control, the court should at least consider this defence.

The issue, then, is the factors that the court should take into consideration; in *Burns* v *Bidder* [1967] 2 QB 227, the Divisional Court allowed an appeal against conviction where the magistrate failed to consider 'mechanical defect' as a defence. The court held that 'a sudden removal of control over the vehicle occasioned by a latent defect of which the driver did not know and could not reasonably be expected to know would render the resulting failure to accord precedence no offence, provided he is in no way at fault himself'. This allows some latitude for courts to consider—it is not simply a case of what the driver *knew*, but it is a case of *either* what they knew, or *what they could reasonably have been expected to know* (making answer A incorrect and answer C correct).

Finally, the question deals with the issue of 'subjective recklessness' which, following the case of *R* v *G and R and another* [2003] UKHL 50, means the approach taken to the interpretation of the word 'reckless' is that it will be 'subjective'. An example of 'subjective recklessness' can be seen in *D* v *DPP* [2005] EWHC 967 (a case dealing with the unreasonable use of force by a police officer). The Divisional Court dismissed the appeal in that case and held that the test of recklessness involved the defendant having *foreseen the risk* that the victim would be subjected to unlawful force and *having gone on to take the risk*. This is a step too far for the defence of 'mechanical defect', which requires the defendant to have *known* about a defect beforehand, or could *reasonably be expected to have known* about it. Indeed, the term 'reckless' has been removed from road policing legislation because of the difficulty in proving the required *mens rea*, when the standard of proof for most offences is slightly lower. Answer D is therefore incorrect.

Road Policing, para. 3.1.14.4 and *Crime*, para. 1.1.4

Answer 1.23

Answer **B** — There is no special exemption for emergency drivers with regard to standards of driving (*R* v *O'Toole* (1971) 55 Cr App R 206), and they will be judged against the standards of care which apply to *all* drivers. There is an exemption which allows emergency drivers to pass through red lights under the Traffic Signs Regulations and General Directions 2002 (SI 2002/3113), reg. 36(1)(b). However, this *does not* exempt emergency drivers from having to drive with due care and attention. Answer A is therefore incorrect.

Answer C is incorrect because of the case of *DPP* v *Harris* [1995] RTR 100, where the driver of a police surveillance vehicle following a suspect drove through a red light. The court held that even though the suspects were being followed to the scene of an armed robbery, the seriousness of the circumstances did not provide an exemption.

Answer D is incorrect (and consequently answer B is correct), because of the ruling in the case of *Keyse* v *Commissioner of the Metropolitan Police* [2001] EWHC Civ 715. This was a case defended on behalf of a police driver, but would presumably apply to other emergency service drivers. The court held that the police driver, who was driving with the vehicle's visual and audible warning equipment in operation, was not liable for the injuries to a pedestrian who stepped off the pavement into the path of the vehicle.

Road Policing, para. 3.1.14.5

Answer 1.24

Answer **A** — In *R* v *Bannister* [2009] EWCA Crim 1571, the Court of Appeal overruled a previous authority (*Milton* v *CPS* [2007] EWHC 532) finding that an advanced police driver with highly developed driving skills was *not* entitled to have that ability taken into account when deciding whether or not the driving in question was dangerous.

The statutory test is based simply on the standard of the competent and careful driver, who is not to be vested with any particular level of skill or ability not found in the ordinary motorist.

Answers B, C and D are therefore incorrect.

Road Policing, para. 3.1.14.5

2 | Key Police Powers

QUESTIONS

Question 2.1

Detective Constable MORENO was on mobile patrol late at night in plain clothes in an unmarked vehicle. There had been a number of burglaries in the area and the officer was on the lookout for suspicious people. The officer saw a vehicle being driven by KNIGHT stop at a set of traffic lights and pulled up alongside. Detective Constable MORENO did not suspect the driver had committed any offences relating to the vehicle, but wanted to ask why the driver was out late at night. The officer produced a warrant card and asked KNIGHT, 'Can you pull over, I just want to have a chat?' KNIGHT immediately got out of the car, ran across the road and entered a dwelling house.

Section 17(1)(c)(iiia) of the Police and Criminal Evidence Act 1984 provides a power of entry for police officers in certain circumstances. Would this power be available to Detective Constable MORENO in these circumstances?

A No, this power may only be used when a person has failed to stop after committing an offence relating to the use of a vehicle on a road.

B No, a police officer must be in uniform to exercise a power of entry under this section.

C No, Detective Constable MORENO could only use this power if KNIGHT had failed to stop for a constable in uniform.

D Yes, Detective Constable MORENO has the power to enter the premises because KNIGHT has failed to stop for a constable.

Question 2.2

Constable ELIAS had been tutoring Constable CHIDIKE for four weeks and had identified that the officer needed more experience in dealing with breathalysers. On a night shift, Constable ELIAS decided to set up a checkpoint on a housing estate with the intention of stopping all vehicles that came along. The plan was for Constable CHIDIKE to speak to the drivers to identify whether they had been drinking and, hopefully, to conduct some breath test procedures.

Would the officers' actions be lawful in these circumstances?

A Yes, it is perfectly acceptable randomly to stop vehicles to train newly appointed officers in traffic procedures.

B No, they must at least anticipate detecting an offence or a crime before stopping the vehicle.

C No, this represents random breath testing, which is unlawful.

D Yes, it is perfectly acceptable to stop vehicles to conduct random breath tests.

Question 2.3

Constable ROBERTS attended a large retail store, where the occupants of a green 4 × 4 vehicle had been captured on closed circuit television (CCTV) as they entered the store and stole two bottles of wine from within. The vehicle was seen to make off immediately prior to Constable ROBERTS's arrival. Constable ROBERTS contacted the control room and asked the duty sergeant to authorise an urgent road check, under s. 4 of the Police and Criminal Evidence Act 1984, for the vehicle and its occupants.

Can the officer's request be granted in these circumstances?

A Yes, but Constable ROBERTS could have authorised the road check himself.

B Yes, provided the sergeant authorises it.

C No, only an inspector may authorise a road check in urgent circumstances.

D No, only a superintendent may authorise a road check in any circumstances.

Question 2.4

Superintendent HAYES has provided written authorisation for a road check to take place. Officers in Superintendent HAYES's area are investigating a case of causing death by dangerous driving and the suspect was believed to have driven away from the scene without stopping in a red Nissan motor vehicle. The superintendent has authorised that all red vehicles of a similar size and colour are to be stopped at the location of the incident, at the approximate time of day, for the next seven days. No useful information was gleaned during the initial period of seven days and the officer in the case has asked Superintendent HAYES to extend the period.

If Superintendent HAYES agrees to extend this period, what would be the maximum period that may be granted beyond the initial seven days?

A One further period of seven days.

B Two further periods of seven days.

C Three further periods of seven days, to a maximum period of 28 days.

D Unlimited period, provided the authorisations are for seven days at a time.

Question 2.5

Constable SWENSEN was on patrol and saw a motor vehicle driving through a 'No Entry' sign. The officer had to turn the police vehicle around and by the time the manoeuvre was completed, the offending vehicle had disappeared. Constable SWENSEN contacted the CCTV operator who replayed the tape and provided the registration number of the vehicle. Following a PNC check, Constable SWENSEN attended the home address of RIVERA, the registered owner of the vehicle. The officer demanded to see RIVERA's driving documents including his driving licence.

Did Constable SWENSEN have the power to demand the production of RIVERA's driving licence, under s. 164(1) of the Road Traffic Act 1988, in these circumstances?

A Yes, RIVERA was obliged to produce both the plastic driving licence and its paper counterpart in these circumstances.

B No, RIVERA was no longer the driver of a motor vehicle on a road and was not obliged to produce his driving licence in these circumstances.

C No, RIVERA had not been involved in a road traffic accident and was not obliged to produce his driving licence in these circumstances.

D Yes, RIVERA was obliged to produce a plastic driving licence only in these circumstances.

Question 2.6

POULTEN has been stopped by Constable GREGORY while driving a motor vehicle on a road. Constable GREGORY conducted a Police National Computer (PNC) check on her BlackBerry, which revealed that POULTEN's vehicle was uninsured. POULTEN had bought the vehicle two days before the stop check and stated that he had received an email from the insurance company, with the certificate of insurance attached. POULTEN offered to show the officer the copy of the certificate on his iPhone.

What is POULTEN required to do, in order to comply with the production of a certificate of insurance, under s. 165 of the Road Traffic Act 1988?

A POULTEN must provide Constable GREGORY with electronic access to a copy of the certificate.

B POULTEN must either produce a legible printed copy of the certificate there and then, or within seven days.

C POULTEN must email the electronic version of the certificate to Constable GREGORY, provided this can be viewed on the BlackBerry.

D POULTEN must produce a legible printed copy of the certificate within seven days.

Question 2.7

BRIARS was involved in a non-injury road traffic accident which the police attended. BRIARS was issued with an HORT/1 form to produce a driving licence and certificate of insurance. BRIARS was due to go on holiday the next day for a week and asked a friend, HAGGER, to take the documents to the station with the HORT/1 form.

In relation to the production of both documents, which of the following statements is correct?

A HAGGER may not produce these documents; they must both be produced by BRIARS.

B HAGGER may produce the driving licence, but BRIARS must produce the certificate of insurance.

C HAGGER may produce both the driving licence and the certificate of insurance.

D HAGGER may produce the certificate of insurance, but BRIARS must produce the driving licence.

Question 2.8

Constable HOLDSWORTH attended a road traffic accident in the High Street. One of the vehicles was being driven by SAUNDERS, a provisional licence holder. The officer was told that another vehicle had driven into the rear of SAUNDERS's car, while it was stationary at a set of traffic lights. At the time, SAUNDERS was being supervised by AMIN, a full licence holder. Both SAUNDERS and AMIN produced driving licences at the scene, but neither could produce a certificate of insurance. Constable HOLDSWORTH issued SAUNDERS with an HORT/1 form for the production of this document.

What is Constable HOLDSWORTH entitled to ask of AMIN, according to s. 165(5) of the Road Traffic Act 1988 (requirement to produce insurance)?

A Constable HOLDSWORTH is entitled to ask for AMIN's name, address and date of birth, and the name and address of the owner of the vehicle.

B Constable HOLDSWORTH is entitled to ask for AMIN's name, address and date of birth, but only if it is suspected that SAUNDERS has committed an offence.

C Constable HOLDSWORTH is entitled to ask AMIN whether or not SAUNDERS was insured to drive the motor vehicle on a road.

D Nothing, the duties under s. 165 only apply to the *driver* of a motor vehicle on a road.

Question 2.9

JORDAN is a designated police community support officer (PCSO) working on a housing estate. Numerous complaints have been received about a motorcycle being ridden around the estate by NEAL. JORDAN saw NEAL sitting astride the motorcycle outside a shopping centre and conducted a Police National Computer (PNC) check on the vehicle, which showed that the vehicle was uninsured.

Does JORDAN have the power to seize NEAL's motorcycle under s. 165A of the Road Traffic Act 1988, in these circumstances?

A No, only a constable has the power to seize vehicles under this section.

B Yes, JORDAN has the power to seize and remove the vehicle in these circumstances.

C No, only a constable in uniform or an authorised vehicle examiner has the power to seize vehicles under this section.

D No, only a constable in uniform has the power to seize vehicles under this section.

Question 2.10

Constable GREEN was on mobile patrol following a vehicle being driven by STONE, who was unaccompanied at the time. The officer conducted a Police National Computer (PNC) check on the vehicle, which showed that it was uninsured. STONE began to make off and, not being pursuit trained, Constable GREEN stood down from following the vehicle. The officer traced the vehicle about two hours later, outside STONE's house. STONE produced a certificate of insurance, which was dated the day before and the officer concluded that PNC had not yet been updated; however, STONE did admit to only being a provisional driving licence holder.

Does Constable GREEN have the power to seize STONE's vehicle under s. 165A of the Road Traffic Act 1988, in these circumstances?

A Yes, the vehicle can be seized because the driver failed to stop, and Constable GREEN has reasonable grounds for believing the vehicle was being driven otherwise than in accordance with a licence.

B No, STONE has produced a valid certificate of insurance, which was the original reason for stopping the vehicle.

C No, STONE is no longer 'driving' the vehicle.

D Yes, the vehicle can be seized simply because the driver failed to stop, without any of the other conditions being met.

Question 2.11

Constable BRIGHT was on mobile patrol and was attempting to stop a vehicle, which made off without stopping. The officer conducted a Police National Computer (PNC) check, which showed that the vehicle did not have insurance. Constable BRIGHT attended the address of the registered owner, HANSON, a short while later and spoke to HANSON, who admitted that the vehicle was uninsured. HANSON stated that the vehicle was parked in the detached garage in the grounds of the house.

Would Constable BRIGHT be entitled to seize the vehicle, under s. 165A(1) of the Road Traffic Act 1988, in these circumstances?

A No, because the vehicle was in a private dwelling house.

B Yes, because the vehicle was not in a private dwelling house.

C Yes, a constable may enter any premises in order to exercise this power.

D No, because the vehicle was on private property.

Question 2.12

A vehicle which is owned by PEARSON was seized by the police under s. 165A of the Road Traffic Act 1988. The vehicle was being driven at the time by McCAULEY. The vehicle is being stored in a garage owned by a firm employed by the local council. PEARSON has been given a seizure notice, but is about to go away on business and is unable to attend to recover the vehicle.

Would PEARSON be able to nominate McCAULEY to recover the vehicle in these circumstances?

A Yes, but PEARSON must first produce a current certificate of insurance and a driving licence at the police station; McCAULEY must then produce such valid documents at the garage.

B No, only PEARSON may recover the vehicle, by producing a current certificate of insurance, first at the police station and then at the garage.

C No, only PEARSON may recover the vehicle, by producing a current certificate of insurance and a driving licence, first at the police station and then at the garage.

D Yes, McCAULEY may recover the vehicle, by producing a current certificate of insurance and a driving licence, first at the police station and then at the garage.

Question 2.13

Constable PIERCE was dealing with a road traffic accident, which involved serious injuries to one driver. The driver of the other vehicle left the scene without stopping. A Police National Computer (PNC) check revealed that the registered keeper of the vehicle, LOWE, lived nearby. Constable PIERCE attended LOWE's address immediately to ascertain who was driving the vehicle.

What does s. 172 of the Road Traffic Act 1988 say in relation to Constable PIERCE's ability to ascertain these details?

A A request may be made verbally by Constable PIERCE, and LOWE has 28 days in which to reply.

B A request may only be made by post, and LOWE would have 28 days in which to reply.

C A request may be made verbally by Constable PIERCE, and LOWE must reply immediately.

D Constable PIERCE may not make the request: this power is restricted to people authorised by the Chief Officer of Police.

Question 2.14

SHARMA was served with a notice under s. 172(2) of the Road Traffic Act 1988, after a vehicle registered to him had driven through a red light and been caught on camera. SHARMA returned the notice with a letter stating that he had lent his car to HOLLAND on the day of the offence; however, HOLLAND had told SHARMA that he in turn had lent the car to another person, but refused to say who that person was. SHARMA stated that he was unable to identify the driver and provided HOLLAND's details in the form.

What options are now open to the police, under s. 172, in these circumstances?

A A notice may only be served on the registered keeper under this section; therefore the police will have to prosecute SHARMA for failing to comply with s. 172 and he has no defence.

B The police should serve a notice on HOLLAND; s. 172 only requires SHARMA to provide details of the actual driver, not a potential driver; since he could not, he has no other liability under this section.

C The police should serve a notice on HOLLAND; however, SHARMA may still be liable under s. 172.

D The police should serve a notice on HOLLAND, but they should also prosecute SHARMA for failing to comply with s. 172 and he has no defence.

ANSWERS

Answer 2.1

Answer **C** — Under s. 163(1) of the Road Traffic Act 1988, a person driving a mechanically propelled vehicle on a road must stop the vehicle on being required to do so by a constable in uniform or a traffic officer. If a person fails to comply with this section he/she is guilty of an offence s. 163(3).

Section 163 carries with it a power of entry under s. 17(1)(c)(iiia) of the Police and Criminal Evidence Act 1984 which states:

> Subject to the following provisions of this section, and without prejudice to any other enactment, a constable may enter and search any premises for the purpose of arresting a person for an offence under...
>
> (iiia) section 4 (driving etc. when under the influence of drink or drugs) or section 163 (failure to stop when required to do so by a constable in uniform) of the Road Traffic Act 1988.

The use of the *power of entry* under this section is not restricted to police officers in uniform; therefore a plain-clothed police officer may exercise this power (answer B is incorrect). However, the suspect must have initially *failed to stop* for a constable in uniform before the power may be used; therefore answer D is incorrect.

There is no requirement for the person to have committed an offence relating to use of a vehicle on a road *and* failed to stop; simply failing to stop when required to do so by a constable in uniform would trigger the use of the power under s. 17. Answer A is therefore incorrect.

Road Policing, para. 3.2.2

Answer 2.2

Answer **A** — Section 163(1) of the Road Traffic Act 1988 states that a person driving a mechanically propelled vehicle on a road must stop the vehicle on being required to do so by a constable in uniform or a traffic officer. This is a power for an officer in uniform randomly to stop vehicles. That said, like any power available to the police its use must be able to be justified. In *Stewart* v *Crowe* 1999 SLT 899, it was said that the power under s. 163 represented a necessary and proportionate response to the prevention of crime and that the only limit on the power is that it should not be used whimsically or oppressively.

In *Chief Constable of Gwent* v *Dash* [1986] RTR 41, vehicles were being randomly stopped in order to give a police officer further experience of the breath test procedure under the supervision of her senior. The court held that the actions of the police were not an abuse of power and did not amount to malpractice; therefore, the requirement of a breath specimen and the subsequent procedure were lawful. Random stopping of cars for the purpose of ascertaining whether their drivers have alcohol in their bodies is perfectly permissible; random breath testing, however, is not. This case adds yet another reason for a police officer to stop a vehicle—to train newly appointed officers in traffic procedure. Answers B and D are therefore incorrect.

In *Miller* v *Bell* 2004 GWD 26–564, it was held that the requirement to stop the vehicle is a legal one and as a result of a response given by the driver and/or the officer's observations, a suspicion may form in the officer's mind that the driver has alcohol in their body and they may require the driver to take a preliminary test. This is a random stop but *not* a random preliminary test. Answer C is therefore incorrect.

Road Policing, para. 3.2.2

Answer 2.3

Answer **A** — Section 4 of the Police and Criminal Evidence Act 1984 states that a road check may be authorised only where the officer has reasonable grounds for believing that the offence committed is an indictable offence. Therefore, as the offence is one of shoplifting, which is indictable, a road check can be authorised. Generally speaking an officer of at least the rank of superintendent must authorise a road check.

In urgent cases the authorising officer may be any rank below the rank of superintendent, and in this case Constable ROBERTS could have authorised the check provided a written record is made and a superintendent informed as soon as possible; answers B, C and D are therefore incorrect as the officer could have authorised the road check himself.

Road Policing, para. 3.2.3

Answer 2.4

Answer **D** — Section 4 of the Police and Criminal Evidence Act 1984 states that a road check may be authorised only where the officer has reasonable grounds for believing that the offence committed is an indictable offence. Generally the authorisation will be given by a superintendent; however, an officer of any rank may authorise the road check in urgent circumstances.

Section 4(11)(a) states that the authorising officer must specify a period, not exceeding seven days, during which the road check may continue. This period may be either continuous, or conducted at specified times during that period. If it appears to a superintendent that the road check ought to continue beyond the initial seven days, he/she may authorise a further period of seven days during which it may continue. There is no limit as to how many road checks may be authorised, provided each period does not exceed seven days. Answers A, B and C are therefore incorrect.

Road Policing, para. 3.2.3.1

Answer 2.5

Answer **D** — Section 164(1) of the Road Traffic Act 1988 provides the power for a constable to demand the production of a driving licence in certain circumstances. The power is divided into three general areas; where the driver:

- *is* driving a motor vehicle on a road (s. 164(1)(a)); or
- is believed (with reasonable cause) to *have been* the driver of a motor vehicle at a time when an accident occurred owing to its presence on a road (s. 164(1)(b)); or
- is believed (with reasonable cause) to *have* committed an offence in relation to the use of a motor vehicle on a road (s. 164(1)(c)).

Section 164(1) allows for the officer to demand the production of a person's driving licence when he/she is reasonably believed to *have been* driving, either when he/she has committed an offence *or* when he/she has been involved in an accident. Answers B and C are incorrect.

Since the paper driving licence counterpart was abolished in June 2015, the requirement to produce both the plastic driving licence *and* its paper counterpart has been removed and answer A is incorrect.

Road Policing, para. 3.2.4.1

Answer 2.6

Answer **A** — Section 165(4)(a) of the Road Traffic Act 1988 states that a person will not be convicted of an offence of failure to produce any certificate if he or she shows that: within seven days after the date on which the production of the certificate or other evidence was required it was produced at a police station that was specified by him at the time when its production was required.

However, s. 165(2B) states that in the case of a certificate transmitted to a person as described in s. 147(1A)(a) of this Act, the person is to be treated for the purposes of this section as producing the relevant certificate of insurance if:

(a) using electronic equipment...he provides the constable or examiner with electronic access to a copy of the certificate, or

(b) he produces a legible printed copy of the certificate.

Therefore, the person *may* comply with this section by simply providing the constable or vehicle examiner with electronic access to a copy of the certificate there and then, without the requirement of producing a legible printed copy of the certificate (at the time or within seven days). Answers B and D are therefore incorrect.

Section 165(2D) states that nothing in subs. (2B) or (2C) requires a constable or examiner to provide a person with electronic equipment for the purpose of compliance with a requirement imposed on the person by this section. Therefore, production in these circumstances is not dependent on the officer having a suitable electronic device to receive the certificate, and for that reason answer C is incorrect.

Road Policing, para. 3.2.5

Answer 2.7

Answer **D** — Under s. 164(8)(a) of the Road Traffic Act 1988, the person must show that within seven days after the production of his or her licence and its counterpart was required, he or she produced them *in person* at a police station that was specified by him or her at the time their production was required.

On the other hand, under s. 165(4)(a), the person must show that within seven days, the certificate of insurance *was produced* at a police station, removing the requirement for it to be produced in person.

Since answer D is the only one containing the correct combination, answers A, B and C are incorrect.

Road Policing, para. 3.2.4.4

Answer 2.8

Answer **A** — Section 165(5) of the Road Traffic Act 1988 states that a person:

(a) who supervises the holder of a provisional licence granted under Part III of this Act while the holder is driving on a road a motor vehicle, or

(b) whom a constable or vehicle examiner has reasonable cause to believe was supervising the holder of such a licence while driving, at a time when an accident occurred owing to the presence of the vehicle on a road or at a time when an offence is suspected of having been committed by the holder of the provisional licence in relation to the use of the vehicle on a road, must, on being so required by a constable or vehicle examiner, give his name and address and the name and address of the owner of the vehicle.

Since the officer may ask the supervisor for these details, answer D is incorrect.

Constable HOLDSWORTH may ask for these details if the vehicle was involved in an accident on the road or if it is suspected that SAUNDERS has committed an offence. Answer B is therefore incorrect.

There is no power under this section to deal with the supervisor in respect of insurance issues. These duties belong to the driver and therefore answer C is incorrect.

Road Policing, para. 3.2.5

Answer 2.9

Answer **D** — Vehicles may be seized under s. 165A of the Road Traffic Act 1988, subject to certain conditions being satisfied. The first condition is where a constable in *uniform* requests that a person produces evidence that a motor vehicle is or was not being driven in contravention of s. 87(1) of the Act (driving otherwise than in accordance with a licence); the second condition is that a similar request is made for evidence that the vehicle was not being driven in contravention of s. 143 (driving without insurance). Where the person fails to produce such evidence, provided the constable has reasonable grounds for believing that the vehicle was being so driven, he or she may seize the vehicle.

The power is restricted to police officers, in uniform, and is not given to authorised vehicle examiners or PCSOs.

Answers A, B and C are therefore incorrect.

Note that PCSOs do have a power to seize a motor vehicle under s. 59 of the Police Reform Act 2002 (using a motor vehicle in an anti-social manner).

Road Policing, para. 3.2.6

Answer 2.10

Answer **A** — Vehicles may be seized under s. 165A of the Road Traffic Act 1988, subject to certain conditions being satisfied. Under s. 165A, the first condition is where a constable in uniform requests that a person produces evidence that a motor vehicle is or was not being driven in contravention of s. 87(1) of the Act (driving otherwise than in accordance with a licence); the second condition is that a similar request is made for evidence that the vehicle was not being driven in contravention of s. 143 (driving without insurance).

There is a third condition attached to s. 165A, which is when a constable in uniform requires a person driving a motor vehicle to stop (under s. 163); the person fails to stop the vehicle, or to stop it for long enough, for the constable to make such lawful enquiries as he or she considers appropriate, and the constable has reasonable grounds for believing that that vehicle is or was being driven in contravention of s. 87(1) or s. 143.

If any of these conditions apply, and the person fails to produce evidence that the vehicle was not being driven in contravention of these two sections, provided the constable has reasonable grounds for believing that the vehicle was being so driven, he or she may seize the vehicle, notwithstanding that the person is no longer driving it. Answer C is therefore incorrect.

The vehicle may be seized if one condition is not met (i.e. the driver has insurance) and the other condition is (i.e. he or she has no driving licence). Answer B is therefore incorrect.

Finally, a vehicle cannot be seized simply because the driver failed to stop. The constable must have reasonable grounds for believing that at least one of the other conditions is met. Answer D is therefore incorrect.

Road Policing, para. 3.2.6

Answer 2.11

Answer **B** — Vehicles may be seized under s. 165A of the Road Traffic Act 1988, subject to certain conditions being satisfied. Under s. 165A(4), where a constable in uniform has required a person to stop a motor vehicle and the person fails to do so, the constable may seize the vehicle where the constable has reasonable grounds for believing the vehicle is or was being driven contrary to s. 143 of the Act.

For the purposes of exercising the power under s. 165A, a constable may enter any premises other than a private dwelling house on which he or she has reasonable grounds for believing the vehicle to be. Answer C is therefore incorrect.

Under s. 165A(9)(d), the definition of a 'private dwelling house' does *not* include any garage or other structure occupied with the dwelling house or land belonging to it. Since a garage is not a private dwelling house, answer A is incorrect.

This exception refers to private dwelling houses and not private property, therefore if the vehicle had been parked on property which was private, but not a dwelling, it could have been seized and therefore answer D is incorrect.

Note that the powers referred to in s. 165A also apply to circumstances where a person is believed to be driving a vehicle contrary to s. 87(1) of the Act (driving otherwise than in accordance with a licence).

Road Policing, para. 3.2.6

Answer 2.12

Answer **D** — The relevant regulations are the Road Traffic Act 1988 (Retention and Disposal of Seized Motor Vehicles) Regulations 2005 (SI 2005/1606) and they set out the procedures to be followed by the police in exercising the seizure power.

The owner or keeper of the vehicle must be given a seizure notice, which must give specified details about the seizure and retention of the vehicle. These details will include an indication that a person must pay any relevant charges and must produce at a specified police station a valid licence and proof of insurance in respect of their use of the vehicle (or nominate a third person who can produce those documents in respect of that person's use of the vehicle to whom the vehicle can be released) (reg. 4(3) to (4)).

Specific provision is made for cases where the person claiming the vehicle can demonstrate that they are the owner and pay the required fee, but they nominate a third person who produces a valid certificate of insurance covering their use of that vehicle and a valid driving licence authorising them to drive that vehicle. In such circumstances, the authorised person must permit that person to remove the vehicle (reg. 5(2)).

Therefore, a nominated person *may* recover the vehicle (answers B and C are incorrect for this reason). The nominated person may also produce the documents at a police station (reg. 4) and subsequently at the place where the vehicle is being held (reg. 5). Answer A is therefore incorrect.

Road Policing, para. 3.2.6.1

Answer 2.13

Answer **C** — Under s. 172(2) of the Road Traffic Act 1988, where the driver of a vehicle has committed an offence to which the section applies (this includes ss. 3 and 170 (accidents)), the keeper of the vehicle shall give information as to the identity of the driver as required by or on behalf of a chief officer of police.

There is no mention of a person having to be authorised to make such a request on behalf of the chief officer and therefore it can be assumed that as Constable PIERCE is acting in the course of his duties, he is acting on behalf of the chief officer. Answer D is therefore incorrect.

When a request is made by post, the keeper has 28 days in which to reply. The 1988 Act does not state that *all* requests must be made by post and answer B is therefore incorrect. On the contrary, the case of *Lowe* v *Lester* [1987] RTR 30 indicates that requests may be made verbally, and the information must be provided within a reasonable time, which may in the prevailing circumstances mean *immediately*. Therefore, answer A is incorrect.

Road Policing, para. 3.2.7

Answer 2.14

Answer **C** — A person is guilty of an offence if they fail to comply with a requirement under s. 172(2) of the Road Traffic Act 1988 to supply the details of the person who was driving a vehicle at the time an offence was committed. A s. 172 notice will be sent by the police to the registered keeper and compliance will be achieved by returning it with details of who was driving. A section of the form allows the registered keeper to enter another person's details if he or she was not the driver at the time of the offence. If the keeper is unable to provide details of the driver, the form asks for reasons for that inability.

Where a registered keeper returned the form with a covering letter stating that he had not completed the form because on the day of the alleged offence more than one person had used the vehicle, he was convicted of failing to comply with the requirement under s. 172. The defendant argued that he had complied with s. 172 because the form only required him to provide details of the actual driver, not a potential driver (which he could not do).

The Divisional Court disagreed, holding that a notice issued pursuant to s. 172 requires an accurate response and not an inaccurate or misleading statement. The defendant's claim was clearly contrary to the legislative intention, as it would frequently be the case that the registered owner of a vehicle would at least suspect who the driver was, even if he or she did not know for certain, e.g. where the owner lent the vehicle to a friend but was not in the vehicle at the time of the alleged offence (*R (On the application of Flegg)* v *Southampton and New Forest Justices* [2006] EWHC 396 (Admin)). Answer B is therefore incorrect.

Answer A is incorrect because s. 172(2) allows for a notice to be sent to the keeper, or any other person who will be required to give 'any information which it is in his power to give and may lead to identification of the driver'. This means that a notice should be sent to HOLLAND regardless of any decision to prosecute SHARMA.

Section 172(4) provides that a person shall not be convicted of this offence if that person can show that he or she did not know and could not have ascertained with reasonable diligence who the driver of the vehicle was. This does not negate the keeper's liability, as seen in *R (On the application of Flegg)*; it will depend whether the prosecution decides to pursue a case against HOLLAND, who would commit the offence if he failed to disclose details of the driver, or both persons. Answer D is therefore incorrect.

Road Policing, paras 3.2.7, 3.2.7.1

3 | Offences Involving Standards of Driving

STUDY PREPARATION

There have been several key changes to the legislation covering offences involving standards of driving to plug the many gaps that existed, such as causing serious injury by dangerous driving, causing death by careless or inconsiderate driving and causing death by careless or inconsiderate driving while under the influence of drugs.

The key to understanding all offences in this chapter—and any relevant defences—lies in knowing:

- the classification of vehicle covered by the offence;
- the *place* in which the offence can be committed;
- the relevant standard breached; *and*
- the mental element required.

It should be noted that there is only one standard of driving that is acceptable of any driver, irrespective of his or her particular driving experience or qualifications.

QUESTIONS

Question 3.1

Fifty cars were gathered in a supermarket car park one evening, racing in an unauthorised 'max power' rally. GLEESON was driving one of the cars at high speed and KRAMER was in the front passenger seat. GLEESON lost control of the car and crashed into a shelter. GLEESON survived the crash, but KRAMER did not. The car park was only open to the public when the supermarket was open. A barrier prevented vehicular access outside these hours, but the people attending the rally damaged it to gain access.

Could GLEESON be found guilty of causing death by dangerous driving, under s. 1 of the Road Traffic Act 1988 in these circumstances?

A No, GLEESON was not driving on a road.

B Yes, because GLEESON was trespassing, the offence could be complete.

C No, GLEESON was not driving on a road or public place.

D Yes, there are no restrictions on where the offence may take place.

Question 3.2

GRAHAM is appearing in court having been charged with an offence under s. 1A of the Road Traffic Act 1988 (causing serious injury by dangerous driving). GRAHAM is accused of driving at high speeds through a housing estate and seriously injuring a pedestrian when the vehicle mounted a pavement. The prosecution has evidence from witnesses that GRAHAM had drunk at least eight pints of lager before driving the vehicle and had staggered out of the pub 15 minutes before the accident; however, they have no evidence of the proportion of alcohol in GRAHAM's body, because the defendant managed to evade arrest for three days after the accident.

Would the evidence that GRAHAM consumed alcohol prior to driving be relevant to the issue in proving dangerous driving?

A No, the prosecution is unable to produce direct evidence of whether GRAHAM was over the limit at the time of the accident.

B Yes, the amount of alcohol consumed before the accident would be sufficient in itself to convict GRAHAM of this offence.

C Yes, the evidence *may* be relevant to the issue of whether GRAHAM drove dangerously.

D No, the evidence is unlikely to be allowed because its prejudicial nature outweighs its probative value.

Question 3.3

JENKINS was a delivery driver and was working in the early hours of the morning while it was still dark and visibility was poor. JENKINS stopped the delivery van on a country road, which had no on-street lighting, to deliver goods to a premises which was situated on a sharp bend. While JENKINS was out of the van, another vehicle driving on the road collided with the van, causing the death of the only occupant. When the police accident investigation team arrived, they noted that the van could not be seen by a person driving towards the bend and that JENKINS had left no warning lights on the vehicle.

In relation to the offence of causing death by dangerous driving, under s. 1 of the Road Traffic Act 1988, could JENKINS be said to have 'caused' the death of the other driver, in these circumstances?

A No, JENKINS was not driving at the time of the accident.

B Yes, there was a causal link between JENKINS parking the van at the location and the fatal accident.

C Yes, in the circumstances the prosecution will be able to show that JENKINS's actions were a substantial cause of the death, which is required in such cases.

D No, the prosecution would have to show that JENKINS's driving fell far below what would be expected of a competent and careful driver which, in the circumstances, would not be possible.

Question 3.4

DALEY was driving her car on the approach to a zebra crossing when some children were crossing the road. When DALEY applied her brakes, they failed and she knocked over a child, injuring her. DALEY's car was examined and it was found that her brake discs were so worn that they did not work. DALEY stated that she had heard the brakes squealing earlier in her journey, but had not realised how bad they were.

What further evidence, if any, would be required in order to convict DALEY of driving dangerously?

A That it would have been obvious to a competent and careful driver that driving the vehicle in that condition would be dangerous.

B No further evidence is required; DALEY may be convicted on these facts alone.

C DALEY could not be convicted of dangerous driving, as she was unaware of the dangerous condition of her car.

D That it should have been obvious to DALEY that driving the vehicle in that condition would be dangerous.

Question 3.5

SCULLY has been arrested for an offence under s. 1A of the Road Traffic Act 1988 (causing serious injury by dangerous driving). SCULLY works for a skip hire company and was driving a vehicle which was carrying a skip full of building materials to a refuse tip. The load was insecure and a large piece of metal fell off the skip, seriously injuring a pedestrian. SCULLY claimed in interview that he was an experienced driver and had securely fastened the load and inspected it before setting off, something which he had done thousands of times before. SCULLY maintained that he had done all he could and that he could not be held liable for a freak accident such as this.

In considering whether or not SCULLY should be charged with this offence, which of the following statements is correct in relation to his 'inspection' of the vehicle before driving?

A It must be shown that had a competent and careful driver inspected the vehicle closely, it should have been obvious to them that the way in which it was loaded would make driving it dangerous.

B It must be shown that had a competent and careful driver seen the load, it should have been obvious to them that the way in which it was loaded would make driving it dangerous.

C It must be shown that it should have been obvious to SCULLY, after careful inspection, that the way in which the vehicle was loaded would make driving it dangerous.

D SCULLY may not be charged under this legislation; an offence under s. 1A may only be charged when the circumstances relate to the standard of a person's driving.

Question 3.6

SHARPE was driving a bus towards a zebra crossing while two people were crossing the road. Witnesses have stated that SHARPE drove into the two people while they were still on the crossing; both persons were taken to hospital but later died of their injuries. SHARPE has been charged with an offence under s. 1 of the Road Traffic Act 1988 (causing death by dangerous driving) but intends pleading not guilty because, on the approach to the crossing, he inadvertently pressed the accelerator pedal instead of the brake which meant that he had no intention to commit the offence.

Which of the following statements is correct in relation to SHARPE's proposed defence to a charge for this offence?

A The fact that SHARPE had no intention to commit the offence is irrelevant; he could be convicted on these facts alone.

B For SHARPE to be convicted of this offence, the prosecution would have to show that he intended his driving to be dangerous.

C The court might not convict SHARPE of this offence because of his lack of intent; however, it may convict him of the alternative charge of causing death by careless driving.

D The court might not convict SHARPE of this offence because of his lack of intent, unless the prosecution can show that he knew his driving was dangerous.

Question 3.7

CALVIN is appearing in Crown Court for an offence of dangerous driving. Witnesses saw CALVIN speeding towards a junction on a housing estate and failing to brake in time. The defendant's vehicle shot through the junction and collided with another vehicle. A nearby resident, REID, has also provided a written statement stating that she saw CALVIN doing handbrake turns in the road shortly before the collision, before the vehicle sped off out of her sight towards the junction where the collision occurred. In her statement, REID has stated that CALVIN was well known on the estate for the dangerous way he drove and she had heard from other residents that there had been several other near misses such as the current case.

Would the prosecution be able to admit REID's evidence in asking the court to decide whether CALVIN is guilty of dangerous driving?

A Yes, the court may hear the evidence of CALVIN's driving immediately before the incident, but the information regarding previous bad driving is hearsay and inadmissible.

B Yes, the court may hear all of REID's testimony—hearsay evidence such as this is admissible in cases of dangerous driving.

C No, only an expert witness could give this evidence and REID will not be regarded as such.

D No, REID's entire evidence is hearsay, which would not be admissible in this case.

Question 3.8

HIGGINSON has been charged with causing death by dangerous driving in relation to a road traffic accident.

In relation to the actual causes of the accident, which of the following is true?

A Any police officer may give an opinion, but it *must* be supported with factual evidence.

B A police officer who has experience in collision investigation may give such opinion.

C A police officer who has experience in collision investigation may give such opinion, but it *must* be supported with factual evidence.

D Only factual evidence in relation to the dangerous driving is allowed. Opinion as to the cause of the accident is not.

Question 3.9

Constable CHAPMAN was dealing with a fatal road traffic accident where the suspected driver of the offending vehicle, LYNCH, had made off. According to witness accounts, LYNCH had caused the accident by driving without due care and attention beforehand. Constable CHAPMAN eventually traced LYNCH some five hours after the accident occurred. LYNCH admitted to have taken drugs since the accident and was exhibiting signs of being unfit. Constable CHAPMAN asked LYNCH to provide a preliminary drug test under s. 6C of the Road Traffic Act 1988, using an approved device; however, LYNCH refused to provide a sample because he had taken drugs after the accident.

Would LYNCH be guilty of an offence under s. 3A(1)(d) of the Road Traffic Act 1988 (causing death by careless driving when under the influence of drink or drugs) in these circumstances?

A Yes, the request was made within the timescale required under s. 3A.

B Yes, the timescale required under s. 3A is not relevant because LYNCH has deliberately attempted to evade arrest.

C No, at this stage an offence is not committed under this section; however, LYNCH could be guilty if he subsequently refuses to provide a sample under s. 7 of the Act.

D Yes, Constable CHAPMAN reasonably suspects that LYNCH is unfit to drive now; therefore the offence is complete.

Question 3.10

CAGE works for a building company and has a drug habit. CAGE turned up for work while under the influence of drugs and was fired. To get revenge, CAGE stole a dumper truck from the site, intending to take it to the head office and cause damage. On the way, CAGE was involved in a road traffic accident, where a pedestrian walked into the road in front of the dumper truck, and was killed. CAGE was still under the influence of drugs at this time.

Has CAGE committed an offence under s. 3A of the Road Traffic Act 1988, in these circumstances?

A No, CAGE was not under the influence of drink at the time of the accident.
B No, it must be shown that CAGE drove without due care and attention or without due consideration to other road users.
C No, he was not driving a motor vehicle at the time of the accident.
D Yes, he was driving a mechanically propelled vehicle on a road while under the influence of drugs.

Question 3.11

TYLER is appearing before the court on a count of careless driving contrary to s. 3 of the Road Traffic Act 1988. TYLER collided with a car in front, while driving in traffic on a motorway. At the time, the police were clearing the scene of a serious accident on the opposite carriageway. TYLER's defence was that he was distracted by the activity and because he was driving at 65 mph, had no time to react.

Which of the following statements is correct, in relation to whether the court should take account of TYLER's claims to have been distracted?
A The court may take account of distraction as a defence, depending on any other hazards on the road at that time.
B The court may only take account of distraction as a defence in a case where the driver was responding to an emergency situation.
C The court may take account of distraction as a defence, but the speed at which a vehicle was travelling will not be a factor for consideration.
D The court may not take account of distraction as a defence; the driver is always responsible for his or her own actions.

Question 3.12

WARE was driving his car on the road in heavy rain in a built-up area. There were several puddles at the side of the road and WARE deliberately drove through these, in order to soak pedestrians who were using the pavement. As a result of WARE's actions, several pedestrians and a pedal cyclist were soaked by water from the puddles; however, the water missed other pedestrians who were protected by a bus shelter.

Against which people, if any, might WARE have committed an offence under s. 3 of the Road Traffic Act 1988 (driving without due consideration to other road users)?
A The pedal cyclist and all pedestrians, as there was potential for them to be affected by WARE's actions.

B None of the people, as no motor vehicles were affected by WARE's actions.

C The pedal cyclist and the pedestrians who were soaked, as they were actually affected by WARE's actions.

D The pedal cyclist only, as the only person 'using' the road.

Question 3.13

FRANCIS was driving a van on a road and was approaching a junction with a side road. FRANCIS indicated to turn left and was in the middle of doing so when, without warning, HASTINGS stepped off the pavement into the path of the vehicle and was knocked over. HASTINGS turned out to be an elderly man who suffered minor injuries; however, he had to be taken to hospital with breathing difficulties and later died of a heart attack. It transpired that FRANCIS had been driving the vehicle without insurance.

Would the fact that FRANCIS did not cause the accident be relevant in relation to an offence under s. 3ZB of the Road Traffic Act 1988 (causing the death of another person)?

A No, the fact that FRANCIS was driving without insurance would be sufficient to prove this offence.

B Yes, there must be evidence that FRANCIS's driving in some way contributed to HASTINGS's death beyond the mere presence of the vehicle on the road.

C No, the mere presence of the vehicle on the road would make FRANCIS guilty of this offence.

D Yes, because HASTINGS's injuries as a result of the collision were not serious, FRANCIS has not 'caused' his death.

Question 3.14

LUTHER is a disqualified driver and was driving his friend's car on a road. Whilst approaching a junction, LUTHER was guilty of a minor lapse in concentration, which resulted in him not seeing a cyclist on his nearside. The wing mirror of the car LUTHER was driving clipped the cyclist, who then fell off the cycle. The cyclist was later taken to hospital, suffering from a broken leg.

Given that LUTHER was not guilty of dangerous or careless driving, could he instead be guilty of an offence under s. 3ZD of the Road Traffic Act 1988 in these circumstances?

A Yes, as a disqualified driver, he meets both requirements under the section (having no driving licence *and* having no insurance).

B Yes, LUTHER has committed this offence simply by being a disqualified driver.

C No, LUTHER has not caused the death of another person.

D Yes, as a disqualified driver, he meets one of the requirements under the section (having no driving licence *or* having no insurance).

Question 3.15

LEIGH was driving a motor vehicle behind FOGG, on the approach to a pelican crossing. LEIGH saw a pedestrian on the pavement next to the crossing, but was in a hurry and hoped to get through the green light before the pedestrian pushed the 'stop' button. FOGG anticipated that the pedestrian might push the button and slowed down, stopping short of the crossing even though the lights were still green. LEIGH was not concentrating and drove into the rear of FOGG's vehicle.

Which of the following statements is correct, in relation to the proof required for an offence of driving without due care and attention, contrary to s. 3 of the Road Traffic Act 1988?

A Any breach of road traffic regulations will provide conclusive evidence for this offence.

B Colliding with another vehicle will provide conclusive evidence for this offence.

C Colliding with another vehicle will not provide conclusive evidence for this offence, but a breach of pedestrian crossing regulations will.

D Neither colliding with another vehicle nor breaching pedestrian crossing regulations will provide conclusive evidence for this offence; further evidence is required.

Question 3.16

KEENAN is appearing in Crown Court for causing death by dangerous driving. KEENAN had been driving on a motorway and had driven into the rear of the car in front. This resulted in a multiple pile-up, during which the occupants of the car in front died. Witnesses stated that KEENAN had caused the accident by driving too close to the vehicle in front and when it braked, KEENAN was unable to react quickly enough.

Would the prosecution be entitled to introduce the stopping distances shown in the Highway Code, to assist in establishing KEENAN's liability for the offence?

A No, the provisions of the Highway Code may only be introduced in proceedings by the defence, to negate the defendant's liability.

B No, the failure by a person to observe a provision of the Highway Code may only be introduced in civil proceedings.

C Yes, the failure by a person to observe a provision of the Highway Code may be introduced in any civil or criminal proceedings.
D Yes, but the failure by a person to observe a provision of the Highway Code may only be introduced in certain criminal proceedings.

Question 3.17

MULLER was riding a bicycle along the road, approaching a junction. In order to avoid stopping at the junction, MULLER decided to ride across the pavement. In doing so, MULLER collided with HOLLAND, a pedestrian. MULLER was in a hurry and started to ride away, but HOLLAND tried to obtain the cyclist's name and address. MULLER refused and rode off.

Has MULLER committed an offence by refusing to provide these details?
A Yes, but only if HOLLAND was injured during the incident.
B Yes, MULLER has committed an offence in these circumstances alone.
C No, this power is only given to police officers.
D Yes, provided it can be shown MULLER was guilty of an offence of dangerous cycling.

Question 3.18

Sergeant AZIZ stopped a vehicle which had been circulated after it had been involved in an incident of dangerous driving. Sergeant AZIZ asked the male driver for his name and address for the purposes of summonsing him for the offence. When asked, the male said nothing and just stood looking at the officer. Sergeant AZIZ eventually arrested the person using powers under s. 24 of the Police and Criminal Evidence Act 1984.

In the circumstances as outlined, has an offence under s. 168 of the Road Traffic Act 1988 been committed?
A No, the offence is only committed by those who refuse to give or give false details and this has not occurred in these circumstances.
B Yes, silence has been held to be a refusal in these circumstances.
C Yes, as failure to give details amounts to refusal.
D No, the offence is only committed by those who refuse to give details and this has not occurred in these circumstances.

ANSWERS

Answer 3.1

Answer **C** — The offence of causing death by dangerous driving under s. 1 of the Road Traffic Act 1988 may be committed by a person driving a mechanically propelled vehicle *on a road or public place*. The Act gives a wide meaning to the types of vehicle that may commit the offence (including dumper trucks, cranes and quad bikes), and the location. Answers A and D are therefore incorrect.

A place will only be public if people are admitted with the permission, express or implied, of the owner of the land in question (see *DPP* v *Vivier* [1991] RTR 205). Because drivers of the vehicles were trespassing, the offence will *not* be complete as it may only take place on a road or public place and therefore answer B is incorrect.

Road Policing, paras 3.3.2, 3.1.11

Answer 3.2

Answer **C** — In some circumstances the condition of the driver will be relevant. In *R* v *Pleydell* [2005] EWCA Crim 1447, the court found that the mere presence of a controlled drug (such as cocaine) in a driver's blood may of itself be relevant to the issue of whether a person drove dangerously—even if there is no specific evidence as to the drug's effect on the person's driving.

Turning to drink-related matters, in *R* v *Woodward* [1995] RTR 130, the courts held that evidence of drink will be admissible in an offence of causing the death of another by dangerous driving (under s. 1 of the Act) where the quantity of it may have adversely affected the quality of the defendant's driving. Answer D is incorrect for this reason.

There is no requirement to prove whether the defendant was above or below the prescribed limit, as that is not an element of the offence (*R* v *Mari* [2010] RTR 192); evidence of the amount of alcohol consumed and said to affect the defendant's ability to drive suffices. Answer A is therefore incorrect.

On the other hand, in *R* v *Webster* [2006] 2 Cr App R 103, it was held that the fact that a driver was adversely affected by alcohol is a circumstance relevant to the issue of dangerous driving, but is not in itself determinative to prove the offence. Answer B is therefore incorrect.

Road Policing, paras 3.3.2, 3.3.2.2

Answer 3.3

Answer **B** — Section 1 of the Road Traffic Act 1988, states that a person who causes the death of another person by driving a mechanically propelled vehicle dangerously on a road or other public place is guilty of an offence.

In this particular scenario, because JENKINS was not actually sitting in the van and 'driving' it in the ordinary sense, the court would have to decide whether or not this impacts on the ability of the defendant to commit the offence. The Court of Appeal have clarified that this offence relates to causing death *by* driving and not causing death *while* driving and therefore the 'driving' does not have to be coextensive (or coterminous) with the accident that resulted in the death. In other words, JENKINS's *earlier* driving was a contributing factor to the victim's death.

In *R v Jenkins* [2012] EWCA Crim 2909 the court held that parking a vehicle to make a delivery, leaving it in conditions of poor visibility, where another vehicle collided with it was certainly a causal link to the fatality that occurred.

Answers A and D are incorrect, because the defendant *has* driven in a way which would fall far below what would be expected of a competent and careful driver.

It is not necessary to show that the driving by the defendant was the sole or even a substantial cause of death; it must only be shown to have been *a* cause of the death (*R v Hennigan* [1971] 3 All ER 133). Answer C is therefore incorrect.

Road Policing, paras 3.3.2.1, 3.3.2.2

Answer 3.4

Answer **A** — Section 2A(2) of the Road Traffic Act 1988 states:

> (2) A person is also to be regarded as driving dangerously for the purposes of sections 1 and 2 above if it would be obvious to a competent and careful driver that driving the vehicle in its current state would be dangerous.

The test is an objective one which looks at the manner of driving and *not* at the defendant's state of mind. It must be proved that:

- the dangerous condition would itself have been obvious to a competent and careful driver; *or*
- the defendant actually *knew* of its condition

(*R v Strong* [1995] Crim LR 428).

Answer B is incorrect as the prosecution has to prove one of these requirements. Answer C is incorrect for the same reason.

Answer D is incorrect as the dangerous driving must have been obvious to a competent and careful driver—not simply to DALEY herself.

However, see the case of *R v Marchant and Muntz* [2003] Crim LR 806, where the prosecution failed to convince the Court of Appeal that a vehicle was dangerous as a result of its being 'manufactured' in that way.

Road Policing, paras 3.3.2.2, 3.3.2.3

Answer 3.5

Answer **B** — Section 2A(2) of the Road Traffic Act 1988 states that a person is to be regarded as driving dangerously for the purposes of ss. 1, 1A and 2 if it would be obvious to a competent and careful driver that driving the vehicle in its current state would be dangerous. Therefore, an offence may be charged under s. 1A when the dangerous driving relates to the current state of the vehicle (answer D is therefore incorrect) and the standard of 'observation' required is what a 'competent and careful' driver would consider to be dangerous, and not the defendant. Answer C is therefore incorrect.

In relation to the dangerous state of a vehicle being 'obvious', no special definition is required and such an observation could arise from an inspection which is something between a fleeting glance and a long look (*R v Marsh* [2002] EWCA Crim 137). Since there is no need for that competent and careful driver to have inspected the vehicle closely, answer A is incorrect.

Road Policing, paras 3.3.2.2, 3.3.2.3, 3.3.3

Answer 3.6

Answer **A** — Section 1 of the Road Traffic Act 1988 states that a person who causes the death of another person by driving a mechanically propelled vehicle dangerously on a road or other public place is guilty of an offence.

Under s. 2A(1) of the Act, a person is to be regarded as driving dangerously if the way he or she drives falls far below what would be expected of a competent and careful driver, and it would be obvious to a competent and careful driver that driving in that way would be dangerous.

The Road Traffic Act 1991 amended previous legislation by replacing the old offence of 'reckless driving' with 'dangerous driving' and this change was significant. Under the original Act, to show that a person was 'reckless' required proof of the defendant's *mens rea* (that he or she foresaw the consequences and carried on regardless). This was updated with an objective test, which focuses on the manner of driving rather than the defendant's state of mind and on what would have been obvious to a hypothetical 'competent and careful driver'. Answer D is incorrect as the prosecution is no longer required to prove any knowledge on the defendant's part.

The Court of Appeal reviewed the requirements of s. 2A in *Attorney General's Reference (No. 4 of 2000)* [2001] EWCA Crim 780, where a bus driver inadvertently pressed the accelerator pedal instead of the brake, killing two pedestrians. The court held that it was no defence to claim that he had not intended to press the accelerator; under s. 2A, the test is an objective one and there is no requirement to show any specific intent to drive dangerously. Answer B is therefore incorrect.

As with dangerous driving, the test for careless driving is entirely objective in nature and focuses on the manner of driving rather than the defendant's state of mind. Answer C is incorrect for this reason.

Road Policing, paras 3.3.2.2, 3.3.6.1

Answer 3.7

Answer **A** — Evidence showing how the particular vehicle was being driven before the incident itself *may* be given in support of the charge of dangerous driving.

However, care needs to be taken by the prosecution not to seek to adduce inadmissible evidence about the defendant's past bad driving (*R v McKenzie* [2008] EWCA Crim 758). Answer B is therefore incorrect.

The evidence REID is able to give of CALVIN's driving immediately before the incident is direct evidence and could be admitted in this case—even though REID is not an expert witness. On the other hand, the information regarding previous bad driving is hearsay and inadmissible. Answers C and D are therefore incorrect.

Road Policing, para. 3.3.4

Answer 3.8

Answer **B** — Whether a witness is properly qualified in the subject calling for expertise is a question for the court. Such competence or skill may stem from formal study or training, experience, or both.

In *R v Oakley* [1979] Crim LR 657, a police officer who had attended a course, passed an exam as a collision investigator, and attended more than 400 accidents was entitled to give expert evidence as to the cause of an accident. Answers A and D are therefore incorrect.

The investigation of road traffic accidents is a science that has professional qualifications attached to it, and mathematical calculations that would not look out of place on a rocket scientist's desk! Although it is likely that factual evidence will be available, a police officer meeting the *Oakley* criteria may give purely an opinion of how the accident occurred. Answer C is therefore incorrect.

Road Policing, para. 3.3.4

Answer 3.9

Answer **C** — Under s. 3A(1) of the Road Traffic Act 1988, if a person causes the death of another person by driving a mechanically propelled vehicle on a road or other public place without due care and attention, or without reasonable consideration for other persons using the road or place, and:

(a) he is, at the time when he is driving, unfit to drive through drink or drugs, or

(b) he has consumed so much alcohol that the proportion of it in his breath, blood or urine at that time exceeds the prescribed limit, or

(ba) he has in his body a specified controlled drug and the proportion of it in his blood or urine at that time exceeds the specified limit for that drug, or

(c) he is, within 18 hours after that time, required to provide a specimen in pursuance of s. 7 of this Act, but without reasonable excuse fails to provide it, or

(d) he is required by a constable to give his permission for a laboratory test of a specimen of blood taken from him under s. 7A of this Act, but without reasonable excuse fails to do so,

he is guilty of an offence.

In the first instance, a person must have driven a mechanically propelled vehicle on a road or other public place without due care and attention, or without reasonable consideration for other persons using the road or place. Once this has been proved, the prosecution would seek to show that one of the circumstances in paras (a) to (d) applies. These require the driver to have been unfit to drive, or over the prescribed limit for drink or drugs, *at the time of the accident* and answer D is incorrect.

There are timescales which are relevant under s. 3A(1)(c); however, these relate to a failure to provide a relevant specimen requested in pursuance of s. 7 of the Act (requests made at the station or hospital) within 18 hours of the accident. Answer C is correct (and answers A and B are incorrect) because LYNCH could only be guilty if he subsequently refuses to provide a sample under s. 7.

Note that LYNCH could have committed offences under s. 6 (failure to provide) and/or s. 2B (causing death by careless or inconsiderate driving); however, the prosecution would seek to prove the offence under s. 3A(1) in the first instance, because it carries a maximum term of imprisonment of 14 years (as opposed to five years under s. 2B).

Road Policing, para. 3.3.5

Answer 3.10

Answer **B** — Under s. 3A(1) of the Road Traffic Act 1988, if a person causes the death of another person by driving a mechanically propelled vehicle on a road or other public place without due care and attention, or without reasonable consideration for other persons using the road or place, and:

(a) he is, at the time when he is driving, unfit to drive through drink or drugs, or
(b) he has consumed so much alcohol that the proportion of it in his breath, blood or urine at that time exceeds the prescribed limit, or
(ba) he has in his body a specified controlled drug and the proportion of it in his blood or urine at that time exceeds the specified limit for that drug, or
(c) he is, within 18 hours after that time, required to provide a specimen in pursuance of section 7 of this Act, but without reasonable excuse fails to provide it, ...
he is guilty of an offence.

In the first instance, a person must have driven without due care and attention, or without reasonable consideration for other persons using the road or place, which is why answer B is correct, and answer D is incorrect.

The offence may be committed by a person driving a mechanically propelled vehicle on a road or other public place, therefore answer C is incorrect.

Finally, the defendant may commit this offence if, at the time, he or she is unfit to drive through drink or drugs, or over the limit due to drink. Answer A is therefore incorrect.

Road Policing, para. 3.3.5

Answer 3.11

Answer **A** — The Administrative Court has accepted that there will be a defence available to a charge of careless driving where the driver can show that for some reason they were distracted (*Plunkett* v *DPP* [2004] EWHC 1937). Answer D is therefore incorrect.

However, each case will be considered on its merits by the courts and certain factors, including the nature and extent of the distraction in question. Among these factors will be:

- how long the distraction was;
- the speed of the vehicle;
- any other hazards present.

This list is not exclusive, but since speed *may* be a factor for consideration by the court, answer C is incorrect.

The *Plunkett* case demonstrates that the court *may* consider distraction as a defence, even when the driver was not responding to an emergency situation. Answer B is therefore incorrect.

Road Policing, para. 3.3.6.1

Answer 3.12

Answer **C** — An offence is committed under s. 3 of the Road Traffic Act 1988 when a person drives a mechanically propelled vehicle on a road or public place, without due care and attention, or without due consideration for other persons using the road or public place.

Other persons using the road or public place can include pedestrians who are deliberately sprayed with water from a puddle, or passengers in a vehicle (*Pawley* v *Wharldall* [1966] 1 QB 373). Answers B and D are therefore incorrect.

It must be shown that another road user was *actually* inconvenienced by the defendant's driving; it is not enough that there was potential for inconvenience (see s. 3ZA(4)). Since the people in the bus shelter were not affected by WARE's actions, answer A is incorrect.

Road Policing, para. 3.3.6.1

Answer 3.13

Answer **B** — Under s. 3ZB of the Road Traffic Act 1988 a person is guilty of an offence if he or she causes the death of another person by driving a motor vehicle on a road, and at the time the circumstances are such that he or she is committing an offence under:

(a) section 87(1) of this Act (driving otherwise than in accordance with a licence); or

(b) ...

(c) section 143 of this Act (using a motor vehicle while uninsured or unsecured against third party risks).

This offence was initially construed as a 'but for' offence, i.e. 'but for' the presence of the person on a road at the time, who was disqualified, had no insurance or no driving licence, a fatality may not have occurred. This was confirmed by the Court of Appeal in *R v Williams* [2010] EWCA Crim 2552, where the deceased walked directly into the path of the uninsured defendant's car. The conviction was upheld despite the lack of any fault in the quality of the defendant's driving.

However, in *R v Hughes* [2013] UKSC 56, their lordships made clear that the 'but for' interpretation 'confuses criminal responsibility for the serious offence of being uninsured with criminal responsibility for the infinitely more serious offence of killing another person'. The following directions should be made to the jury where such an offence is charged:

> ... it is not necessary for the Crown to prove careless or inconsiderate driving, but there must be something open to proper criticism in the driving of the defendant, beyond the mere presence of the vehicle on the road, and which contributed in some more than minimal way to the death.

Answers A and C are therefore incorrect.

The elements in relation to 'causing the death of' and 'another person' are, generally, the same as those under s. 1. In *R v Hennigan* [1971] 3 All ER 133, it was held that the driving by the defendant must be shown to have been a cause of the death; it is not necessary to show that it was the sole or even a substantial cause of death. It is irrelevant whether or not the person killed contributed to the incident which resulted in his/her death (*R v Girdler* [2009] EWCA Crim 2666). The heart attack, which arguably occurred as a result of the collision, *could* result in a person being charged in these circumstances (provided all the other elements of the offence are present); therefore, answer D is incorrect.

Road Policing, paras 3.3.7, 3.3.2.1

Answer 3.14

Answer **B** — Under s. 3ZD of the Road Traffic Act 1988, a person is guilty of an offence if he or she:

(a) causes serious injury to another person by driving a motor vehicle on a road, and
(b) at that time, is committing an offence under section 103(1)(b) of this Act (driving while disqualified)...

Causing the *death* of another person, whilst committing an offence under s. 103(1)(b), is a separate offence under s. 3ZC; since the offence under s. 3ZD may be committed by causing a serious injury to another person, answer C is incorrect.

There is no offence of causing serious injury to another person whilst committing an offence under s. 143 of the Act (driving without insurance); this behaviour is covered in s. 3ZB, where a driver must cause the death of a person. Answers A and D are therefore incorrect.

Road Policing, para. 3.3.7

Answer 3.15

Answer **D** — Breaching certain road traffic regulations will always be *potentially* relevant evidence of poor driving, but will not always be conclusive of the issue. Answer A is therefore incorrect.

Also, colliding with another vehicle has been held *not* to amount to sufficient evidence in itself of careless driving and therefore answer B is incorrect.

Finally, simply breaching the regulations at a pedestrian crossing is not of itself proof that the person's driving fell below the required standard (*Gibbons* v *Kahl* [1956] 1 QB 59). Answer C is therefore incorrect.

It should be noted that the fact that a traffic signal is showing a green light does *not* mean that a driver is entitled to assume that no other person or vehicle might be proceeding from another direction and it may be that, in the circumstances, a reasonably careful driver would have anticipated that a pedestrian or other road user might still move into his or her path (see *Goddard and Walker* v *Greenwood* [2002] EWCA Civ 1590). However, this case still does not support the point that a person may be prosecuted for a s. 3 offence, without further evidence.

Road Policing, para. 3.3.8.1

Answer 3.16

Answer **D** — Under s. 38(7) of the Road Traffic Act 1988, a failure on the part of a person to observe a provision of the Highway Code shall not of itself render that person liable to criminal proceedings of any kind. However, any such failure may be introduced into civil *or* criminal proceedings. Answer B is therefore incorrect.

The stopping distances shown in the Highway Code are not admissible in proving speeding cases in court, as they amount to hearsay (*R* v *Chadwick* [1975] Crim LR 105). Answer C is incorrect, because such evidence may not be introduced into *all* civil and criminal proceedings.

The failure to observe a provision of the Highway Code may be introduced to establish *or* negate any liability as to a person's driving, therefore, it may be introduced by the prosecution or the defence, and therefore answer A is incorrect.

Road Policing, para. 3.3.9

Answer 3.17

Answer **B** — Under s. 168(b) of the Road Traffic Act 1988, the rider of a cycle who is alleged to have committed an offence under s. 28 or s. 29 of this Act (dangerous or careless cycling), who refuses, on being so required by any person having reasonable grounds for so requiring, to give his or her name or address, or gives a false name or address, is guilty of an offence.

Since the rider must give these details to *any person having reasonable grounds for so requiring,* answer C is incorrect.

The offences to which this section applies include dangerous *and* careless cycling; therefore, answer D is incorrect.

Finally, there is no requirement for a person to be injured as a result of the driving and therefore answer A is incorrect.

Road Policing, para. 3.3.11

Answer 3.18

Answer **A** — Under s. 168 of the Road Traffic Act 1988, the driver of a mechanically propelled vehicle who is alleged to have committed an offence under s. 2 or s. 3 of the Act, who refuses, on being so required by any person having reasonable grounds for so requiring, to give his name or address, or gives a false name or address, is guilty of an offence. Since the offence applies to those who refuse *or* those who give false details, answer D is incorrect.

The section uses the word 'refuses', but makes no mention of a failure to provide the required details. Section 11 of the Road Traffic Act 1988 states:

(1) The following provisions apply for the interpretation of sections 3A to 10 of this Act.
(2) In those sections—'drug' includes any intoxicant other than alcohol, 'fail' includes refuse...

The interpretation of 'fail' in s. 11 of the Road Traffic Act 1988 only applies to ss. 3A to 10 of the Act, and not to s. 168, and although subs. (2) makes provision for a 'failure' to include a 'refusal' (in relation to drink-driving offences), the Act says nothing about a vice versa situation. Given that omission, together with the fact that the courts have held (albeit in an employment law case) that 'failure' is not synonymous with 'refusal' (see *Lowson* v *Percy Main & District Social Club and Institute Ltd* [1979] ICR 568), it would seem that a mere failure to provide the details required under s. 168 will not amount to the offence. Answers B and C are therefore incorrect.

Don't forget that the original offence is still committed and there is existing legislation to take the offender to court to answer that charge.

Road Policing, para. 3.3.11

4 | Reportable Accidents

STUDY PREPARATION

The law relating to road traffic 'accidents' is primarily concerned with obligations on the drivers involved and the offences for failing to comply with those obligations.

You need to be able to recognise from the fact pattern of a question whether an 'accident' has happened. Then you need to know what obligations the law imposes and upon whom. You also need to know any offences which may apply, along with the attendant police powers.

QUESTIONS

Question 4.1

YEW was riding a pedal cycle along the road late at night without lights and, failing to see a car parked at the side of the road, collided with it. As a result of the collision, YEW was injured and damage was caused to the cycle and the car. YEW knocked on the door of the nearest house and woke up PRICE, who turned out to be the owner of the car. YEW demanded to know PRICE's insurance details.

What will be PRICE's liability in relation to providing these details or reporting the accident to the police, under s. 170 of the Road Traffic Act 1988?

A An accident has occurred owing to the presence of a motor vehicle on a road, which means that PRICE must provide details, including insurance, to YEW.

B PRICE does not have to provide any details to YEW, but must report the accident to the police as soon as reasonably practical.

C PRICE has no obligations at all under s. 170, in these circumstances.

D PRICE has no obligations under s. 170, provided the car was lawfully parked.

Question 4.2

The police were called to an incident in a large public park, in which members of the public were allowed to drive vehicles in certain areas on tarmac 'roads'. The roads lacked the usual signage and were single-tracked. A member of staff, PEARCE, reported that a car had been in a queue, but being impatient, the driver had over-taken several vehicles to get out of the park quickly. In doing so the person had driven over some flower beds, causing damage to the plants and the grass adjacent to the beds. PEARCE had taken the registration number of the car, which had driven off without stopping.

Would this amount to a 'reportable accident', under s. 170 of the Road Traffic Act 1988?

A Yes, damage has been caused to property growing on land.

B Yes, but only in relation to the flower beds; grass would not amount to 'property' for the purposes of s. 170.

C No, plants and grass would not amount to 'property' for the purposes of s. 170.

D No, the 'accident' did not occur on a road.

Question 4.3

JIMENEZ was driving a Motorhome on the motorway and was towing a Smart car behind the Motorhome, which the family would use as a runaround when they reached their holiday destination. As JIMENEZ was driving, the tow hitch attaching the Smart car to the Motorhome broke and the car detached itself, falling away from the towing vehicle. The Smart car collided with another car which was driving behind JIMENEZ, causing damage to both vehicles.

Considering s. 170 of the Road Traffic Act 1988, which of the following statements is correct, in respect of 'reportable accidents'?

A The Smart car was not a mechanically propelled vehicle as it was being towed; therefore, a reportable accident has not occurred in these circumstances.

B The Smart car was not a mechanically propelled vehicle as it was not being 'driven' while it was being towed; therefore, a reportable accident has not occurred in these circumstances.

C The Smart car was neither a mechanically propelled vehicle nor a trailer while it was being towed; therefore, a reportable accident has not occurred in these circumstances.

D An accident has occurred owing to the presence of a mechanically propelled vehicle on a road; therefore, it is irrelevant whether the Smart car was being towed or not.

Question 4.4

While driving his car, DAWSON was involved in a road traffic accident with a motorcycle being ridden by WINTER. WINTER suffered cuts and grazes as a result. The drivers exchanged details and WINTER asked DAWSON for his insurance certificate. DAWSON did not have it with him, but gave WINTER the name of his insurance company and promised to show him the certificate the next day.

Has DAWSON complied with the requirements of s. 170 of the Road Traffic Act 1988 in these circumstances?

A Yes, he is not obliged to produce his insurance certificate to another driver, provided he gives the name of his insurance company.

B No, he must report the accident to the police as soon as reasonably practicable, and produce his insurance certificate within seven days.

C No, he must report the accident to the police as soon as reasonably practicable, and produce his insurance certificate at the same time.

D Yes, provided he produces his insurance certificate to WINTER within 24 hours.

Question 4.5

PARKS was involved in a road traffic accident, having pulled out of a side street and collided with a car being driven by ZIMMERMAN; damage was caused to both vehicles. The drivers stopped and exchanged mobile telephone numbers at the scene. They decided they would not exchange their names and addresses until they had taken their cars to their own garages to obtain estimates for the amount of damage caused. They arranged to contact each other in the next couple of days to decide what to do.

Considering a driver's duty to stop and report accidents, under s. 170 of the Road Traffic Act 1988, which of the following statements is correct in respect of PARKS' and ZIMMERMAN's actions?

A They have exchanged details at the scene of the accident and have complied with s. 170 in these circumstances.

B Because they have not exchanged the correct details, they have not complied with s. 170 and both commit an offence.

C They have not complied with s. 170 in these circumstances, but would commit no offence if they report the accident to the police.

D They have not complied with s. 170 in these circumstances, but would commit no offence if PARKS reports the accident to the police, as the person who was at fault.

Question 4.6

DERBYSHIRE was driving a motor vehicle on a road when she received a mobile phone call. DERBYSHIRE answered the call but did not have a hands-free kit and she pulled over to the side of the road, continuing the conversation. While on the phone, DERBYSHIRE realised she needed some information that was in a briefcase in the back of the car. She opened the driver's door, intending to get her briefcase. However, she was unaware that BEVAN was passing her vehicle at the time on a pedal cycle. DERBYSHIRE's actions caused BEVAN to collide with the car door and BEVAN was injured, falling off the cycle.

Because of her actions, does DERBYSHIRE attract any responsibility under s. 170 of the Road Traffic Act 1988 (duty of a driver to stop and exchange details) in these circumstances?

A Yes, provided the engine of DERBYSHIRE's vehicle was still running when she opened the door.

B No, DERBYSHIRE was not driving when the accident occurred.

C Yes, provided it can be shown that DERBYSHIRE was at fault for the accident.

D Yes, whether or not the engine was still running, or whether or not she was at fault for the accident.

Question 4.7

MILLER drove a bus with 16 passenger seats and was employed by the local authority to drive children to school. The bus was approaching a set of traffic lights near the school at which there was a queue of vehicles. MILLER had lost concentration and had to brake sharply on the approach. This resulted in one of the school children falling over and banging their head. MILLER was told that one of the children was injured, but decided to carry on driving to the school, which was about 100 metres away.

Considering the driver's duty to stop, under s. 170(2) of the Road Traffic Act 1988, which of the following statements is correct in respect of MILLER's actions?

A The driver is required to stop at or near the scene and 100 metres away is not an unreasonable distance.

B The driver is required to stop at the scene and MILLER has failed to do so in these circumstances.

C The driver is required to stop at the scene; however, because damage has not been caused to another vehicle, MILLER's actions are not unreasonable in these circumstances.

D Because the injury was to a passenger in the bus, the bus could be considered to be the scene and MILLER's actions are not unreasonable in these circumstances.

Question 4.8

McLEOD appeared in court, having been charged with driving whilst over the limit for alcohol and other offences relating to a road traffic accident. It was alleged that the defendant had been driving along a narrow street with cars parked on both sides, and had scraped the rear wing of one of the cars, before driving away without stopping. McLEOD pleaded guilty to drink-driving and driving without due care and attention, but not guilty to failing to stop and failing to report the accident. McLEOD claimed he did not know he had been involved in an accident, having had too much to drink.

In relation to any possible defence McLEOD may have for failing to stop at the scene of an accident, which of the following statements is correct?

A The prosecution would have to prove beyond reasonable doubt that an accident had occurred and that McLEOD was aware he had been involved in it.

B McLEOD would have to prove on the balance of probabilities that he was not aware he had been involved in an accident; he may have a defence in these circumstances.

C McLEOD would have to prove on the balance of probabilities that he was not aware he had been involved in an accident, but he would have no defence in these circumstances.

D A driver is responsible for their own actions and there is no specific defence for failing to stop at an accident.

Question 4.9

SAKI was involved in a road traffic accident, having driven into a stationary car in a rural area, late at night. SAKI tried to find the owner, but was unsuccessful. SAKI then found a police station nearby, but the station was closed. Finally, SAKI drove home, intending to report the accident in the morning.

Which of the following is correct in respect of SAKI's duty to report the accident under s. 170 of the Road Traffic Act 1988?

A SAKI has made reasonable efforts to report the accident; provided it is reported within 24 hours, s. 170 will have been complied with.

B Although SAKI has made efforts to report the accident, it must still be reported as soon as practicable, in person to a constable.

C Although SAKI has made efforts to report the accident, it must still be reported as soon as practicable, in person to a constable or at a police station.

D SAKI may report the accident by telephone, having made reasonable efforts to report it in person, provided this is done as soon as practicable.

Question 4.10

NEWENT was driving a car on the road. Due to a lack of concentration, NEWENT collided with a trailer, which had been left at the side of the road, unattached to a motor vehicle. Damage was caused to both NEWENT's car and the trailer.

Which of the following statements is correct in respect of NEWENT's duty to comply with the requirements of s. 170 of the Road Traffic Act 1988 (stopping and reporting an accident)?

A The trailer is not a vehicle, as it was not being drawn by a motor vehicle; therefore, s. 170 does not apply in these circumstances.

B The trailer is not a vehicle as it was not attached to a motor vehicle; therefore, s. 170 does not apply in these circumstances.

C The trailer is a vehicle; therefore, s. 170 does apply in these circumstances.

D The trailer is not a vehicle, but is property; therefore, s. 170 does apply in these circumstances.

Question 4.11

HULL is employed as a care worker for the elderly. HULL had taken BROOKFIELD (aged 85 years) to a shopping centre and on the way home was involved in a road traffic accident. BROOKFIELD (seated in the front passenger seat) suffered shock and HULL suffered whiplash as a consequence of the accident. HULL was concerned about her position as a care worker and decided not to report the accident, hoping that BROOKFIELD would not tell anyone and no one would notice that she had suffered from shock. Two days later, BROOKFIELD's daughter found out about the incident and contacted the police. By then, however, BROOKFIELD had recovered from her shock.

Would HULL be guilty of an offence under s. 170(4) of the Road Traffic Act 1988 (failing to report) in these circumstances?

A Yes, the offence is complete.

B No, because the personal injuries were caused to people in HULL's car only.

C No, the shock suffered by BROOKFIELD is not classed as a personal injury.

D No, the shock suffered by BROOKFIELD was not a permanent or lasting injury.

Question 4.12

OXLADE was driving a car on a road at 2 am in icy conditions when she lost control of the vehicle resulting in it colliding with a set of bollards. The bollards were completely demolished and there was damage to OXLADE's car, but it was still driveable. Unknown to OXLADE, a witness was watching from a shop doorway and saw her get out of the car, examine the damage caused and wait at the scene for a little while, before getting back into the car and driving off. The witness took the registration number.

Which of the following statements is correct, in relation to OXLADE's actions?

A OXLADE will be guilty of failing to stop and giving details to anyone at the scene.

B OXLADE has not failed to stop at this stage, provided she reports the accident to the police as soon as reasonably practicable.

C Because she has damaged property and is unlikely to be able to give details to the owner, OXLADE should have contacted the police from the scene.

D OXLADE has not failed to stop at this stage, provided she reports the accident to the police within 24 hours.

Question 4.13

SANDHURST was driving along a country lane which led to a popular beach. There were cars parked on either side of the lane and SANDHURST clipped the side of a vehicle, causing damage to it. There were people in the vicinity walking to the beach, none of whom appeared to be connected to the parked vehicle. SANDHURST was concerned about causing an obstruction to the lane and, after a few minutes, left a note under the windscreen wiper of the vehicle with a contact telephone number.

Which of the following statements is correct, in relation to SANDHURST's duties under s. 170(2) of the Road Traffic Act 1988 (requirement to stop after an accident)?

A SANDHURST was required to remain at the scene for such a time as would allow her to give her details to the owner of the vehicle.

B SANDHURST was required to remain at the scene for such a time as would allow anyone having a right or reason for doing so to ask for her details.

C SANDHURST was required to remain at the scene for such a time as would allow any person to ask for her details.

D SANDHURST was required to remain at the scene for such a time as would allow her to give her details to the owner of the vehicle, or alternatively, for her to make enquiries to find such a person.

Question 4.14

JORDAN was involved in a road traffic accident when he drove into a parked vehicle, causing damage to it. JORDAN sustained a head injury during the accident and was taken to the nearest hospital by BRUIN, a passenger in his vehicle at the time. JORDAN was detained at the hospital, eventually being released 12 hours after the accident.

Which of the following statements is correct, in relation to s. 170(3) of the Road Traffic Act 1988 (duty to report an accident)?

A JORDAN must report the accident within 24 hours; however, s. 170(3) allows for a reasonable time in which to comply, when the *defendant* is unable to make the report.

B JORDAN has up to 24 hours to report the accident; therefore, he has another 12 hours in which to comply with s. 170(3).

C JORDAN must report the accident within 24 hours; it does not matter what the reason for the non-provision of the information is.

D JORDAN must report the accident within 24 hours; however, s. 170(3) allows for a reasonable time in which to comply, where the *police* are unavailable to take the report.

Question 4.15

MOLINA was involved in a road traffic accident late at night and made off from the scene. Constable HAMPTON managed to trace MOLINA the next day, and during interview she admitted failing to stop after the accident, stating that she had done so because she had been drinking beforehand and thought she may have been over the prescribed limit. Constable HAMPTON conducted a breath test procedure which was negative and then consulted with the Crown Prosecution Service (CPS), to discuss whether there was sufficient evidence to charge MOLINA with perverting the course of justice, alongside the offences under s. 170 of the Road Traffic Act 1988 (failing to stop and failing to report an accident).

Which of the following statements is correct, in relation to the offence of perverting the course of justice in these circumstances?

A MOLINA's actions amounted to an omission, which was sufficient to convict her of this offence.

B By leaving the scene and allowing passage of time to dissipate the level of alcohol in her body, MOLINA avoided a conviction for drink-driving and was guilty of this offence.

C MOLINA's actions amounted to a positive act, which was sufficient to convict her of this offence.

D Although MOLINA left the scene of the accident to avoid a conviction for drink-driving, without more evidence she was unlikely to be convicted of this offence.

ANSWERS

Answer 4.1

Answer **C** — Under s. 170(2) of the Road Traffic Act 1988, the driver of a mechanically propelled vehicle involved in an accident must stop and, if required to do so by any person having reasonable grounds for so requiring, give his or her name and address and also the name and address of the owner and the identification marks of the vehicle.

Since it is the *driver* of a vehicle who has obligations following an accident, and PRICE was asleep in bed when it occurred, s. 170 does not apply in these circumstances even though, technically, a road traffic 'accident' has occurred under the definition. Answers A and B are therefore incorrect.

It is irrelevant whether or not the vehicle was lawfully parked—this does not alter the obligations of a driver under s. 170, and answer D is incorrect.

Road Policing, para. 3.4.2

Answer 4.2

Answer **A** — Under s. 170(1)(b)(iii) of the Road Traffic Act 1988, if owing to the presence of a mechanically propelled vehicle on a road or other public place, an accident occurs by which damage is caused to any other property constructed on, fixed to, growing in or otherwise forming part of the land on which the road or place in question is situated or land adjacent to such land, there will be a requirement on the driver to stop and report the accident.

This duty applies to accidents on a road *or* a public place. This addition was unsuccessfully contested in the courts (*R (On the Application of Parker) v Crown Court at Bradford* [2006] EWHC 3213 (Admin)). Answer D is therefore incorrect.

Damage has been caused to both the plants *and* the grass growing in or otherwise forming part of the land in the public place; therefore, the accident is 'reportable' in relation to both items of property and answers B and C are incorrect.

Road Policing, para. 3.4.2

Answer 4.3

Answer **D** — When a motor vehicle is towing another motor vehicle, the latter still falls within the category of motor vehicle, but can also be regarded as a 'trailer'

(*Milstead* v *Sexton* [1964] Crim LR 474) and it is irrelevant whether the towed vehicle is being 'driven' at the time. Answers A, B and C are therefore incorrect.

However, the issue of whether the Smart car was a motor vehicle, a mechanically propelled vehicle or a trailer is irrelevant. The duties to stop and report accidents under s. 170 of the Road Traffic Act 1988 apply where, owing to the presence of a mechanically propelled vehicle on a road or other public place, an accident occurs by which personal injury is caused to a person other than the driver of that mechanically propelled vehicle, or damage is caused:

- to a vehicle other than that mechanically propelled vehicle or a trailer drawn by that mechanically propelled vehicle; or
- to an animal other than an animal in or on that mechanically propelled vehicle or a trailer drawn by that mechanically propelled vehicle; or
- to any other property constructed on, fixed to, growing in or otherwise forming part of the land on which the road or place in question is situated or land adjacent to such land.

The accident in these circumstances occurred owing to the presence of a mechanically propelled vehicle on a road, the Motorhome, and damage was caused to another vehicle. The presence of the Motorhome on the road, towing the Smart car, was the cause of the accident and it would be no different, for example, if a roof box had fallen off the Motorhome and damaged the vehicle behind it—damage would still have occurred to another vehicle, owing to the presence of the Motorhome on a road.

Road Policing, para. 3.4.2

Answer 4.4

Answer **C** — If a driver is involved in an accident where injury is caused to another person, he or she must, at the time of the accident, produce a certificate of insurance to a constable *or* any person having reasonable grounds for requiring it (s. 170(5) of the Road Traffic Act 1988). Answer A is therefore incorrect.

If the driver does not produce his or her insurance certificate as required, he or she *must* report the accident to the police *and* produce an insurance certificate as soon as practicable, and in any case within 24 hours (s. 170(6)).

Answer D is incorrect as once a driver fails to produce a certificate at the scene to the other driver, the requirement moves to reporting the accident and producing the certificate to the police.

Answer B is incorrect as the requirement is to report the accident *and* produce the insurance certificate as soon as practicable and within 24 hours. Under s. 170(7) of the 1988 Act, a person will escape prosecution for failing to produce insurance at the time of the accident, or later at the police station, if he or she produces it within seven days from the accident (usually as a result of the issue of an HORT/1). Therefore, although answer B may appear correct, the *first* process must be to report the accident and produce the certificate as soon as practicable.

Road Policing, paras 3.4.2, 3.4.3

Answer 4.5

Answer **C** — Under s. 170(2) of the Road Traffic Act 1988, the driver of a mechanically propelled vehicle involved in an accident must stop and, if required to do so by any person having reasonable grounds for so requiring, give his/her name and address and also the name and address of the owner and the identification marks of the vehicle. If for any reason the driver of the mechanically propelled vehicle does not give his or her name and address under subs. (2), he or she must report the accident (s. 170(3)).

Clearly, neither of the drivers involved in this accident has fully complied with the requirements of s. 170, because of the details they have exchanged. A failure to provide any details because they have not been requested, e.g. because no one asks for them or no one is at the scene of the accident, would not constitute an offence. However, if, *for any reason whatsoever*, the driver does not provide his/her name and address to anyone, the driver must report the accident to the police. Therefore, even though they have agreed not to exchange these details, they are obliged to report the matter to the police and answer A is incorrect.

The offence under this section is not complete unless the driver, having failed to exchange details correctly at the scene, also fails to report the matter to the police. Answer B is therefore incorrect.

Section 170 of the Act does not distinguish between drivers who are at fault and those who are not; drivers have their own duties to exchange details and report the matter to the police if they have been involved in a reportable accident. Answer D is therefore incorrect.

In practical terms, the police may be quite happy for drivers to sort out accidents such as this between themselves; however, according to the Act, the drivers should have reported the matter to the police because they did not exchange the correct details at the scene.

Road Policing, paras 3.4.2, 3.4.2.2

Answer 4.6

Answer **D** — It has been held that even though a driver may not have been to blame for an accident, he or she will still attract the duties imposed by s. 170 of the Road Traffic Act 1988 (*Harding* v *Price* [1948] 1 All ER 283). Answer C is therefore incorrect.

For the purposes of some road traffic offences, the person who takes out the vehicle remains the 'driver' of it until they have finished that journey. Therefore, even if the vehicle is stationary and has been for some time, a person may still be the 'driver' of it if they have not completed the journey (see *Jones* v *Prothero* [1952] 1 All ER 434, where the driver sitting in a parked car opened the offside door causing injury to a passing pedal cyclist).

A further example was seen in *Cawthorn* v *DPP* [2000] RTR 45, where the defendant stopped his car on a hill in order to post a letter and activated the hazard warning lights. While he was away from the vehicle, it started to roll down the hill and hit and damaged a wall. The roll was started by a passenger releasing the handbrake. The defendant left the scene and was subsequently convicted of failing to stop and exchange details and failing to report an accident. The Divisional Court said that, although there had been a break in the driving, the appellant was still making his journey as evidenced by the use of the hazard warning lights. The intervening act by the passenger did not make that passenger the driver.

Both *Jones* and *Cawthorn* relate to the obligations of a 'driver' under s. 170 of the Road Traffic Act 1988 and confirm that a person in DERBYSHIRE's circumstances *could* still have been driving when the accident occurred, and could have been so whether the engine of the vehicle was running or not. Answers A and B are therefore incorrect.

Road Policing, paras 3.4.2, 3.1.6

Answer 4.7

Answer **B** — The requirement to stop under s. 170(2) of the Road Traffic Act 1988 means to stop safely and remain *at the scene* for such a time as would allow anyone having a right or reason for doing so to ask for information from the driver (*Lee* v *Knapp* [1967] 2 QB 442). Whether or not the vehicle stops at the appropriate point is a question of fact; where a driver chose to drive on for 80 yards before stopping and returning to the scene of the accident, the Divisional Court was not prepared to interfere with a decision finding that this constituted a failure to stop as required (*McDermott* v *DPP* [1997] RTR 474). The offence is complete as soon as the failure to stop occurs. Answer A is therefore incorrect.

Where a bus driver braked hard, causing injury to one of his passengers, the Divisional Court held that he had a duty to stop at the place and the time that the passenger was caused to be injured. It was not open to the driver to claim that the bus itself was the scene of the accident. The fact that the driver failed to stop immediately meant that he was guilty of an offence under s. 170(4) (*Hallinan* v *DPP* [1998] Crim LR 754)—this is regardless of whether any other vehicles are involved and therefore answers C and D are incorrect.

Road Policing, paras 3.4.2, 3.4.2.1

Answer 4.8

Answer **C** — In order to attract the duties under s. 170(2) of the Road Traffic Act 1988, the driver must know of the accident (*Harding* v *Price* [1948] 1 KB 695). Answer D is incorrect, because it *is* possible to raise a defence if the driver did not know he/she had been involved in the accident.

Once the prosecution has proved that an accident to which s. 170 applies has occurred, it is for the *driver* to show (on the balance of probabilities) that they were unaware of its occurrence (*Selby* v *Chief Constable of Avon and Somerset* [1988] RTR 216). Answer A is therefore incorrect.

Finally, the Divisional Court has held that a driver cannot rely on the fact that they were drunk as to whether they were aware an accident had occurred or not. The court stated that even if it could properly find that the appellant was unaware of the accident because of their drunken state, they could not rely upon that as a defence. The defendant would have been able to rely on it had they been sober, but not where they were voluntarily intoxicated (*Magee* v *Crown Prosecution Service* [2014] EWHC 4089 (Admin)). Answer B is therefore incorrect.

Road Policing, para. 3.4.2

Answer 4.9

Answer **C** — Under s. 170(2) of the Road Traffic Act 1988, the driver of a mechanically propelled vehicle involved in an accident must stop and, if required to do so by any person having reasonable grounds for so requiring, give his or her name and address and also the name and address of the owner and the identification marks of the vehicle.

If for any reason the driver of the mechanically propelled vehicle does not give his or her name and address under subs. (2), he or she must report the accident (s. 170(3)).

Under s. 170(6), to comply with this duty, the driver:

(a) must do so at a police station or to a constable, and
(b) must do so as soon as is reasonably practicable and, in any case, within twenty-four hours of the occurrence of the accident.

Section 170(6)(a) allows for the accident to be reported *either* at a police station *or* to a constable. Therefore, if the accident is reported at a police station, the provisions of s. 170(6) will be met even if the person receiving the report is a police staff member—which reflects the reality of modern policing, where most station enquiry offices are staffed by police staff members and not police officers. Alternatively, the accident can be reported to a police officer (either at a police station or anywhere else). Answer B is therefore incorrect.

This must also be done *in person*; telephoning (and presumably sending a fax or email to) a police station is not enough (*Wisdom* v *McDonald* [1983] RTR 186). Answer D is therefore incorrect.

The driver is not given 24 hours to report the accident—in most circumstances there is no reason for an accident not to be reported as soon as practicable because of the availability of police officers 24 hours a day. Therefore, even though the person in the question has tried to contact the police, there is still a requirement to report the accident as soon as practicable. Answer A is therefore incorrect.

Road Policing, paras 3.4.2, 3.4.2.4

Answer 4.10

Answer **C** — The duties to stop and report accidents under s. 170 of the Road Traffic Act 1988 apply where, owing to the presence of a mechanically propelled vehicle on a road or other public place, an accident occurs by which personal injury is caused to a person other than the driver of that mechanically propelled vehicle, or damage is caused:

- to a vehicle other than that mechanically propelled vehicle or a trailer drawn by that mechanically propelled vehicle; or
- to an animal other than an animal in or on that mechanically propelled vehicle or a trailer drawn by that mechanically propelled vehicle; or
- to any other property constructed on, fixed to, growing in or otherwise forming part of the land on which the road or place in question is situated or land adjacent to such land.

In the first instance, the trailer cannot be 'property'; therefore, answer D is incorrect.

A 'trailer' is defined under s. 185(1) of the Act as a vehicle drawn by a motor vehicle. However, the definition under this section applies to circumstances when the trailer is being drawn by a motor vehicle (the 'offending vehicle') and damage is caused to something other than that trailer. The definition under s. 185(1) is irrelevant for the purposes of this question.

The next thing to establish is whether the trailer is a 'vehicle' in its own right, because s. 170 applies when damage is caused to a vehicle other than that mechanically propelled vehicle or a trailer drawn by that mechanically propelled vehicle. 'Vehicle' is not defined in the Act; the *Oxford English Dictionary* defines a 'vehicle' as a 'carriage or conveyance of any kind used on land'. In addition, the courts have ruled that virtually anything is capable of amounting to a vehicle under the right circumstances, even a chicken shed on wheels (see *Garner* v *Burr* [1951] 1 KB 31) or a hut (*Horn* v *Dobson* [1933] JC 1). In *Ellis* v *Nott-Bower* (1896) 60 JP 760, the court held that damage caused under the circumstances set out at s. 170(1)(b) applies to any vehicle (such as bicycles) and not just one which is mechanically propelled.

It follows, therefore, that a trailer parked at the side of the road will be a vehicle, even though it is not being drawn by, or is not attached to, a motor vehicle, and if damage is caused to it during a reportable accident, s. 170 will apply. Answers A and B are therefore incorrect.

Road Policing, paras 3.4.2, 3.1.3

Answer 4.11

Answer **A** — If the driver of the vehicle is the only person injured, it will not be a 'reportable' accident; it will, however, be reportable if the passenger in the vehicle is injured. Answer B is therefore incorrect.

Injury under s. 170 has been held to include shock and, given the developments in the area of assaults, it would appear that psychological harm may well amount to an 'injury' for these purposes. Answer C is therefore incorrect.

It is immaterial whether the injury was 'permanent or lasting' and for that reason answer D is incorrect.

Road Policing, paras 3.4.2, 3.4.2.3

Answer 4.12

Answer **B** — Under s. 170(2) of the Road Traffic Act 1988, the driver of a mechanically propelled vehicle involved in an accident must stop and, if required to do so by any person having reasonable grounds for so requiring, give his or her name and address and also the name and address of the owner and the identification marks of the vehicle.

If for any reason the driver of the mechanically propelled vehicle does not give his or her name and address under subs. (2), he or she must report the accident (s. 170(3)).

Under s. 170(6), to comply with this duty, the driver:

(a) must do so at a police station or to a constable, and
(b) must do so as soon as is reasonably practicable and, in any case, within twenty-four hours of the occurrence of the accident.

'Stop' under s. 170(2) means to stop safely and remain at the scene for such a time as would allow anyone having a right or reason for doing so to ask for information from the driver (*Lee* v *Knapp* [1967] 2 QB 442); it does not require the driver to make enquiries of his or her own to try and find such a person (see *Mutton* v *Bates* [1984] RTR 256). OXLADE has actually stopped at the scene in these circumstances and when no one required any details, she was entitled to leave the scene. Answer A is therefore incorrect.

The driver's duties are the same whether they have been involved in an accident with another vehicle, a person, an animal or property. The onus is still on OXLADE to report the matter as described in s. 172(6). Of course, the police may well attend the scene if the witness reports the matter, but OXLADE cannot rely on the police attending to enable her to report the matter as they may be busy elsewhere. Answer C is incorrect.

The first duty is to report the accident to the police as soon as reasonably practicable—the 24 hours is a maximum time period. In modern times, it should be possible to report a matter at any time of the day and OXLADE should do this straight away. Answer D is therefore incorrect.

Road Policing, paras 3.4.2, 3.4.2.1

Answer 4.13

Answer **B** — Section 170(2) of the Road Traffic Act 1988 states that:

the driver of the mechanically propelled vehicle must stop and, if required to do so by any person having reasonable grounds for so requiring, give his name and address and also the name and address of the owner and the identification marks of the vehicle.

'Stop' under s. 170(2) means to stop safely and remain at the scene for such a time as would allow anyone having a right or reason for doing so to ask for information from the driver (*Lee* v *Knapp* [1967] 2 QB 442). The requirement under s. 170(2) is not so narrow that the driver must remain at the scene to only provide details to the *owner* of the vehicle (answer A is therefore incorrect); conversely, the requirement is not so wide that the driver must remain to provide details to *any person*. Answer C is therefore incorrect.

Section 170(2) does *not* require the driver to make enquiries of his or her own to try and find such a person (see *Mutton* v *Bates* [1984] RTR 256) and for that reason answer D is incorrect.

Note that this duty also appears to require the driver to stay with his or her vehicle for a reasonable time (see *Ward* v *Rawson* [1978] RTR 498), but it does not require the driver to remain there indefinitely (*Norling* v *Woolacott* [1964] SASR 377).

Road Policing, para. 3.4.2.1

Answer 4.14

Answer **C** — Under s. 170(3) of the Road Traffic Act 1988, if there are no other persons in the vicinity to whom the information may be given, then the matter must be reported to a police officer or at a police station as soon as is reasonably practicable and, in any case, within 24 hours of the occurrence of the accident.

Section 170(3) does not allow for a reasonable time in which to comply, when the defendant is unable to make the report, or where the police are unavailable to take the report; therefore, answers A and D are incorrect.

The report must be made as soon as reasonably practicable (which will be a question of fact for the court to decide in each circumstance) and in any case within 24 hours of the occurrence of the accident. This requirement does *not* give the driver up to 24 hours to report the accident; that report must be made as soon as is reasonably practicable. Answer B is therefore incorrect.

It is possible that, given the requirement that the report must be made as soon as reasonably practicable, the person in this scenario might have a defence for not doing so. However, the section is prescriptive in that if the driver does *not* give his or her name and address, it does not matter what the reason for the non-provision of the information is, even if it is not practicable, or possible, to do so within that time limit (see *Bulman* v *Lakin* [1981] RTR 1).

Road Policing, para. 3.4.2.4

Answer 4.15

Answer **D** — The Court of Appeal refused to accept that a driver who failed to stop and report an accident for fear of being breathalysed did not, without more, commit an offence of perverting the course of justice (*R* v *Clark* [2003] EWCA Crim 991). While it is true that driving home and remaining there allowed the passage of time to dissipate the level of alcohol in the driver's body and thereby avoid conviction for a drink-driving offence, the court was not convinced that this was enough to justify being charged with this offence. Answer B is therefore incorrect.

The court held that the failure to report an accident did *not* amount to a positive act by the defendant (which is required under this statute), which means that answer C is incorrect. On the other hand, even though failing to report an accident may amount to an 'omission' (as opposed to a positive act), the decision in *Clark* clearly outlined the court's unwillingness to convict a person for such a serious offence. Answer A is therefore incorrect.

Road Policing, para. 3.4.3

5 | Drink, Drugs and Driving

> ## STUDY PREPARATION
>
> This is a big one. The areas of law and procedure covered in this chapter are extensive. You will need to know the elements of each of the main drink-driving offences first. Entwined with those offences is a range of police powers such as the powers to require preliminary samples. Failure or refusal to comply with such requirements can lead to further offences and further powers.
>
> It should be noted that the Road Traffic Act 1988 makes references to the availability in law of two devices—one to carry out a preliminary drug test and the other to obtain what is termed as a 'roadside evidential specimen of breath' (not to be confused with a preliminary roadside *screening* test). While this legislation has been in force for some time, it is important to stress that these devices are not widely available for operational use. However, as these provisions are an integral part of the Road Traffic Act 1988, they are both dealt with within this chapter in order to provide the reader with the most complete picture of the current *legislative framework* that exists in relation to drink-drive matters.
>
> This subject area is generally divided into roadside, police station and hospital procedures.
>
> The evidential issues are also important and there is a great deal of established case law to clarify this area of the legislation.

QUESTIONS

Question 5.1

SPEDDING has been convicted in court for driving whilst over the prescribed limit and has been disqualified from driving for 12 months. SPEDDING's defence solicitor has indicated that she would be prepared to attend a drink-drive rehabilitation course, to negotiate a reduction in the disqualification period.

If the court agrees to this course of action, which of the following statements is correct, under the Road Traffic Offenders Act 1988?

A The reduced disqualification period can be no less than three months and no more than nine months.

B The period may only be reduced by three months for a 12-month disqualification.

C The court may reduce the disqualification for any period, provided SPEDDING is disqualified for at least one month.

D The period may only be reduced by six months for a 12-month disqualification.

Question 5.2

Constable BOTAN was walking past a public car park when PALMER called him over. PALMER pointed out HODGES, who was driving around the car park on a quad bike and being cheered on by a group of teenagers. PALMER had seen HODGES drinking cans of lager earlier and was concerned for the safety of people using the car park. Constable BOTAN managed to stop the vehicle and on speaking to HODGES, formed the opinion that he was drunk.

Given that the quad bike was a mechanically propelled vehicle (and not a motor vehicle), has HODGES committed an offence under either s. 4(1) (unfit to drive through drink or drugs) or s. 5(1) (driving while over the prescribed limit) of the Road Traffic Act 1988?

A Yes, under s. 4(1), as HODGES was driving a mechanically propelled vehicle in a public place.

B Yes, under either section, as HODGES was driving a mechanically propelled vehicle in a public place.

C No, HODGES was not driving a motor vehicle on a road.

D No, HODGES was not driving a motor vehicle or a mechanically propelled vehicle on a road.

Question 5.3

Constable LANGLEY was following a vehicle being driven by FORSYTHE. The officer observed the vehicle being driven erratically, swerving across the road. Constable LANGLEY lost sight of the vehicle but, following a computer check, attended FORSYTHE's home address. On arrival, Constable LANGLEY saw FORSYTHE asleep inside the vehicle, which was inside a detached garage, a building adjacent to FORSYTHE's house. The garage door was open.

Given that the officer may have formed a reasonable suspicion that FORSYTHE was drunk, did Constable LANGLEY have the power to enter the garage or the vehicle, under s. 4 of the Road Traffic Act 1988?

A No, because the vehicle was inside a detached garage, which is not a dwelling for the purposes of s. 4.

B Yes, because the vehicle was inside a garage, which is a dwelling for the purposes of s. 4.

C Yes, but only the garage, as a vehicle is not a 'premises' for the purposes of s. 4.

D Yes, both the garage and the vehicle are 'premises' for the purposes of s. 4.

Question 5.4

Constable DERECK attended the Fox and Hounds public house as a result of a call from the licensee, BELL. BELL had seen MEARS enter the premises from the car park in a drunken condition with some friends. They had bought two rounds of drinks when it had been brought to BELL's attention that MEARS had driven to the premises. Constable DERECK spoke to MEARS who admitted he had driven to the premises, but stated that he had only drunk two pints, which had been bought since he'd arrived. BELL was adamant that MEARS had been drunk when he'd arrived and that he was too intoxicated for someone who had only drunk two pints.

Considering the offence under s. 4 of the Road Traffic Act 1988, which of the following statements is correct, in relation to the evidence BELL has provided so far?

A BELL could give an opinion of MEARS's impairment and his ability to drive a vehicle on a road, which would provide sufficient evidence for Constable DERECK to arrest him for this offence.

B BELL's suspicion that MEARS had been drunk when he'd arrived would provide sufficient evidence for Constable DERECK to arrest him for this offence.

C BELL's opinion of MEARS's impairment would not be sufficient; Constable DERECK must formulate a separate reasonable suspicion of the defendant's condition before arresting him.

D BELL's opinion of MEARS's impairment would only provide sufficient evidence for Constable DERECK to arrest him for this offence if BELL was an expert on such matters.

Question 5.5

Constable SATO stopped HENSON who was driving a motor vehicle on a road at night. Constable SATO noticed that HENSON smelled of intoxicants and requested a sample of breath. The screening test proved negative; however, as HENSON was returning to her car, Constable SATO noticed that she was staggering, which gave the officer reason to believe that she was unfit to drive through drink, despite the negative screening test. Constable SATO then arrested HENSON under s. 4 of the Road Traffic Act 1988 (unfit to drive through drink or drugs).

Did Constable SATO act correctly in these circumstances?

A Yes, the officer was entitled to arrest HENSON in these circumstances alone.

B No, Constable SATO should have required HENSON to provide a further sample of breath before making this decision.

C No, Constable SATO could not have formed a reasonable suspicion that HENSON was unfit to drive through drink, as the screening test was negative.

D No, the arrest would only have been lawful if Constable SATO had suspected HENSON was unfit to drive through drugs.

Question 5.6

BEDFORD is appealing against a conviction for driving a motor vehicle on a road, while over the prescribed limit. The circumstances were that BEDFORD was on a night out and was bought several alcoholic drinks by friends. BEDFORD claims that she had told her friends to buy her soft drinks and she was unaware that the drinks she had consumed contained alcohol.

Which of the following statements is correct, regarding the responsibility BEDFORD had in relation to the proportion of alcohol in her body?

A BEDFORD had some positive duty to enquire whether the drinks contained alcohol before consuming them.

B BEDFORD had an absolute duty to enquire whether the drinks contained alcohol before consuming them.

C BEDFORD had no particular duty to enquire whether the drinks contained alcohol before consuming them.

D If BEDFORD's claim is correct, her friends had an absolute duty to inform her that the drinks contained alcohol before she consumed them.

Question 5.7

SHELLEY was charged with an offence of being in charge of his motor vehicle on a road, while over the prescribed limit, having been found asleep at the wheel of the vehicle one night. At his court hearing, SHELLEY claimed that he would not have driven the vehicle while he was still unfit to do so.

Who is responsible for proving or disproving SHELLEY's claim, that he was unlikely to drive the vehicle while unfit to do so?

A SHELLEY must demonstrate an arguable case that there was no likelihood of his driving while unfit to do so.

B The prosecution must demonstrate beyond reasonable doubt that there was a likelihood of SHELLEY driving while unfit to do so.

C SHELLEY must demonstrate on the balance of probabilities that there was no likelihood of his driving while unfit to do so.

D The prosecution must demonstrate on the balance of probabilities that there was a likelihood of SHELLEY driving while unfit to do so.

Question 5.8

RICHMOND is appearing in court, having been charged with driving a motor vehicle on a road when there was a specified controlled drug in her body and the proportion of the drug in her blood exceeded the specified limit. The drug in question is Diazepam and RICHMOND is claiming a defence, because the drug was prescribed by her GP.

Section 5A of the Road Traffic Act 1988 provides a 'medical defence' to such a charge. Would this defence be available to RICHMOND in these circumstances?

A No, Diazepam is a controlled drug under the Misuse of Drugs Act 1971; this defence is not available for such a drug.

B Yes, provided the drug was lawfully prescribed to RICHMOND, this defence may be available.

C Yes, provided the drug was lawfully prescribed and it was taken in accordance with advice given by the person who prescribed it.

D Yes, but only if RICHMOND can demonstrate that the drug was prescribed to her in error and that she was unaware that she had taken that particular drug.

Question 5.9

CHANEY works for a building company which was contracted to conduct work in a supermarket car park. In his lunch break, CHANEY took cocaine and when he returned to work, he drove a dumper truck erratically around the car park. Several customers complained and Constable CHUNG was called to deal with the incident; the officer immediately suspected CHANEY had been taking drugs because of his behaviour. Constable CHUNG worked in a force area that was piloting an approved hand-held device able to carry out a preliminary drugs test.

Given that the dumper truck was not intended or adapted for use on the road, would Constable CHUNG be able to request a preliminary drugs test from CHANEY under s. 6 of the Road Traffic Act 1988, in these circumstances?

A Yes, CHANEY was driving a mechanically propelled vehicle in a public place at the time of the incident.

B No, CHANEY was not driving a motor vehicle on a road or other public place at the time of the incident.

C No, CHANEY was not driving a motor vehicle on a road at the time of the incident.

D No, CHANEY was not driving a mechanically propelled vehicle on a road at the time of the incident.

Question 5.10

Detective Constable PARR was in plain clothes on enquiries in the Fox and Hounds public house. The officer saw BAKER stumble through the bar to the exit door, leave the pub and get into a car outside. Detective Constable PARR left the premises and got into a police vehicle as BAKER was driving away. At the end of the street, BAKER failed to observe a stop sign, turned into a main road and then collided with the rear of another car, which was stationary at a red traffic light.

Would Detective Constable PARR have been entitled to require BAKER to cooperate with one of the preliminary tests, under s. 6(1) of the Road Traffic Act 1988?

A Yes, when BAKER first got into the car.

B Yes, but only when BAKER drove through the stop sign.

C Yes, but only when BAKER collided with the rear of the other car.

D No, Detective Constable PARR was in plain clothes and had no power to require BAKER to submit to one of the preliminary tests.

Question 5.11

WHEELAN attended a police station to report a crime and spoke to Constable BLOOM. As they were speaking, the officer suspected that WHEELAN may have been drinking and asked whether she had been. WHEELAN stated she had and the officer asked whether or not she had driven to the station. Again, WHEELAN stated she had. Constable BLOOM requested a sample of breath from WHEELAN, which proved to be positive. WHEELAN was charged with the offence, but pleaded not guilty in court, stating that Constable BLOOM should have cautioned her prior to administering the breath test as their conversation constituted an interview.

Is the court likely to accept WHEELAN's defence in these circumstances?

A Yes, as the conversation occurred prior to the breath test, Constable BLOOM had formed the suspicion that WHEELAN had committed an offence and a caution was required.

B No, Constable BLOOM only formed the suspicion an offence had been committed after the breath test was administered, therefore a caution was not required.

C Yes, the questions asked by Constable BLOOM were preliminary to a breath test and designed to establish whether an offence had taken place, therefore a caution was required.

D Yes, Constable BLOOM knew that WHEELAN had been drinking, therefore the question as to whether she had driven there constituted an interview and a caution was required.

Question 5.12

Constable STANTON works in a force area that was piloting an approved hand-held device able to carry out a preliminary drugs test. Constable STANTON used this device to obtain a sample of saliva, having stopped McPHERSON who was driving a motor vehicle on a road and the test produced positive results. However, it took two attempts for the officer to obtain a sample from McPHERSON because the device stated that the first sample taken was insufficient to provide a result.

Has Constable STANTON acted lawfully in these circumstances, by taking more than one sample?

A Yes, Constable STANTON was allowed to administer up to two tests to obtain a sample which was sufficient.

B Yes, Constable STANTON was allowed to administer up to three tests to obtain a sample which was sufficient.

C Yes, there are no limits as to how many tests may be administered to ensure that a sample is sufficient.

D No, Constable STANTON was only allowed to administer one test to obtain a sample which was sufficient.

Question 5.13

Constable COURT was conducting her first breath test procedure, having stopped KAY, who was driving with a defective light. During the test, Constable COURT failed to hold down a button on the breath test device for the recommended amount of time. However, the reading still showed a positive breath result and Constable COURT arrested KAY.

Has Constable COURT acted correctly in these circumstances?

A Yes, Constable COURT has acted correctly in the circumstances and the arrest is lawful.

B No, the arrest is unlawful, as Constable COURT made a mistake with the procedure.

C No, the arrest is unlawful, but this would not affect the result of the case if KAY provided a positive sample at the station.

D No, the arrest is unlawful, and KAY should have been made to take the test again.

Question 5.14

Constable CLEMENT attended a road traffic accident, involving two vehicles. One of the drivers, MARINER, smelled of intoxicants, but the other driver, McCLAREN, did not. Constable CLEMENT requested both drivers to cooperate with a preliminary breath test. However, the officer's breath test machine was defective; after several attempts to get another officer to attend the scene with a machine that worked, Constable CLEMENT realised that the rest of the team was too busy to assist. The officer considered whether or not to take MARINER and McCLAREN to the nearest police station to conduct the test.

Is Constable CLEMENT empowered to take the drivers to a police station, in these circumstances?

A Yes, both drivers may be taken to the police station to conduct the test, as they have been involved in a road traffic accident.

B Yes, but only in respect of MARINER, who is suspected to have alcohol in his breath or body.

C No, this power is only available in respect of a person who is suspected to be unfit to drive through drugs.

D Yes, this power is available in respect of any person who is required to cooperate with one of the preliminary tests.

Question 5.15

Constable PENG is trained to conduct preliminary impairment tests. He was called to assist another officer who had stopped a motor vehicle, which was being driven erratically by WENGER. The officer had administered a breath test, which was negative; however, WENGER's behaviour led the officer to believe that he was under the influence of either drink or drugs. On his arrival, Constable PENG gave instructions to WENGER as part of the test, but WENGER was not able to complete the test because of his condition.

Would the officer be able to arrest WENGER now, for failure to complete the impairment test?

A Yes, provided the officer suspects the presence of alcohol or drugs.

B No, as he has not refused to take the impairment test.

C Yes, regardless of whether the officer suspects the presence of alcohol or drugs.

D No, the officer would have to arrest him under s. 4 of the Act.

Question 5.16

Constable TAYLOR was called to an accident in a shopping centre car park, which was open to the public. SINGH had reversed his car into the path of a dumper truck being driven by WALSH. WALSH was working on an adjacent building site and the dumper truck he was driving was not manufactured for use on roads.

From whom, if anyone, may Constable TAYLOR require a breath test, in these circumstances?

A SINGH only, provided she suspects he has alcohol in his body.

B Neither driver, as the accident did not occur on a road.

C Both drivers, as they have been involved in an accident.

D SINGH only, whether or not she suspects he has alcohol in his body.

Question 5.17

Constable CAREY was investigating an incident that occurred outside a public house one night. HALL had been found lying in a gutter with blood coming from a head wound. Witnesses had seen PRIOR driving away from the scene, but could not say how HALL had sustained the injury. Constable CAREY attended PRIOR's address and saw a vehicle parked outside matching the description of the one that had driven away from the scene. PRIOR was at home but refused to open the door. Suspecting that an accident involving injury had taken place, Constable CAREY entered the premises by force and administered a breath test, which was positive.

Has Constable CAREY acted correctly in these circumstances?

A No, there was no power of entry as Constable CAREY did not know for certain that an accident involving injury had taken place.

B Yes, Constable CAREY had a reasonable *belief* that an accident involving injury had taken place.

C Yes, Constable CAREY had a reasonable *suspicion* that an accident involving injury had taken place.

D Yes, Constable CAREY had a reasonable *suspicion* that an accident involving a motor vehicle on a road had taken place.

Question 5.18

BALL drove his car into a garden wall and, without stopping, made his way home. He was uninjured, alone in the car and no other people were involved. Constable DAWE arrived at the scene and, following a Police National Computer (PNC) check, attended BALL's home address. Constable DAWE found BALL in the front garden of his house and asked him for a sample of breath, as the officer suspected he had been involved in a road traffic accident. BALL refused and was arrested by the officer. BALL refused to go with Constable DAWE and told him to leave his property.

Does Constable DAWE have the power to continue with his arrest now that he has become a trespasser?

A Yes, BALL was arrested before Constable DAWE became a trespasser.

B Yes, Constable DAWE had a power to enter premises, as BALL had been involved in an accident.

C No, the arrest was unlawful, as Constable DAWE was trespassing as soon as he entered the garden.

D No, Constable DAWE has now become a trespasser and must leave the property.

Question 5.19

TAYLOR was in custody in a force area that was piloting an approved hand-held device able to carry out a preliminary drugs test. TAYLOR had provided a saliva sample at the roadside which tested positive for the presence of drugs. TAYLOR was arrested for an offence under s. 5A of the Road Traffic Act 1988. Sergeant VINES was considering requesting a blood sample from TAYLOR.

Which of the following statements is correct, in relation to Sergeant VINES's obligations under s. 7(3) of the Act?

A Sergeant VINES must consult with a medical practitioner or a registered health care professional before requesting a blood sample, because of the offence TAYLOR has been arrested for.

B Sergeant VINES may consult with a medical practitioner or a registered health care professional before requesting a blood sample, but this is not absolutely necessary because TAYLOR provided a positive drugs sample at the roadside.

C Sergeant VINES must consult with a medical practitioner or a registered health care professional before requesting a blood sample; this must be done for every occasion when such a sample is to be taken.

D Sergeant VINES is not required to consult with anyone before requesting a blood sample; this need only be done when it is suspected that the person cannot provide a breath sample for medical reasons.

Question 5.20

Constable WEAR was on mobile patrol and saw BALE driving through a red traffic light. The officer stopped BALE and requested a preliminary breath sample, which proved to be positive. Constable WEAR was working in a force area that was piloting an approved hand-held device able to obtain evidential specimens of breath. The officer arrested BALE and a colleague arrived with the hand-held evidential device. BALE provided two further samples of breath; however, the device produced zero readings. Because the preliminary sample had proved positive, Constable WEAR suspected that the hand-held device may be defective. Constable WEAR arrested BALE on suspicion of driving with excess alcohol, based on the preliminary breath sample.

Can BALE be asked to provide two further evidential samples of breath at the police station?

A No, BALE has provided two samples and must now be asked to provide a sample of blood or urine.

B No, a constable may only make this request if there was no device available at the scene. BALE should now be asked to provide a sample of blood or urine.

C Yes, but only if it can be shown that it was impracticable to use a device at the scene.

D Yes, the police can request a further two samples of breath at the station under these circumstances alone.

Question 5.21

Constable CAMPBELL stopped CAMERON, who was driving a motor vehicle on a road. The officer suspected that CAMERON had been drinking and requested a sample of breath. The sample proved positive; however, it transpired that CAMERON had consumed a non-alcoholic drink approximately ten minutes before the request was made. Constable CAMPBELL had forgotten to ask whether CAMERON had consumed anything in the previous 20 minutes, prior to administering the test.

Would the validity of the breath test have been compromised in these circumstances?

A Yes, it is mandatory that the officer asks whether anything has been consumed in the 20 minutes prior to the breath test.

B No, provided the officer did not know, or had no reason to suspect that any substance had been consumed in the 20 minutes prior to the breath test.

C No, it is mandatory that the officer asks whether any alcohol has been consumed in the previous 20 minutes, but CAMERON had consumed a non-alcoholic drink.

D No, a test would only be compromised in these circumstances if the officer had actually known that a substance had been consumed in the 20 minutes prior to the breath test.

Question 5.22

GRANT was arrested and taken to a police station after failing to provide a specimen of breath at the roadside. At the station, it was decided that for medical reasons GRANT should provide a urine sample.

Which of the following statements is correct in relation to the provision of the urine sample, under s. 7(5) of the Road Traffic Act 1988?

A GRANT must provide two separate samples within an hour of being requested to do so.

B GRANT must provide two samples from the same act of urinating, within an hour of being requested to do so.

C GRANT must provide two separate samples within an hour of providing the second breath sample.

D GRANT must provide two samples, which may or may not be from the same act of urinating, within an hour of providing the second breath sample.

Question 5.23

RADCLIFFE was taken to hospital from a custody office, having been in police detention following a positive breath test. RADCLIFFE had suffered a suspected heart attack while about to provide samples for the station breath test procedure. Following tests, it was decided that RADCLIFFE had most likely suffered an anxiety attack, but would need to remain on a ward in hospital for observation. The arresting officer, Constable SAMPSON, spoke to the medical practitioner in charge of the ward about the breath test procedure. Constable SAMPSON was told that obtaining a sample of blood may be detrimental to RADCLIFFE's medical health. The officer decided to contact the custody officer for advice about how to proceed.

Considering s. 7 of the Road Traffic Act 1988, which of the following statements is correct, in respect of the options open to Constable SAMPSON?

A A police medical practitioner should be called to the hospital to take a sample of urine from RADCLIFFE.

B A police medical practitioner should take the urine sample, but if one is not available, a medical practitioner at the hospital who is not in immediate charge of RADCLIFFE's case should take it.

C A sample of urine may not be requested in these circumstances; such a sample may only be requested at a police station.

D A sample of urine may be requested in these circumstances and it may be taken by a police officer.

Question 5.24

Constable COLE attended a road traffic accident involving a car which had struck a wall. There were two occupants in the vehicle: PEARSON, the owner, and his friend, STUART. Constable COLE could smell intoxicants on both persons, but neither admitted being the driver of the vehicle at the time of the accident. PEARSON and STUART provided screening samples of breath, which were both positive. They were arrested and taken to the police station.

From whom, if either, could a specimen of breath for analysis be requested, under s. 7 of the Road Traffic Act 1988 (provision of specimens for analysis)?

A Both, provided it is believed one of them was driving.

B PEARSON only, as the owner of the vehicle.

C Both, regardless of who was suspected to be the driver.

D Neither, Constable COLE should not have breathalysed both persons.

Question 5.25

Sergeant CLARIDGE was conducting the station breath test procedure for CATTON, who had failed to provide a roadside specimen of breath. CATTON agreed to provide an evidential specimen under s. 7 of the Road Traffic Act 1988; however, after five attempts to blow into the Intoximeter machine, the sergeant halted the procedure and asked CATTON for a sample of blood; the defendant refused to provide a blood sample and was charged with the offence. CATTON pleaded not guilty, alleging that Sergeant CLARIDGE had no reason to believe that there was a medical reason to ask for a sample of blood.

What would the prosecution need to show in order to contest CATTON's defence in court?

A That after failing to provide a sample five times, it was reasonable to assume that there was a medical reason for this inability.

B That Sergeant CLARIDGE actually believed that a medical reason existed to ask CATTON to provide a sample of blood.

C That Sergeant CLARIDGE's reasonable cause to believe that medical reasons existed was based on expert medical advice.

D That there was evidence that Sergeant CLARIDGE had consulted with CATTON before asking for a sample of blood.

Question 5.26

FOSTER was arrested under s. 4 of the Road Traffic Act 1988 and was taken to the police station. FOSTER provided one specimen of breath, but then the machine malfunctioned. The custody officer, Sergeant CANNON, considered transferring FOSTER to another police station to complete the station procedure.

Would Sergeant CANNON be able to transfer FOSTER to another station, in these circumstances?

A Yes, FOSTER may be transferred and may be required to supply two further specimens of breath.

B No, FOSTER must now be asked to provide a sample of blood or urine at the current station, to replace the specimen of breath.

C Yes, FOSTER may be transferred and may only be required to supply one specimen of breath.

D No, a person may only be transferred to another station if there is no one available to conduct the station procedure.

Question 5.27

BOBIN pleaded not guilty in court to an offence of failing to provide a urine sample, citing that the police had failed to properly issue a warning under s. 7(7) of the Road Traffic Act 1988 (failure to provide the specimen may render a person liable to prosecution). Whilst in custody, it had been decided that for medical reasons, the defendant should provide a specimen of urine. Sergeant HAYES commenced the procedure and issued a warning under s. 7(7); however, the sergeant was called away to other duties before the specimen was taken and the procedure was passed over to Constable PIERCE, who did not issue a further warning before requesting the sample. However, BOBIN failed to provide a specimen and was charged with the offence.

Since Constable PIERCE did fail to issue a warning, would BOBIN's defence be successful?

A No, the warning was not required in these circumstances.
B Yes, the warning should have been given by the person conducting the procedure.
C No, the warning under s. 7(7) only relates to the provision of samples of breath.
D No, the warning under s. 7(7) only relates to the provision of specimens of breath or blood.

Question 5.28

KHAN has been arrested for being unfit to drive through drink. Sergeant WILSON formed the opinion that KHAN could not provide a breath sample because he had severe asthma and informed him that he would have to provide blood instead. KHAN stated that he would prefer not to give blood, as he had a fear of needles. Sergeant WILSON has been informed that a medical practitioner is available by telephone only and will not attend immediately.

What action should Sergeant WILSON now take in respect of KHAN?

A Speak to the medical practitioner on the telephone and proceed as advised by him or her.
B Request a sample of blood; a fear of needles is not a medical reason for not giving blood.
C Take a sample of urine from KHAN; he has the choice as to which sample is to be taken.
D Wait until the medical practitioner arrives and proceed as advised by him or her; such advice may not be taken by telephone.

Question 5.29

Sergeant DONELLY was conducting the station breath test procedure for BEECH, who had provided one sample of breath. However, BEECH stated that he was tired, and fell asleep before providing a second sample. Sergeant DONELLY tried to wake BEECH, without success, and in the end placed him in a cell. BEECH was later charged with driving with excess alcohol, based on the reading provided, which was 150 microgrammes of alcohol in 100 millilitres of breath.

Has Sergeant DONELLY acted correctly in these circumstances?

A Yes, Sergeant DONELLY has acted correctly in these circumstances as BEECH has driven with excess alcohol.

B No, BEECH should have been charged with failing to provide a sample, but his drunken condition may provide a defence.

C No, BEECH should have been given the opportunity to provide a sample of blood or urine when he was sober enough.

D No, BEECH should have been charged with failing to provide a sample and would have no defence arising from his drunken condition.

Question 5.30

LONSDALE was stopped by Constable McMAHON for driving through a red traffic light and the officer requested a preliminary breath test; however, LONSDALE stated that he was not able to provide a sample, claiming to suffer from bronchitis. Constable McMA-HON arrested LONSDALE for failing to provide a specimen; however, during the booking in procedure, the officer did not mention LONSDALE's medical excuse given at the scene. During the station procedure, LONSDALE made no effort to provide a sample and nor did he mention his condition. He was charged with failing to provide a specimen of breath but pleaded not guilty, claiming that the custody officer had reasonable cause to believe that a specimen of breath should not be required for medical reasons and should have consulted a police medical practitioner.

Considering the offence under s. 7(6) of the Road Traffic Act 1988, would LONS-DALE have a reasonable excuse for failing to provide a specimen?

A Yes, Constable McMAHON should have informed the custody officer of LONS-DALE's alleged medical condition.

B No, the offence is complete in these circumstances alone.

C Yes, the custody officer should have made enquiries of LONSDALE as to whether he had a medical condition.

D Yes, LONSDALE was not required to declare the reasonable excuse at the time, but it may be raised subsequently.

Question 5.31

ASKEW was involved in a road traffic accident during which she received head injuries, and was taken to hospital. The officer dealing with the accident, Constable LEE, was told by witnesses that ASKEW's driving was erratic immediately prior to the accident. Constable LEE attended the hospital to interview ASKEW and require her to provide a sample of breath. On his arrival, Constable LEE was told that ASKEW was unconscious due to her injuries. Constable LEE considered that a sample of blood should be taken from ASKEW without her permission.

Who would be able to take such a sample from ASKEW, under s. 7A of the Road Traffic Act 1988?

A A police medical practitioner or the medical practitioner in charge of the patient only.

B A police medical or health care practitioner or any other medical practitioner, but not the one in charge of the patient.

C A police medical or health care practitioner only.

D A police medical or health care practitioner, or the medical practitioner in charge of the patient.

Question 5.32

WICKS was involved in a road traffic accident and was taken to hospital with a suspected heart attack and a possible broken leg. After dealing with the accident, Constable GABBIDON attended the hospital to deal with WICKS. The officer intended requiring WICKS to submit to a preliminary breath test and spoke to Doctor WELCH, a cardiologist. Doctor WELCH confirmed that WICKS had not suffered a heart attack and was now in the care of the doctor in charge of A&E. When asked, Doctor WELCH expressed the opinion that there was no medical reason preventing Constable GABBIDON from requiring WICKS to cooperate with a preliminary breath test.

Has Constable GABBIDON complied with s. 9(1) of the Road Traffic Act 1988 (hospital procedures), in these circumstances?

A No, Constable GABBIDON did not seek permission from the medical practitioner in immediate charge of WICKS's case.

B Yes, Constable GABBIDON was required to consult with a medical practitioner who was *not* in immediate charge of WICKS's case.

C No, Constable GABBIDON did not consult with a medical practitioner in immediate charge of WICKS's case, to allow them an opportunity to object to the requirement.

D Yes, Constable GABBIDON consulted with a medical practitioner in immediate charge of WICKS's case, to allow them an opportunity to object to the requirement.

Question 5.33

WEBBER was at a hospital, having been involved in a road traffic accident. Having consulted with the medical practitioner in immediate charge of WEBBER's case, Constable O'SHEA required WEBBER to provide a specimen of breath, but she refused. Constable O'SHEA arrested WEBBER for failing to provide a specimen. After further consultation with the medical practitioner, Constable O'SHEA asked WEBBER to supply a specimen of blood.

Has Constable O'SHEA complied with the requirements of s. 9 of the Road Traffic Act 1988?

A No, because WEBBER was under arrest, the request for blood should have been made at a police station.

B No, Constable O'SHEA should not have arrested WEBBER while she was still a patient at the hospital.

C Yes, as the medical practitioner has agreed to both specimens being requested, Constable O'SHEA has complied with the Act.

D Yes, but there was no need to ask permission on the second occasion, as permission had already been granted.

Question 5.34

PELLOW was involved in a road traffic accident with another vehicle driven by CASE. As they were exchanging details, CASE noticed that PELLOW smelled strongly of intoxicants. CASE asked PELLOW to remain at the scene for the police. PELLOW refused, stating she had an out-patient's appointment at the local hospital. After PELLOW left, CASE contacted the police and gave details of her vehicle. Constable GRADY attended the local hospital intending to breathalyse PELLOW. The officer found her in the out-patient's department—she had been seen by a medical practitioner and had been discharged, to return for another appointment the following week.

Which of the following statements is correct, in relation to PELLOW's status as a 'patient' when she was seen by Constable GRADY, in respect of s. 9 of the Road Traffic Act 1988?

A PELLOW was an out-patient at the hospital; therefore she was not a 'patient' according to s. 9.

B PELLOW was still a 'patient', as she had to return to the hospital for further treatment.

C PELLOW was still a 'patient' as she was within the precincts of the hospital.

D PELLOW was not a 'patient' as she had been discharged.

Question 5.35

PEARCE has been charged with an offence of driving with excess alcohol (under s. 5 of the Road Traffic Act 1988) and is still in custody. Sergeant REVERS is considering whether or not to detain PEARCE at the custody office, because the lowest reading of the sample provided by PEARCE was 130 microgrammes of alcohol in 100 millilitres of breath.

What matters should Sergeant REVERS take into consideration, before detaining PEARCE under s. 10(1) of the Road Traffic Act 1988?

A Sergeant REVERS has a statutory power to confiscate PEARCE's car keys under this subsection, to prevent her from committing an offence under s. 5 or s. 4 of the Act.

B Sergeant REVERS has a statutory power to detain PEARCE until she has provided a negative screening test, to prevent her from committing an offence under s. 5 or s. 4 of the Act.

C PEARCE may be detained, provided Sergeant REVERS has reasonable grounds to believe she will commit an offence under s. 5 or s. 4 if she were to drive a motor vehicle on a road.

D PEARCE may be detained, provided Sergeant REVERS has reasonable grounds to believe she will commit an offence under s. 5 or s. 4 if she were to drive a mechanically propelled vehicle on a road.

Question 5.36

NEWMAN is in custody and is suspected of being unfit to drive through taking drugs. NEWMAN has provided a specimen of blood, which the custody officer, Sergeant BURKE, intends to submit for analysis. NEWMAN will not be charged until the results of the analysis are known and, therefore, Sergeant BURKE intends to release him on bail for the period. However, NEWMAN has stated his intention to drive when released. Sergeant BURKE suspects that NEWMAN would still be unfit if he were to drive a motor vehicle on a road.

What does s. 10 of the Road Traffic Act 1988 say, in relation to the advice Sergeant BURKE should seek, before detaining NEWMAN further until he is fit to drive a motor vehicle on a road?

A Sergeant BURKE may make this decision herself; she does not need to seek advice from anyone.

B Sergeant BURKE may seek advice from a police medical practitioner, and must act on any advice given.

C Sergeant BURKE may not detain NEWMAN under this section, as he has not been charged or reported for an offence.

D Sergeant BURKE must seek advice from a police medical practitioner, and must act on any advice given.

Question 5.37

Constable TREEN was dealing with a road traffic accident and one of the drivers, BENSKIN, was taken to hospital with a leg injury, which was not serious. While at the hospital, Constable TREEN received permission from the medical practitioner in charge of BENSKIN's clinical care to request a breath specimen, which proved to be positive. Constable TREEN's force was piloting an approved hand-held device able to obtain evidential specimens of breath. BENSKIN provided two evidential specimens using this device, which were also positive. Following initial treatment, the medical practitioner discharged BENSKIN; however, Constable TREEN believed that BENSKIN was likely to drive a motor vehicle on a road while unfit to do so.

Given that Constable TREEN's belief was reasonable, did the officer have authority to detain BENSKIN under s. 10 of the Road Traffic Act 1988, to prevent the defendant from driving a motor vehicle on a road while unfit to do so?

A No, Constable TREEN would only have had the power to arrest BENSKIN if it was necessary, under s. 24 of the Police and Criminal Evidence Act 1984.

B Yes, provided it would not be prejudicial to BENSKIN's proper care and treatment as a patient.

C No, the power to detain people under s. 10 only applies to people who have been arrested and detained at a police station.

D No, the power to detain people under s. 10 only applies to people who have been required to provide a blood sample under s. 7 of the Act.

ANSWERS

Answer 5.1

Answer **A** — Sections 34A to 34C of the Road Traffic Offenders Act 1988 allow drink-drive offenders who are disqualified from driving to have the period of disqualification reduced if they complete a drink-drive rehabilitation course.

These reductions must be not less than three months, and not more than one quarter of the unreduced period (this equates to a range from a three-month to a nine-month disqualification for a 12-month imposed disqualification sentence).

Answers B, C and D are therefore incorrect.

Road Policing, para. 3.5.1

Answer 5.2

Answer **A** — Under s. 5(1)(a) of the Road Traffic Act 1988, a person who drives or attempts to drive a motor vehicle on a road or other public place after consuming so much alcohol that the proportion of it in his breath, blood or urine exceeds the prescribed limit is guilty of an offence. There can be no offence, therefore, under s. 5, and answer B is incorrect.

However, under s. 4(1) of the Act, a person who, when driving or attempting to drive a *mechanically propelled vehicle* on a road or *other public place*, is unfit to drive through drink or drugs is guilty of an offence. There *can* be an offence, therefore, under s. 4, and answers C and D are incorrect.

Road Policing, paras 3.5.2, 3.5.3

Answer 5.3

Answer **D** — The power of entry in connection with an offence under s. 4 is found in s. 17(1)(c)(iiia) of the Police and Criminal Evidence Act 1984, which states:

> Subject to the following provisions of this section, and without prejudice to any other enactment, a constable may enter and search any premises for the purpose of...
> (iiia) section 4 (driving etc. when under influence of drink or drugs) or section 163 (failure to stop when required to do so by constable in uniform) of the Road Traffic Act 1988.

Since the power is given to enter a 'premises', as opposed to a 'dwelling', answers A and B are therefore both incorrect.

'Premises' is not defined, but would include a vehicle; answer C is therefore incorrect.

Note that the power of entry under this section is only exercisable if the constable has reasonable grounds for believing that the person whom he is seeking is on the premises (s. 17(2)(a)).

Road Policing, para. 3.5.2

Answer 5.4

Answer **B** — This question deals with whether a 'reasonable suspicion' would provide sufficient evidence to arrest a person and prove an offence under s. 4 of the Road Traffic Act 1988, when that evidence is provided by a 'lay' witness. In *R* v *Lanfear* [1968] 2 QB 77, it was held that while evidence of impairment must be produced by the prosecution, that evidence *may* be provided by a 'lay' witness, who would not need to be an expert on such matters (see also *R* v *Davies* [1962] 3 All ER 97). Answers C and D are therefore incorrect.

However, that witness *may* not be required to give expert testimony or to *comment on the defendant's ability to drive*. Answer A is therefore incorrect.

Road Policing, paras 3.5.2, 3.5.2.2

Answer 5.5

Answer **A** — The circumstances in this question are similar to those in *DPP* v *Robertson* [2002] EWHC 542 (Admin). In that case, the officers had breathalysed the defendant who produced a negative result. However, on talking to the officers further, the defendant slurred his speech when giving the name of his solicitor. The officers then arrested the defendant under s. 4 and took him to a police station where he provided an evidential sample of breath which was over the prescribed limit.

The magistrates held that the defendant had been unlawfully arrested and the prosecutor appealed on a number of grounds. However, the Administrative Court held that it was quite conceivable to have a case where, notwithstanding that a driver had given a negative screening breath test, he or she was seen moments later staggering in a way that gave rise to a suspicion of unfitness. In such a case the law (s. 4) clearly gave a constable a power to arrest if what he or she had witnessed amounted to reasonable cause to suspect that the person was impaired, regardless of whether the impairment was due to drink or drugs. Answers C and D are therefore incorrect.

There would be no requirement for the police to require a further breath sample from the driver in these circumstances; therefore, answer B is incorrect.

Road Policing, para. 3.5.2.2

Answer 5.6

Answer **A** — The Divisional Court has held that there is some positive duty on a person to enquire whether a drink contains alcohol before drinking it if that person intends to drive afterwards (see *Robinson* v *DPP* [2003] EWHC 2718 (Admin)).

Answers B, C and D are therefore incorrect.

Road Policing, para. 3.5.3

Answer 5.7

Answer **A** — Section 5(2) of the Road Traffic Act 1988 provides a defence for a person charged with an offence under s. 5(1)(b) (in charge of a motor vehicle while over the prescribed limit), provided there was no likelihood of him or her driving the vehicle while unfit.

The situation was examined in the Divisional Court, in the case of *Sheldrake* v *DPP* [2003] 2 All ER 497. The defendant claimed that the application of s. 5(2) was contrary to Art. 6(2) of the European Convention on Human Rights (presumption of innocence). The court held that s. 5(2) did not breach Art. 6(2), and that a person charged with an offence under s. 5(1)(b) must demonstrate from the evidence an *arguable case* that there was no likelihood of him driving while unfit to do so. Answer C is therefore incorrect.

The prosecution *does* have some responsibilities under s. 5(2); these are to show that the defendant was, in fact, in charge of the vehicle and was unfit through drink or drugs. Once these elements are proved, it will be for the *defence* to show that there was no likelihood of the defendant driving whilst unfit to do so. Answers B and D are therefore incorrect.

The case came before the House of Lords as *Attorney General's Reference (No. 4 of 2002) Sheldrake* v *DPP* [2004] UKHL 43. There it was held that, although s. 5(2) did in fact infringe the presumption of innocence under Art. 6, the burden placed on the defendant was reasonable because it was in pursuance of a legitimate aim.

The likelihood of the defendant's driving was so closely linked to his or her own knowledge at the relevant time that it made it much more appropriate for the defendant to prove—on the balance of probabilities—that he or she would not have been likely to drive (as opposed to the prosecution being required to prove the opposite beyond reasonable doubt).

Road Policing, para. 3.5.3.1

Answer 5.8

Answer **C** — Section 5A(3) of the Road Traffic Act 1988 states that it is a defence for a person ('D') charged with an offence under this section to show that:

(a) the specified controlled drug had been prescribed or supplied to D for medical or dental purposes,
(b) D took the drug in accordance with any directions given by the person by whom the drug was prescribed or supplied, and with any accompanying instructions (so far as consistent with any such directions) given by the manufacturer or distributor of the drug...

As part of the defence, the defendant would also have to show that he/she was not in unlawful possession of the controlled drug (according to s. 5(1) of the Misuse of Drugs Act 1971), a condition a defendant should be able to satisfy if the drug was prescribed.

Therefore, provided the defendant is able to demonstrate that he/she followed any advice given when the drug was prescribed (e.g. the amount of time that should elapse between taking the drug and driving a motor vehicle) and followed any manufacturer's instructions accompanying the drug, the defence may be available even if the drug is listed in the 1971 Act as a controlled drug. Answer A is therefore incorrect.

This is a slightly more testing defence than simply being able to prove that the drug was lawfully prescribed; therefore, answer B is incorrect.

These are the only two requirements for this statutory defence (of course, if a person can show that the drug was prescribed in error or that they were unaware they had taken a particular drug, then a court would be bound to take this into consideration). Answer D is therefore incorrect.

Note that the court must assume that the defence is satisfied unless the prosecution proves beyond reasonable doubt that it is not (s. 5A(5)).

Road Policing, paras 3.5.3, 3.5.3.1

Answer 5.9

Answer **B** — Section 5A of the Road Traffic Act 1988 deals with driving or being in charge of a motor vehicle with a concentration of a specified controlled drug above the specified limit. Where a person drives, attempts to drive or is in charge of a motor vehicle on a road or other public place and there is in that person's body a specified controlled drug (which includes cocaine), he or she is guilty of an offence if the proportion of the drug in his or her blood or urine exceeds the specified limit for that drug (s. 5A(1)–(2)).

Under s. 6(2), a constable may require a person to cooperate with any one or more preliminary tests (including the test to detect drugs) if he or she reasonably suspects that the person has been driving, attempting to drive or in charge of a motor vehicle on a road or other public place while having alcohol or a drug in his or her body or while unfit to drive because of a drug, and still has alcohol or a drug in his or her body or is still under the influence of a drug.

However, as with the power to require a preliminary breath test, a request for a preliminary drugs test will only be lawful if the person is or has been driving etc. a *motor vehicle* on a road or other public place. Of course, the officer could still arrest the person for an offence under s. 4 of the Act in these circumstances since that section *does* apply to mechanically propelled vehicles.

Answers A, C and D are incorrect for this reason.

Road Policing, paras 3.5.4, 3.5.4.2

Answer 5.10

Answer **A** — This is a bit of a trick question—no apologies for that! Section 6 of the Road Traffic Act 1988 outlines the circumstances in which a person may be required to cooperate with any one of the preliminary tests, e.g. where the person is reasonably suspected:

- to be driving, attempting to drive or in charge of a motor vehicle on a road or other public place and has alcohol or a drug in his or her body, or is under the influence of a drug (s. 6(2)); or
- *has been* driving etc. in these circumstances and *still* has alcohol or a drug in his or her body or is still under the influence of a drug (s. 6(3)); or
- *is* or *has been* driving etc. in these circumstances and has committed a traffic offence while the vehicle was in motion (s. 6(4)).

In each of these circumstances, the officer *making the requirement* does not have to be in uniform; however, the officer *administering the test* must be in uniform (s. 6(7)).

Under s. 6(5), where an accident occurs owing to the presence of a motor vehicle on a road or other public place, and it is reasonably believed that the person was driving, attempting to drive or in charge of the vehicle at the time of the accident, the officer making the requirement *and* administering the test does not have to be in uniform.

Therefore, the *earliest point* at which Detective Constable PARR would have been entitled to require BAKER to cooperate with one of the preliminary tests was when the person sat in the car, and was in charge of a motor vehicle on a road and had alcohol or a drug in his or her body.

Answers B, C and D are therefore incorrect.

Road Policing, paras 3.5.4, 3.5.4.3

Answer 5.11

Answer **B** — The facts in the question are similar to the case of *Ridehalgh* v *DPP* [2005] RTR 26. In this case, the defendant (a police officer) argued that the questions asked prior to the breath test procedure constituted an interview and as he had not been cautioned, Code C, paras 10.1 and 11.1(A) of the Codes of Practice had been breached. It was held that no interview had taken place and that there had been no breach of Code C. It was held that the questions regarding driving and whether he had been drinking first were merely preliminary and had been made with the intention of finding the possibility of whether an offence had been committed. On appeal, the Divisional Court held that a necessary precondition of the giving of a caution was that there had to be grounds for the suspicion of a criminal offence and that the magistrates were correct. The police officers merely suspected that the defendant had been drinking alcohol; they had no indication as to how much alcohol had been consumed, or whether he had actually driven. The ruling followed an earlier, similar decision in the case of *Whelehan* v *DPP* [1995] RTR 177. Answers A, C and D are therefore incorrect.

Road Policing, para. 3.5.4.1

Answer 5.12

Answer **B** — Under s. 6C(1) of the Road Traffic Act 1988, a preliminary drug test is a procedure by which a specimen of sweat or saliva is obtained by means of an approved device to provide an indication whether the person has a drug in his/her body and if so:

whether it is a specified controlled drug and

(i) if it is, whether the proportion of it in the person's blood or urine is likely to exceed the specified limit for that drug.

A preliminary drug test may be administered at or near the place where the requirement to cooperate with the test is imposed or, if the constable who imposes the requirement thinks it expedient, at a police station specified by him/her (s. 6C(2)).

According to s. 6C(3), up to *three* preliminary drug tests may be administered to ensure the sample is sufficient.

Answers A, C and D are therefore incorrect.

Road Policing, para. 3.5.4.2

Answer 5.13

Answer **A** — It has been held that where a constable innocently fails to follow the manufacturer's instructions, it will not render the test nor any subsequent arrest unlawful (*DPP* v *Kay* [1999] RTR 109). Answer B is therefore incorrect. Answer C is also incorrect, as the arrest was not unlawful.

In addition to the case of *Kay*, it was decided in *DPP* v *Carey* [1970] AC 1072, that failing to comply with the manufacturer's instructions on the use of an approved device will mean that the person *has not provided* a preliminary breath test and *may* be asked to provide another; refusing to do so will be an offence. Answer D is incorrect as the case is not the authority for the view that a person *must* be made to take another test. Since the purpose of the test is to indicate whether there is a *likelihood* of an offence being committed, an arrest in these circumstances is appropriate, as the test did show a positive result.

Road Policing, para. 3.5.4.2

Answer 5.14

Answer **A** — The three tests that the driver may be required to cooperate with under s. 6 of the Road Traffic Act 1988 are:

- preliminary breath test (s. 6A);
- preliminary impairment test (s. 6B); and
- preliminary drug test (s. 6C).

A preliminary breath test under s. 6A may only be administered at or near the place where the requirement to cooperate with the test is imposed. The other two tests, under ss. 6B and 6C may be administered at or near the place where the requirement to cooperate is imposed, *or* if the constable imposing it thinks it expedient, at a police station specified by the constable. Answers C and D are therefore incorrect.

There are separate provisions under s. 6(5) relating to drivers, where an accident occurs owing to the presence of a motor vehicle on a road or other public place, and a constable reasonably believes that the person was driving, attempting to drive or in charge of the vehicle at the time of the accident. In such cases, a preliminary *breath* test (under s. 6A) may be administered:

(a) at or near the place where the requirement to cooperate with the test is imposed; or
(b) if the constable who imposes the requirement thinks it expedient, at a police station specified by the constable (see s. 6A(3)).

This provision applies to *any* driver who has been involved in such an accident, regardless of whether or not that person is suspected to have alcohol in his or her breath or body, and answer B is therefore incorrect.

Road Policing, paras 3.5.4.2, 3.5.4.3

Answer 5.15

Answer **A** — Under s. 6B of the Road Traffic Act 1988, an appropriately trained officer has the power to require the driver of a motor vehicle on a road or public place to submit to a preliminary impairment test, to observe the driver's behaviour. Such observations may be used as evidence in any subsequent court cases—but will not provide absolute proof of a person's guilt.

A person who fails to cooperate with a preliminary impairment test commits an offence under s. 6(6) of the Act. A person does not cooperate unless his or her cooperation is sufficient to allow the test to be carried out (s. 11(3)). In the question, the driver's behaviour meant that the test could not be carried out, even though he did not refuse to take it. Answer B is therefore incorrect.

A constable may arrest a person who has failed to cooperate with a test under this section, *provided* the constable reasonably suspects that the person has alcohol or drugs in his or her body, or is under the influence of drugs (s. 6D(2)). Answers C and D are therefore incorrect.

Road Policing, paras 3.5.4.2, 3.5.4.4, 3.5.4.5

Answer 5.16

Answer **D** — The power to conduct a breath test under s. 6(5) of the Road Traffic Act 1988 applies where an accident has occurred owing to the presence of a motor vehicle on a road or public place. Since WALSH was driving a mechanically propelled vehicle and not a motor vehicle, there is no power to request a breath test from him. Answer C is therefore incorrect. As s. 6 applies to accidents that occur in a public place as well as on a road, answer B is also incorrect.

There is no need for the officer making the enquiry to suspect or believe that the driver has been drinking, nor that he has committed an offence in order to require a breath test following an accident. Answer A is therefore incorrect.

Road Policing, para. 3.5.4.3

Answer 5.17

Answer **A** — Under s. 6E(1)(a) of the Road Traffic Act 1988, a constable may enter any place using reasonable force for the purpose of requesting a preliminary breath test following an accident involving an injury. Answer D is therefore incorrect. However, before the power is used, there are four criteria that must apply. The officer must:

- know that an accident has taken place (mere suspicion is not enough);
- have reasonable cause to believe that the person had been driving or attempting to drive, or had been in charge of the vehicle (mere suspicion is not enough);
- have reasonable cause to suspect that the accident involved injury to another person (here suspicion is enough); and
- have reasonable cause to suspect that the person he or she is seeking is in the place to be entered (again suspicion is enough).

Since Constable CAREY did not know for certain that an accident had taken place, there was no power to enter the premises. Answers B and C are therefore incorrect.

Road Policing, para. 3.5.4.6

Answer 5.18

Answer **A** — Generally, where an officer is trespassing on a defendant's property, he or she is not entitled to require a breath test (*R* v *Fox* [1986] AC 281). Also, if officers are trespassing, any subsequent arrest made by them is unlawful (*Clowser* v *Chaplin* [1981] RTR 317). However, any requirement for a sample of breath properly made and any subsequent arrest remains lawful until the officer becomes a trespasser.

A police officer, like any other citizen, has an implied licence to go on to certain parts of property (which might include a garden), unless and until that licence is withdrawn. It is when the licence is withdrawn that the officer may become a trespasser. Therefore, if a police officer is on the defendant's property and has not been told to leave, any requirement for a breath test and subsequent arrest is lawful (*Pamplin* v *Fraser* [1981] RTR 494). This would still be the case even if the licence were withdrawn later. Answer D is therefore incorrect.

In the scenario given, the officer was not a trespasser until the defendant told him to leave the garden. Answer C is therefore incorrect.

Constable DAWE has no statutory power to enter the premises under s. 6E of the Road Traffic Act 1988, as this section only affords a power of entry following an accident involving injury to any person other than the driver. Answer B is incorrect as the scenario did not involve an injury.

Road Policing, para. 3.5.4.7

Answer 5.19

Answer **B** — Generally, people who are in detention under this legislation will be asked to provide evidential samples of breath. However, if the person has provided a preliminary sample which has tested positive for the presence of drugs, there is no requirement to then ask that person for a sample of breath, to test for the presence of alcohol, and the police can move straight to requesting a sample of blood to confirm the presence of drugs (see s. 7(3)(bc) of the Road Traffic Act 1988).

However, if it is believed that the person's intoxication is due to some drug and the person has *not* been tested at the roadside for the presence of drugs (e.g. if they were arrested under s. 4), a request may be made under s. 7(3)(c) for a sample of blood or urine. There are two conditions which must precede this decision:

(a) the constable making the requirement has been advised by a medical practitioner or a registered health care professional that the condition of the person required to provide the specimen might be due to some drug; and
(b) the suspected offence is one under s. 3A, 4 or 5A of the Act.

Therefore, if the request for blood is being made under s. 7(3)(bc), there will be no requirement for the police to consult with a medical practitioner before making the request (answer A is incorrect).

On the other hand, if the person has *not* provided a positive drug sample during a preliminary test and he/she has been arrested under different circumstances (e.g. they were exhibiting signs of being unfit and were arrested under s. 4 for being unfit to drive through drugs), the officer must consult with a medical practitioner beforehand. Answer D is incorrect because it is not true that the police *only* need to consult with a medical practitioner if it is suspected that the person cannot provide a breath sample for medical reasons.

Answer C is incorrect because police do not need to consult with a medical practitioner *every* time they make a request for a blood sample—they are only required to do so in the circumstances outlined above.

Road Policing, para. 3.5.5.1

Answer 5.20

Answer **D** — Section 7 of the Road Traffic Act 1988 (the obtaining of evidential samples) permits the police to carry out an evidential breath test (following a positive preliminary test) away from a police station when an approved device is available to the officer. Section 7(2D) of the Road Traffic Act 1988 states that if a requirement has been made under s. 7(1)(a) at a place other than a police station, a *further* requirement may subsequently be made at a police station if (but only if):

(a) a device or a reliable device was not available at that place or it was for any other reason impracticable to use such a device, or
(b) the constable who made the previous requirement had reasonable cause to believe that the device used there has not produced a reliable indication of the proportion of alcohol in the breath of the person concerned.

Since the request can be made either if a device is not available or it was impracticable to use the device or the device was defective, answers B and C are incorrect.

A requirement may be made for a sample of blood or urine, under s. 7(3) of the Act. Section 7(3)(bb) states that a requirement may be made for such a sample if a device has been used at the police station or elsewhere, but the constable who required the specimens of breath has reasonable cause to believe that the device has not produced a reliable indication of the proportion of alcohol in the breath of the person concerned. In theory, therefore, the defendant in the scenario could have been asked to provide a blood or urine sample at the station, or evidential breath samples. However, it is not mandatory to request a sample of blood or urine in these circumstances, therefore answer A is incorrect.

Note that while the officer has acted correctly in these circumstances, s. 5A of the Act allows a police officer to proceed directly to an evidential breath test at the roadside if in possession of a portable evidential device, without the need to carry out a preliminary test and arrest the person if they fail to provide.

Road Policing, para. 3.5.5.1

Answer 5.21

Answer **B** — It is common for device manufacturers to issue guidelines that require a 20-minute period free from consumption of alcohol or other substances prior to the administration of the test. In *DPP* v *Carey* [1970] AC 1072, the House of Lords ruled that if an officer has no knowledge or reason to suspect consumption of any substances within the relevant 20-minute period, the test remains valid even if it later transpires that some substance was actually consumed during that 20-minute period.

The 20-minute rule is guidance and not part of legislation, therefore, answers A and C are incorrect. This is true whether the person has consumed alcohol or any other substance.

The ruling in *Carey* demonstrates that the test could be compromised if the officer administers the breath test and either knows *or* has reason to suspect a substance has been consumed in the 20 minutes prior to the test. This is less prescriptive than the answer given in D, which is why the answer is incorrect.

Road Policing, para. 3.5.5.1

Answer 5.22

Answer **A** — Urine samples must be provided within an hour *from the time the request is made* (s. 7(5)). Answers C and D are therefore incorrect.

The defendant must provide two distinct samples (as opposed to two samples taken during the same act of urinating) (*Prosser* v *Dickeson* [1982] RTR 96). Answers B and D are incorrect for this reason also.

Note that the defendant must be given the opportunity to provide the urine within the one-hour period (see *Robertson* v *DPP* [2004] EWHC 517).

Road Policing, para. 3.5.5.1

Answer 5.23

Answer **D** — Under s. 7(3) of the Road Traffic Act 1988, a requirement to provide a specimen of blood or urine can only be made at a police station or at a hospital. Answer C is therefore incorrect.

Urine samples do not need to be taken by a medical practitioner. The samples will be admissible as long as they are provided within the time set out under s. 7(5) and may be taken by a police officer. Answers A and B are therefore incorrect.

Road Policing, para. 3.5.5.1

Answer 5.24

Answer **A** — It was held in the case of *Pearson* v *Metropolitan Police Commissioner* [1988] RTR 276 that the requirement under s. 7 may be made of more than one person (in this instance three people were involved), in respect of the same vehicle. Answers B and D are therefore incorrect. However, it must be believed that one of them was driving the vehicle, and for that reason answer C is incorrect.

Road Policing, para. 3.5.5.2

Answer 5.25

Answer **A** — There are three defining cases on this particular breathalyser issue, each of which confirms the sergeant in this scenario acted lawfully.

In *Bodhaniya* v *CPS* [2013] EWHC 1743 (Admin), the officer (rather generously) made a requirement for a sample of blood after five failed attempts by the defendant to provide an evidential breath sample. The officer's generosity was rewarded by the defendant appealing the conviction stating that the request for blood was unlawful. The officer contended that by failing to provide an evidential breath sample five times the only reasonable inference was that there had been a medical reason for him not doing so; the appeal was dismissed.

In another case, it was held that for the officer making the requirement to have 'reasonable cause to believe' that medical reasons exist, there is no need to seek medical advice first (*Dempsey* v *Catton* [1986] RTR 194). Answer C is therefore incorrect.

Whilst consulting the defendant on his or her medical ability to provide a sample may provide useful evidence later on, there is nothing in s. 7 of the Road Traffic Act 1988 that actually *requires* this consultation before an officer can formulate the reasonable cause to believe that the medical reason in fact existed. Answer D is therefore incorrect.

Finally, it is the objective cause of the officer's belief which will be considered by the courts, not whether the officer actually did believe that a medical reason existed (see *Davis* v *DPP* [1988] RTR 156). Answer B is therefore incorrect.

Road Policing, para. 3.5.5.3

Answer 5.26

Answer **A** — If the machine being used at one station is unreliable, by virtue of the fact that it will not calibrate the reading correctly, it will be 'unavailable'. In this case, the driver may be taken to another station, where another machine is available, even if the driver has already provided two specimens on the inaccurate machine (*Denny* v *DPP* [1990] RTR 417). Answer B is incorrect for this reason.

When a person is transferred in such a way, the procedure will start again and the defendant may be required to provide two further specimens (logically, the sample from the first station could not be used as the machine has malfunctioned). Answer C is therefore incorrect.

A person *may* be transferred to another station if there is no trained officer to operate the machine (see *Chief Constable of Avon and Somerset* v *Kelliher* [1986] Crim LR

635). However, this is not the only circumstance in which a person can be transferred and answer D is therefore incorrect.

Road Policing, para. 3.5.5.4

Answer 5.27

Answer **A** — Under s. 7(7) of the Road Traffic Act 1988, when a constable is requesting the provision of a specimen under s. 7(3), a warning must be given that a failure to provide the specimen may render a person liable to prosecution. This warning is generally critical to a successful prosecution for failing to provide a specimen.

Answers C and D are incorrect because the warning relates to *any* specimen requested under s. 7 (breath, blood or urine).

In *Bobin* v *DPP* [1999] RTR 375, it was held that as long as the information is provided by a police officer, it does not matter which police officer. Therefore, the warning under s. 7(7) might be given by, for instance, the arresting officer or by the custody officer who makes the requirement for the relevant specimen. There was no requirement in these circumstances to provide a further warning and answer B is incorrect.

Road Policing, paras 3.5.5.5, 3.5.5.6

Answer 5.28

Answer **A** — Under s. 7(4) of the Road Traffic Act 1988, the question of whether it is to be a specimen of blood or a specimen of urine shall be decided by the constable making the requirement. Answer C is therefore incorrect.

The possibility of medical reasons for not providing blood *must* be considered (see s. 7(4A)) and an alleged fear of needles by the driver is a relevant consideration when making this decision (*DPP* v *Jackson*; *Stanley* v *DPP* [1999] 1 AC 406 and also *Johnson* v *West Yorkshire Metropolitan Police* [1986] RTR 167). Answer B is therefore incorrect.

The medical advice may be given to the officer over the telephone if appropriate (*Andrews* v *DPP* [1992] RTR 1). Answer D is therefore incorrect.

Note the extended power given to registered health care professionals to take blood.

Road Policing, paras 3.5.5.6, 3.5.5.11

Answer 5.29

Answer **D** — Sergeant DONELLY has not acted correctly in these circumstances. Where a driver provides one specimen only, and fails without a reasonable excuse to provide the second sample, he or she has committed the offence of 'failing to provide' a sample (*Cracknell* v *Willis* [1988] AC 450). Answers A and C are incorrect for this reason.

'Mental impairment' may provide a reasonable excuse for failing to provide a sample. However, being drunk or under stress is not in itself enough to provide a 'reasonable excuse' for failing to provide a specimen (*DPP* v *Falzarano* [2001] RTR 14). This is confirmed by the case of *DPP* v *Beech* [1992] Crim LR 64, where it was decided that where the defendant's mental capacity to understand the warning was impaired by his or her drunkenness, this was not a 'reasonable' excuse. Answer B is therefore incorrect.

Road Policing, para. 3.5.5.11

Answer 5.30

Answer **B** — A case similar to this one was heard by the Administrative Court in *DPP* v *Lonsdale* [2001] EWHC Admin 95. In this case, the driver alleged at the roadside that he suffered from bronchitis and therefore could not provide a breath sample. The arresting officer did not tell the custody officer of this alleged condition, but neither did the motorist himself. As a result, the court held that no objective observer could say that the custody officer had 'reasonable cause to believe that for medical reasons a specimen of breath should not be required' and therefore the defendant should have been convicted for failing to provide a specimen. Answers A and C are therefore incorrect.

In *DPP* v *Furby* [2000] RTR 181, it was held that if a police officer required a motorist to provide a breath specimen at the police station and the motorist made no effort at all to blow into the machine, they could not subsequently argue that they had a reasonable excuse for failing to do so. Any such reasons should be raised promptly and where a driver clearly declined the option of replacing the breath specimen with a blood or urine sample, he was not permitted to claim later that a phobia of needles had caused him to decline the opportunity (*R (On the application of Ijaz)* v *DPP* [2004] EWHC 2635 (Admin)). Answer D is therefore incorrect.

Road Policing, para. 3.5.5.11

Answer 5.31

Answer **B** — The power under s. 7A of the Road Traffic Act 1988 allows a sample of blood to be taken from a person without his or her consent, at a hospital. It may be taken if the driver has been 'involved' in an accident and is incapable of giving consent because he or she is incapacitated due to medical reasons.

Section 7A(2)(a) states that a request under this section shall not be made to a medical practitioner 'who for the time being has any responsibility for the clinical care of the person concerned'. Note, however, that the medical practitioner in charge of the patient must still be consulted under s. 9 of the Act, as he or she will still be concerned with the physical well-being of the patient. This means that both medical practitioners must be consulted—one under s. 7A and one under s. 9. Answers A and D are incorrect as the question referred to who *could* take a sample under s. 7A.

Section 7A(2)(b) states that the request must be made to a police medical or health care practitioner unless this is not reasonably practicable, in which case the request may be made to any other medical practitioner (other than the one clinically responsible for the patient). Answer C is therefore incorrect.

Road Policing, paras 3.5.5.8, 3.5.6

Answer 5.32

Answer **D** — Under s. 9(1) of the Road Traffic Act 1988, while a person is at a hospital as a patient, he or she shall not be required to cooperate with a preliminary test or to provide a specimen of breath for a breath test or to provide a specimen under section 7 of this Act unless the medical practitioner in immediate charge of his/her case has been notified of the proposal to make the requirement; and:

(a) if the requirement is then made it shall be for co-operation with a test administered, or for the provision of a specimen, at the hospital, but
(b) if the medical practitioner objects on the ground specified in subsection (2) below, the requirement shall not be made.

The first thing that should be considered here is that the constable is not required to *ask the permission* of a medical practitioner to make a request of a suspect to cooperate with a preliminary test. This may seem like semantics, but the officer has the power to request such a test under the Road Traffic Act 1988 and s. 9(1)(a) requires the constable to consult with the medical practitioner in immediate charge of the case and allow them the opportunity to object (on medical grounds). Answer A is incorrect for this reason.

The next thing to consider is whether or not the constable in this question has consulted with the correct person (i.e. the 'medical practitioner in immediate charge of the case'). This issue was examined in *Cherpion* v *DPP* [2013] EWHC 615 (Admin), where, in similar circumstances, the defence sought to claim that the doctor who gave permission for the specimen to be taken could not have been in immediate charge, as she was a specialist. Although the person was not an A&E doctor she was the medical practitioner the officer first saw at the hospital. The High Court held that the magistrates were correct in taking a common-sense view that this doctor was in immediate charge even though she was an orthopaedic surgeon. Consider the circumstances in this question; the specialist cardiologist makes no objection because there is no medical reason to prevent a request being made for a preliminary breath test, as the suspect has suffered a leg injury and not a cardiac arrest. Because of the *Cherpion* case, answer C is incorrect.

The constable *is* required to consult with a medical practitioner who is in immediate charge of the suspect's case; therefore, answer B is incorrect.

Road Policing, para. 3.5.6

Answer 5.33

Answer **B** — While a person is at a hospital as a patient, he or she shall not be required to cooperate with a preliminary test or to provide a specimen under s. 7 of the Road Traffic Act 1988, unless the medical practitioner in immediate charge of his or her case agrees. Section 7 applies to both breath samples and samples of blood/urine.

However, if a patient provides a positive reading or fails to provide a sample at a hospital, he or she cannot be arrested while still a 'patient' (s. 6(5)). Answer B is therefore correct and answer C is incorrect as, even though the officer sought permission to take the second sample, the arrest that preceded it was unlawful.

Since the arrest was unlawful, answer A is incorrect, as the patient should not have been taken to a police station in these circumstances. However, if the person had been arrested after ceasing to be a patient, she could have been taken to the station to provide a sample (see *Webber* v *DPP* [1998] RTR 111).

Answer D is incorrect as permission must be sought from a medical practitioner for each sample that is required under s. 9(1).

Road Policing, para. 3.5.6

Answer 5.34

Answer **D** — Under s. 9 of the Road Traffic Act 1988:

(1) While a person is at a hospital as a patient, he or she shall not be required to co-operate with a preliminary test or to provide a specimen of breath for a breath test or to provide a specimen under section 7 of this Act unless the medical practitioner in immediate charge of his/her case has been notified of the proposal to make the requirement; and—

(a) if the requirement is then made it shall be for co-operation with a test administered, or for the provision of a specimen, at the hospital, but

(b) if the medical practitioner objects on the ground specified in subsection (2) below,
the requirement shall not be made.

A 'hospital' will include an institution providing medical treatment for in-patients or
out-patients (s. 11(2) of the Road Traffic Act 1988). Answer A is therefore incorrect.

If a person has been treated and then discharged from the hospital, he or she ceases
to be a 'patient' for these purposes, even if he or she has to return at a future date for
further, related treatment (e.g. to have stitches removed). Therefore, even though
PELLOW was still within the precincts of the hospital, she had been discharged and
was no longer a 'patient'. Answers B and C are therefore incorrect.

Road Policing, para. 3.5.6

Answer 5.35

Answer **D** — Section 10(1) of the Road Traffic Act 1988 states that a person required
to provide a specimen of breath, blood or urine may afterwards be detained at a
police station (or if the specimen was provided otherwise than at a police station,
arrested and taken to and detained at a police station) if the constable has reasonable
grounds for believing that, were the person to drive or attempt to drive a *mechanically
propelled* vehicle on a road, he or she would commit an offence under s. 4, 5 or 5A of
the Act. Answer C is therefore incorrect.

Although the provision of a negative screening test would be a good indication
that the person would not commit an offence under s. 4, 5 or 5A, there is no specific
power to demand such a sample. Answer B is therefore incorrect. Similarly, there is
no statutory power to retain a person's car keys to prevent them from driving
(although this is common practice) and therefore answer A is incorrect.

Road Policing, para. 3.5.7

Answer 5.36

Answer **D** — Section 10 of the Road Traffic Act 1988 allows for the detention of a
person who has provided a specimen of breath, blood or urine, until it appears to a
constable that were the person to drive a mechanically propelled vehicle on a road,
he or she would not be committing an offence. The power does not apply if it appears
to a constable that there is no likelihood of the person driving such a vehicle on a
road. There is no mention of a person having been charged or reported for an offence,

merely that they have been required to provide the relevant sample. Answer C is therefore incorrect.

Under s. 10(3), a constable *must* consult a medical practitioner on any question arising under this section whether a person's ability to drive properly is or might be impaired through drugs. The constable must act on such advice. This is mandatory; therefore, both answers A and B are incorrect.

Road Policing, para. 3.5.7

Answer 5.37

Answer **B** — Section 10 of the Road Traffic Act 1988 states:

(1) Subject to subsections (2) and (3) below, a person required under section 7 or 7A to provide a specimen of breath, blood or urine may afterwards be detained at a police station (or, if the specimen was provided otherwise than at a police station, arrested and taken to and detained at a police station) if a constable has reasonable grounds for believing that, were that person then driving or attempting to drive a mechanically propelled vehicle on a road, he would commit an offence under s. 4, 5 or 5A of this Act.

Therefore, subs. (1) allows for a person to be arrested and taken to a police station if the specimen under s. 7 was obtained otherwise than at a police station. Answers A and C are incorrect.

Section 10(1) refers to occasions where a person was required to provide a specimen of breath, blood or urine under s. 7 or s. 7A (and not just blood), therefore answer D is incorrect.

Note that under s. 10(2), a person may not be detained if it ought reasonably to appear to the constable that there is no likelihood of his driving or attempting to drive a mechanically propelled vehicle while his ability to drive properly is impaired or while the proportion of alcohol in his breath, blood or urine exceeds the prescribed limit.

Also, a person who is at a hospital as a patient shall not be arrested and taken from there to a police station in pursuance of this section if it would be prejudicial to his proper care and treatment as a patient (s. 10(2A)).

Road Policing, para. 3.5.7

6 | Insurance

QUESTIONS

Question 6.1

PERRY has just bought a new vehicle and has applied for a new certificate of insurance from an insurance company. PERRY completed the application on the Internet and was informed at the end of the process that the certificate of insurance would be made available online in approximately two hours, due to the number of applications being administered. The message also informed PERRY that a copy of the certificate of insurance would be sent by email within 24 hours, and a hard copy would be delivered by post within two days.

At which point, according to s. 147 of the Road Traffic Act 1988, was PERRY insured to drive the new vehicle?

A When the online application process was completed.
B When the certificate of insurance was made available online.
C Only when the certificate of insurance was emailed to PERRY.
D Only when PERRY received the certificate of insurance by post.

Question 6.2

SILVA owned a caravan and had just driven into a motorway services car park when the hitch attaching the caravan to the car broke. SILVA received permission to leave the caravan in the car park while he arranged to have it repaired and returned with a new part two days later. While SILVA was fitting the part, the caravan rolled backwards in the parking space; the caravan collided with a parked car, causing damage to it. At the time, the caravan was not attached to SILVA's car.

Which of the following statements is correct, in relation to the insurance requirements for SILVA's caravan, under s. 143 of the Road Traffic Act 1988?

A A caravan is a trailer and therefore cannot be included in the definition of motor vehicle when charging an offence under s. 143.

B A caravan would be classed as a motor vehicle for insurance purposes.

C A caravan is a vehicle and may be included in the definition of motor vehicle when charging an offence under s. 143.

D A caravan is a vehicle and may be included in the definition of motor vehicle when charging an offence under s. 143; however, this section only applies to vehicles on roads.

Question 6.3

SIMPSON owned a car and lent it to MARKS one day. MARKS told SIMPSON that he had a certificate of insurance and SIMPSON took his word for it. Whilst driving the vehicle on a road, MARKS was involved in a road traffic accident; it transpired that MARKS had lied to SIMPSON and did not have a certificate of insurance that covered him to drive the vehicle on a road.

Which of the following statements is correct, in relation to SIMPSON and MARKS's liability for an offence under s. 143 of the Road Traffic Act 1988?

A MARKS has used the vehicle without insurance and SIMPSON has permitted its use.

B MARKS has used the vehicle without insurance; however, SIMPSON has committed no offence because MARKS lied to her.

C MARKS has used the vehicle without insurance; for SIMPSON to be found guilty, the prosecution would have to show that she did not reasonably believe that MARKS was insured.

D Both MARKS and SIMPSON have used the vehicle without insurance in these circumstances.

Question 6.4

MARCEAUX was a French national who was staying in this country for three months with her friend, FULTON, who was a UK national. MARCEAUX was a full licence holder in France and had a motor vehicle in that country which was insured there, but she did not bring it to this country. FULTON allowed MARCEAUX to drive her home from the pub one night, as she'd had too much to drink. They were stopped by the police while MARCEAUX was driving. FULTON stated that she thought MARCEAUX might be insured through her own policy in France; MARCEAUX herself was not sure if this was the case. Both persons were later prosecuted for using a vehicle without insurance.

Considering the requirements of s. 143(1) of the Road Traffic Act 1988, in respect of which defendant, if either, would the prosecution have to prove knowledge of the fact that MARCEAUX was uninsured?

A In respect of MARCEAUX only, as the driver of the vehicle.

B In respect of neither; there is no requirement to prove guilty knowledge in these circumstances.

C In respect of FULTON only, as the owner of the vehicle.

D In respect of FULTON and MARCEAUX, as the owner and driver of the vehicle.

Question 6.5

BECKER was stopped by Constable CADDICK while driving a medium-sized van containing a large quantity of gaming CDs. BECKER produced a valid certificate of motor insurance, permitting social domestic and pleasure use of the van. Constable CADDICK believed that the certificate was invalid and that BECKER was using the vehicle for business purposes.

Which of the following statements is correct, as to the proof required that BECKER was driving the van without insurance?

A BECKER would have to demonstrate that the van was not being used for business purposes.

B The prosecution would simply have to prove that the van was being used on a road; it is for BECKER to prove that it was not being used for business purposes.

C The prosecution would have to prove that the van was being used on a road and that it was being used for business purposes.

D There is no further burden of proof; this offence is one of strict liability and BECKER has clearly committed an offence.

Question 6.6

THORNTON was stopped by the police while driving a motor vehicle on a road. As a result of checks, it appeared that the insurance for the vehicle had expired. THORNTON stated that the vehicle was owned by his employer, BIGGINS, and that he was using it in the course of his employment.

Which of the following statements is correct, in relation to any defences available to THORNTON or BIGGINS to an offence of using a motor vehicle on a road without insurance?

A As the driver, THORNTON may have a defence and he only has to prove that he was not aware that the insurance had expired; as the owner, BIGGINS cannot use this defence in these circumstances.

B As the driver, THORNTON may have a defence if he can prove that he was not aware that the insurance had expired and that he was acting in the course of his employment; as the owner, BIGGINS cannot use this defence in these circumstances.

C Both persons may have a defence to this offence; they would both have to prove that they were not aware that the insurance had expired and that THORNTON was acting in the course of his employment.

D Both persons may have a defence to this offence; THORNTON would have to prove that he was not aware that the insurance had expired and BIGGINS must prove that THORNTON was acting in the course of his employment.

Question 6.7

GRIFFITHS owned a small van, which was insured for social, domestic and pleasure purposes only. His friend, LONGMAN, was moving house and GRIFFITHS helped him by moving furniture in the van, to LONGMAN's new house. Because this entailed several trips, LONGMAN reimbursed GRIFFITHS's petrol costs.

Would GRIFFITHS be covered by his insurance policy for the use of the van in these circumstances?

A No, the use of the van would amount to a business arrangement, regardless of whether money was paid to GRIFFITHS.

B No, because money was paid to GRIFFITHS and the van was being used for purposes other than social, domestic or pleasure.

C No, either because money was paid to GRIFFITHS, or because the van was being used for purposes other than social, domestic or pleasure.

D Yes, this will not amount to a business arrangement, regardless of whether payment was paid to GRIFFITHS.

Question 6.8

SAGGERS owned a 2.0 litre Rover motor vehicle and one day the crankshaft on the vehicle failed, causing catastrophic damage to the engine. SAGGERS bought a similar Rover which was being sold for parts, which had a 2.5 litre engine that could be reconditioned and fitted to SAGGERS's car. SAGGERS paid a friend to fit the engine and then took out a new insurance policy on the vehicle; however, he failed to tell the insurance company about the increased engine capacity, despite being asked directly whether any modifications had been made to the vehicle. A week later, SAGGERS was involved in a road traffic accident, in which he was to blame, and which resulted in the Rover suffering serious damage. When the vehicle was examined by the loss adjustor, it was discovered that the engine had been modified and the insurance company declared the policy void.

Considering the requirements of s. 143(1) of the Road Traffic Act 1988, would SAGGERS's vehicle have been insured at the time of the accident?

A No, SAGGERS's false representation to the insurance company would make the policy invalid.

B Yes, unless it can be shown that SAGGERS intended to gain an advantage by making false representations to the insurance company.

C No, SAGGERS's modification to the vehicle without informing the insurance company means that the policy may be declared void retrospectively.

D Yes, the policy may not be declared void retrospectively: despite SAGGERS's false representation to the insurance company, the policy was valid at the time of the accident.

Question 6.9

Constable FENTON is a Neighbourhood Officer, who arranged to take a group of school children to the police station to take part in a community meeting. Constable FENTON had arranged for a minibus owned by the police to pick up the children; however, the vehicle broke down before arriving at the school. Fortunately, the officer owned a people carrier and offered to take the children to the police station in it. However, Constable FENTON's vehicle was only insured for social, domestic and pleasure purposes.

Would Constable FENTON's vehicle qualify for an exemption from the requirement for insurance, as outlined in s. 144 of the Road Traffic Act 1988?

A Yes, this exemption applies to on-duty officers using their vehicles for police purposes.

B No, Constable FENTON's vehicle would need to be insured for journeys to and from work.

C Yes, Constable FENTON's vehicle was being used for police purposes.

D No, the exemption would only apply if the vehicle was being used for operational purposes, such as the prevention or detection of crime.

Question 6.10

STRICKLAND suffered serious spinal injuries during an accident whilst in a vehicle being driven by CARSON. CARSON was arrested at the scene when the officer dealing with the accident discovered that the car was stolen. STRICKLAND made a claim to the Motor Insurers' Bureau (MIB) for damages as a result of the accident.

Which of the following statements is correct, in relation to the MIB's liability for STRICKLAND's claim?

A The MIB is required to make compensation in these circumstances, because STRICKLAND was a passenger in the vehicle and not the driver.

B The MIB is not required to make compensation under any circumstances to drivers or passengers in stolen vehicles.

C The MIB is required to make compensation in these circumstances, because STRICKLAND's behaviour does not amount to a deliberate criminal act, such as an assault.

D The MIB is not required to make compensation if STRICKLAND voluntarily allowed himself to be carried in a stolen vehicle.

ANSWERS

Answer 6.1

Answer **B** — Under s. 143(1)(a) of the Road Traffic Act 1988, a person must not use a motor vehicle on a road or other public place unless there is in force in relation to the use of the vehicle by that person such a policy of insurance or such a security in respect of third party risks as complies with the requirements of this Part of this Act.

Compliance with s. 143(1) requires a certificate of insurance to be 'delivered' to the owner/user of the vehicle. Anyone using, or causing or permitting to be used, a motor vehicle on a road or other public place before the delivery of such a certificate, commits this offence (s. 147(1)).

Delivery may now also take place electronically—so a certificate of insurance transmitted from the insurer to the insured by email or made available for access on a website is sufficient (s. 147(1A)(a) and (b)). Answer D is incorrect for this reason.

Therefore, in this particular question, delivery had not been made when the person completed the application process online, as they were told the certificate would be made available two hours after completion. Answer A is therefore incorrect. However, it was made when the certificate was made available online, before it was emailed to PERRY, and so answer C is incorrect.

Road Policing, para. 3.6.2

Answer 6.2

Answer **C** — Under s. 143(1)(a) of the Road Traffic Act 1988, a person must not use a motor vehicle on a road *or other public place* unless there is in force in relation to the use of the vehicle by that person such a policy of insurance or such a security in respect of third party risks. Answer D is therefore incorrect.

Although the question of whether or not a policy applies to the particular vehicle will not usually present a problem, trailers (which would include caravans) can create difficulties, in relation to both the vehicles covered by the policy, and the use to which they are being put. Trailers are themselves 'vehicles' (and not motor vehicles) and answer B is incorrect.

However, trailers *may* be included in the definition of motor vehicle when charging an offence under s. 143 (*Rogerson* v *Stephens* [1950] 2 All ER 144). Answer A is therefore incorrect.

Road Policing, paras 3.6.2, 3.6.2.3

125

Answer 6.3

Answer **A** — Generally the offence under s. 143 is one of strict liability, that is, you need not prove any intent or guilty knowledge by the defendant in order to convict (*Tapsell* v *Maslen* [1967] Crim LR 53). Answer C is therefore incorrect.

If a person allows another to use his or her vehicle on the express condition that the other person insures it first, the lender cannot be convicted of 'permitting' (*Newbury* v *Davis* [1974] RTR 367). However, this defence is available when the person makes it a condition of driving the motor vehicle on a road; simply accepting someone's word that they have insurance would not be enough to convince the court that this defence is applicable. Answer B is therefore incorrect.

The offence of 'permitting' is more appropriate than 'use' in these circumstances and answer D is therefore incorrect.

Road Policing, paras 3.6.2, 3.6.2.1

Answer 6.4

Answer **B** — Generally, the offence under s. 143(1) of the Road Traffic Act 1988 is one of strict liability, that is, you need not prove any intent or guilty knowledge by the defendant in order to convict, especially in these circumstances (*Tapsell* v *Maslen* [1967] Crim LR 53).

Answers A, C and D are therefore incorrect.

Road Policing, para. 3.6.2.1

Answer 6.5

Answer **C** — Generally the offence under s. 143 of the Road Traffic Act 1988 is one of strict liability, that is, you need not prove any intent or guilty knowledge by the defendant in order to convict (*Tapsell* v *Maslen* [1967] Crim LR 53).

However, there is still a burden of proof on the Crown to prove that the use of the vehicle had not been in accordance with the terms of use permitted by that policy of insurance. In *DPP* v *Whittaker* [2015] EWHC 1850 (Admin) the defendant was stopped by police whilst driving a van containing a large number of DVDs. There was limited questioning by the police officer about the use of the vehicle and the defendant subsequently produced a valid certificate of motor insurance permitting social domestic and pleasure use of the van. The defendant was charged with using a motor vehicle without insurance on the basis the van was used for the business of mobile

DVD sales which was not permitted under the terms of insurance. The Justices found no case to answer which was supported by the High Court holding that the *prosecution* still had to provide evidence that the vehicle was being used for a business use to discharge their burden of proof.

Answers A, B and D are therefore incorrect.

Road Policing, para. 3.6.2.1

Answer 6.6

Answer **B** — Under s. 143(3) of the Road Traffic Act 1988, a person charged with using a motor vehicle in contravention of this section shall not be convicted if he/she proves:

(a) that the vehicle did not belong to him and was not in his possession under a contract of hiring or of loan,

(b) that he was using the vehicle in the course of his employment, *and*

(c) that he neither knew nor had reason to believe that there was not in force in relation to the vehicle such a policy of insurance or security as is mentioned in subsection (1) above.

While the defence is open to a person who is 'using' the motor vehicle on a road without insurance (which in a legal sense includes the owner, BIGGINS), the defendant is required to prove all three elements under s. 143(3). Therefore, as the owner of the vehicle, BIGGINS could not use this subsection as a defence (because of the requirements in s. 143(3)(a)) and answers C and D are incorrect.

On the other hand, the defence may be available to THORNTON (as the driver and not the owner) provided he can prove *both* elements under s. 143(3)(b) and (c), i.e. that he was not aware that the insurance had expired *and* that he was acting in the course of his employment. Answer A is therefore incorrect.

Road Policing, para. 3.6.2.2

Answer 6.7

Answer **D** — Lending a vehicle to a friend in return for payment reimbursing petrol costs has been held *not* to contravene s. 143 of the Road Traffic Act 1988, even when the vehicle was insured only for social, domestic and pleasure purposes (see *Lee* v *Poole* [1954] Crim LR 942). Answers B and C are incorrect for this reason. In the same case, it was held that using the vehicle to help a friend to move house will still amount to using the vehicle for social, domestic and pleasure purposes, therefore answer A is also incorrect.

Road Policing, para. 3.6.2.3

Answer 6.8

Answer **D** — Section 148(1) of the Road Traffic Act 1988 makes the effects of some restrictions in a policy void in relation to s. 143. This means that, if a policy purports to restrict the extent of its cover by reference to any of these features, breach of them by the insured person will *not* affect the validity of that policy for the purposes of s. 143. Those features will include, under s. 148(2)(f), 'the horsepower or cylinder capacity or value of the vehicle'.

It was held in *Durrant* v *MacLaren* [1956] 2 Lloyd's Rep 70 that an insurance policy obtained by false representations will be valid for the purposes of s. 143; therefore, SAGGERS's vehicle was covered by his insurance at the time of the accident despite the false representations to the insurance company and regardless of whether he intended to gain an advantage. Answers A and B are therefore incorrect.

Also, while the insurance company was entitled to declare the policy void, the vehicle remains insured until the contract has been 'avoided' (ended) by the insurer (see *Durrant*) and answer C is therefore incorrect.

Road Policing, paras 3.6.2.3, 3.6.2.4

Answer 6.9

Answer **C** — Section 144 of the Road Traffic Act 1988 sets out occasions where vehicles will be exempt from the requirement for having insurance. Such occasions include police authority vehicles and vehicles being used for police purposes. Since the officer in the scenario would be using the vehicle for police purposes, the vehicle would be exempt and no additional insurance would be required. Answer B is therefore incorrect.

The exemption will include an off-duty police officer using his or her own vehicle for police purposes (*Jones* v *Chief Constable of Bedfordshire* [1987] RTR 332). However, the exemption is not restricted to *on-duty* officers using their vehicles for police purposes and for this reason answer A is incorrect.

There is nothing in the Act which states that the vehicle must be used for operational purposes, such as the prevention or detection of crime. Answer D is therefore incorrect.

Road Policing, para. 3.6.2.5

Answer 6.10

Answer **D** — All insurers in Great Britain are required to be members of the Motor Insurers' Bureau (MIB) (s. 145 of the Road Traffic Act 1988).

The purpose of the MIB is to provide compensation where someone is unable to pursue a valid claim against another following a road traffic accident because the other party is:

- not insured;
- not known/traceable;
- insured by a company now in liquidation.

The MIB has drawn up an agreement with the Secretary of State which sets out its terms of operation. Under the terms of the agreement, the MIB is not required to compensate claimants if they voluntarily allowed themselves to be carried in a stolen vehicle and either before the commencement of the journey, or after the commencement, the person could reasonably have been expected to have alighted from it, or knew or ought to have known that the vehicle had been stolen or unlawfully taken. Answers A and C are therefore incorrect.

Since there *are* circumstances when the MIB may have to compensate passengers in stolen vehicles (e.g. if they didn't know the vehicle was stolen), answer B is incorrect.

Road Policing, para. 3.6.3

7 | Legislation for the Protection of Road Users

STUDY PREPARATION

This chapter examines the legislation aimed at protecting all users of the roads.

Once again this is a pretty straightforward area.

QUESTIONS

Question 7.1

PRENTON was driving along a road and was stopped by Constable DENT for not wearing a seat belt. PRENTON's 15-year-old daughter was sitting in the front of the vehicle and her 13-year-old son was sitting in the rear; neither was wearing a seat belt. The vehicle had seat belts fitted in the front and the rear.

Which of the following statements is true in relation to any possible offences committed by PRENTON under s. 14(3) of the Road Traffic Act 1988 (provisions for wearing seat belts)?

A PRENTON was guilty of not wearing her own belt and aiding and abetting the two children, who also commit offences under this section.

B PRENTON was guilty of not wearing her own belt and committed separate offences under this section in relation to her two children.

C PRENTON was guilty of not wearing her own seat belt and a separate offence under this section relating to her son; she committed no offence in relation to her daughter.

D PRENTON was guilty of not wearing her own seat belt and a separate offence under this section relating to her son; she is also guilty of aiding and abetting her daughter, who also commits the offence.

Question 7.2

DECKER was driving a two-year-old motor vehicle on a road and had three passengers in the vehicle, all of whom were his children. PAUL, aged 14, was sitting in the rear nearside passenger seat and was not wearing a seat belt; MANDY, aged 10, was 1 metre in height and was sitting in the rear offside passenger seat wearing a normal adult seat belt; DANNY, aged 2, was sitting in a rear-facing child safety seat in the front passenger seat. DECKER was wearing a seat belt himself and the front passenger airbag was deactivated.

Which of the following statements is true in relation to the wearing of seat belts?
A DECKER commits an offence in respect of all three children in these circumstances.
B DECKER commits no offence in these circumstances; however, PAUL would commit an offence.
C DECKER commits an offence in respect of MANDY only in these circumstances; however, PAUL would also commit an offence.
D DECKER commits an offence in respect of MANDY and DANNY in these circumstances; however, PAUL would also commit an offence.

Question 7.3

Constable FARRELL has stopped BALE while driving a motor vehicle on a road, for failing to wear a seat belt. BALE claimed an exemption to wearing a seat belt for medical reasons. Constable FARRELL has decided to issue BALE with an HORT/1 to produce a driving licence, certificate of insurance and test certificate, together with proof of the exemption from wearing a seat belt.

What are BALE's responsibilities to produce documents in these circumstances?
A BALE must be in possession of a certificate of exemption and produce it on request, immediately, and produce the other documents at a police station within seven days.
B BALE must produce a certificate of exemption on request, or at a police station within seven days, with the other documents.
C BALE must produce a certificate of exemption within a reasonable time, or at a police station within seven days, with the other documents.

D BALE need only produce a driving licence, certificate of insurance and test certificate at a police station within seven days; the exemption from wearing a seat belt should be indicated on the driving licence.

Question 7.4

WEBSTER works for a delivery company and visits ten shops in a shopping precinct, in a small goods vehicle. WEBSTER delivers fresh fruit, vegetables and flowers to various shops in the morning from a market situated half a mile from the precinct. The shops were situated just under 100 metres apart. One Saturday morning, WEBSTER took his son, aged 14, to help him. That day, they drove to the shops from the market without their seat belts fastened and then delivered the goods, again while not wearing seat belts.

Which of the following statements is correct in relation to whether WEBSTER or his son would qualify for the exemption from wearing seat belts, under s. 14(2)(b)(i) of the Road Traffic Act 1988?

A Only WEBSTER would qualify for the exemption, his son cannot qualify because of his age.

B Both would qualify for the exemption as they were on a journey to deliver goods.

C They would only qualify for the exemption when they were in the shopping precinct; they committed an offence while driving there.

D They would not qualify for the exemption at any time in these circumstances.

Question 7.5

MICHAELS was riding a motorbicycle combination on the road. At the time, KEANE was a pillion passenger and ANDERSEN was sitting in the side-car. MICHAELS was wearing a crash helmet that did not bear a British Standard kite mark, but which was substantial enough to meet British Standard requirements. KEANE was wearing an old-style motorcycle helmet, which had a chin strap and cup attached, which was not fastened. ANDERSEN was wearing a helmet that said 'Not for Motorbike Use' but appeared to be just as substantial as MICHAELS's helmet. All people on the motorbicycle combination were over 18.

Who, if anyone, has committed an offence of not wearing protective headgear, under s. 16(4) of the Road Traffic Act 1988?

A MICHAELS and KEANE.

B KEANE only.

C MICHAELS and ANDERSEN.
D MICHAELS only.

Question 7.6

HEALEY, aged 22, has a full licence to ride motorcycles. One day, HEALEY gave WORTH, aged 15, a ride on a motorcycle as a pillion passenger. They were stopped while riding on the road by Constable MALLOY and at the time, WORTH was not wearing a helmet.

Who, if either, would commit an offence in these circumstances (because of WORTH's failure to wear a helmet)?
A Both, because of WORTH's age.
B WORTH only, because of his age.
C Both, regardless of WORTH's age.
D HEALEY only, because of WORTH's age.

Question 7.7

HAMILTON is the holder of a full licence to ride motorcycles. One day, HAMILTON gave STEWART a ride on a motorcycle as a pillion passenger. As a joke, STEWART sat astride the motorcycle, behind HAMILTON, facing the rear. HAMILTON was fully aware of what STEWART was doing. They were stopped by Constable CHOI while riding on the road.

Who, if either, would commit an offence in these circumstances (because of STEWART's seating position), under s. 23 of the Road Traffic Act 1988?
A Both HAMILTON and STEWART commit the full offence because STEWART was not sitting properly astride the motorcycle.
B HAMILTON commits the full offence because STEWART was not sitting properly astride the motorcycle. STEWART is guilty of aiding and abetting HAMILTON.
C Neither; there is no requirement for a pillion passenger to face the front, provided they are sitting astride the motorcycle.
D STEWART commits the full offence of not sitting properly astride the motorcycle. HAMILTON is guilty of aiding and abetting STEWART.

Question 7.8

Constable BASTABLE was conducting a speeding operation on a main road, using a hand-held speed detection camera. The officer was positioned on a long stretch of road, which led to a bend and was pointing the camera towards the bend. BETTS was travelling in a vehicle in the opposite direction, away from the officer. Upon negotiating the bend, BETTS attempted to warn other drivers approaching Constable BASTABLE by flashing the headlights of the vehicle. BETTS was seen by another police officer who was driving a police vehicle towards Constable BASTABLE.

Would BETTS's actions amount to an offence of obstructing a police constable in the execution of their duty, in these circumstances?

A Yes, merely giving such a warning can amount to an offence.

B Yes, provided it can be shown that the other drivers were exceeding the speed limit.

C No, warning drivers in such a way does not amount to an offence.

D Yes, provided it can be shown that the other drivers were exceeding the speed limit or were likely to do so.

Question 7.9

COOMBES is pleading not guilty to a speeding offence, having been caught by a mobile speed detection vehicle driving at 47 mph in a 40 mph area. COOMBES has produced photographic evidence in court showing that the traffic sign at the commencement of the area was badly maintained and has claimed that it did not conform to the Traffic Signs Regulations and General Directions 2002 (TSRGD) and the Traffic Signs Manual 2008 (TSM). The prosecution, on the other hand, has produced evidence that there were ample 'repeater' signs at the side of the road that *did* conform to the TSRGD and TSM, which they claim provided adequate guidance as to the speed limit.

Which of the following statements is true in relation to COOMBES's defence?

A Even though the sign may not have conformed to the Regulations, COOMBES could still be guilty if the court finds that adequate guidance was provided as to the speed limit.

B If the court finds the sign did not conform to the Regulations, it must find COOMBES not guilty of the offence.

C The Regulations are merely guidelines; it is for the driver to familiarise themselves with speed limits and COOMBES is guilty of the offence regardless of the condition of the sign.

D Speeding is an absolute offence; it is for the driver to familiarise themselves with speed limits and COOMBES is guilty of the offence regardless of the condition of the sign.

Question 7.10

OLSEN is appearing in Crown Court, having been charged with causing death by dangerous driving. OLSEN was driving along an unfamiliar country road and failed to negotiate a sharp right-hand bend. OLSEN's car collided with a stone wall and the front seat passenger, CROWLEY, was killed outright. OLSEN is pleading not guilty to the offence, claiming that there were no warning signs or chevrons on the approach to the sharp bend. OLSEN's defence will be that the liability for the accident lay with the local authority, as it had failed in its statutory duty to maintain the highway, under s. 41 of the Highways Act 1980.

Which of the following statements is correct in relation to OLSEN's claim?

A The local authority has committed an offence under this section and could be liable.

B The local authority has not committed an offence, but it has a common law duty to promote road safety and has failed in this case.

C The local authority has not committed an offence; drivers bear their own responsibility to protect themselves and their passengers and OLSEN is liable.

D The local authority has not committed an offence, but the absence of road signs may provide OLSEN with a defence in these circumstances.

Question 7.11

Constable MACINTYRE was a Roads Policing Officer and was driving a police vehicle fitted with specialist speed measuring equipment along a restricted road. The road normally had a set speed limit of 50 mph; however, roadworks were being conducted at the location and a temporary speed restriction was in place, reducing the speed limit to 30 mph. Constable MACINTYRE stopped GRETTON, who had been travelling at 49 mph and reported her for exceeding the speed limit.

Is Constable MACINTYRE required to give GRETTON a notice of intended prosecution (NIP), in these circumstances?

A Yes, an NIP is required for this offence on a restricted road, even when there is a temporary speed restriction in place.

B No, an NIP is not required for this offence on a restricted road, when there is a temporary speed restriction in place.

C Yes, an NIP is required for all speeding offences, regardless of where they are committed.

D No, an NIP is not required for speeding offences committed on restricted roads or motorways.

Question 7.12

EMMERICH works in the Fire and Rescue Service and is on a training course to learn how to drive fire tenders. EMMERICH has been given instructions by the instructor to drive at speeds above the statutory speed limits.

Would EMMERICH be exempt from the laws in relation to speed limits in these circumstances, under s. 87 of the Road Traffic Regulation Act 1984?

A No, the exemption does not apply to such vehicles being used on training courses.

B Yes, provided EMMERICH has been previously trained in driving at high speeds.

C Yes, the exemption applies to EMMERICH regardless of any previous training received.

D Yes, provided EMMERICH does not exceed any speed limit by more than 30 mph.

Question 7.13

Constable WOODS and Constable HUSSEIN were on duty in a marked police vehicle, which was not equipped with specialist speed measuring equipment. They were driving along a restricted road, which had a speed limit of 30 mph. They followed DICKSON, who was driving at 40 mph in his car, for about a mile. The officers stopped DICKSON and spoke to him.

Would the officers be able to give evidence of DICKSON's speed, in order to prosecute him for the offence of speeding?

A No, their evidence does not amount to corroboration, and would not be accepted in court.

B Yes, provided it can be shown that they saw the vehicle at exactly the same time.

C Yes, the evidence that they both saw the vehicle speeding is sufficient alone to prosecute.

D Yes, corroboration is not required, as the offence took place on a restricted road.

Question 7.14

Constable NOBLE was a Roads Policing Officer on patrol in a marked police vehicle single crewed. The officer was trialling the latest speed measuring equipment, which was fitted to the vehicle, but was yet to be approved for operational use by the Association of Chief Police Officers (ACPO). The intention was that Constable NOBLE would record vehicle speeds for testing purposes, not to prosecute drivers; however, the officer was driving on a road with a speed limit of 40 mph behind MONCRIEFF, who was travelling at 70 mph. Constable NOBLE stopped and reported MONCRIEFF for the offence, due to the vehicle's excessive speed.

If MONCRIEFF were to be prosecuted for speeding, could the prosecution rely on the reading provided by the device being tested?

A Yes, the opinion of the police officer could be supported by reference to the reading on the device, even though it is not approved by ACPO.

B No, the officer's evidence and a calibration certificate of the speed detection device are required in all cases.

C No, a person prosecuted for exceeding the speed limit cannot be convicted solely on the evidence of one witness.

D No, the court will only accept the evidence provided by a device approved by ACPO.

Question 7.15

Constable BURNS stopped McCABE, who was driving a motor vehicle on a road. The officer had seen McCABE smoking a cigarette in the vehicle and had noticed that there was a child sat in the back seat of the car.

How old must the child be for McCABE to be guilty of a breach of the Smoke-free (Private Vehicles) Regulations 2015?

A The child must be at least under 10.

B The child must be at least under 14.

C The child must be at least under 17.

D The child must be at least under 18.

Question 7.16

LEVESQUE was sat in the front passenger seat of a motor vehicle which was parked at the side of the road; Constable HOOFMAN was walking past and saw that the front passenger door was open and that LEVESQUE was smoking a cigarette. At the time, MORTON was sat in the driver's seat and was not smoking and there were two young children under 10 sat in the rear passenger seats.

Could either LEVESQUE or MORTON be guilty of a breach of the Smoke-free (Private Vehicles) Regulations 2015, in these circumstances?

A Yes, both could be guilty in these circumstances.

B No, the vehicle was not being driven on a road.

C Yes, but only LEVESQUE, who was actually smoking.

D No, the door to the vehicle was open, which meant that it was not 'enclosed'.

Question 7.17

NEWMAN and DUNN lived on a housing estate and were continually disturbed by local youths on motorcycles on a field behind their houses. The only access to the field was via a bridleway, which was used by horse riders and ramblers. The motorcyclists used the bridleway to get onto the field, usually in the evenings. In an attempt to try to stop the motorcyclists, NEWMAN and DUNN tied a length of rope across the bridleway at waist height, hoping that it would unseat the riders. They were not particularly bothered if the riders were injured or their vehicles damaged, they were merely trying to prevent access to the field and stop the disturbance they created.

Considering the location of the obstruction created by NEWMAN and DUNN, could they have committed an offence under s. 22A of the Road Traffic Act 1988 (causing danger to other road users)?

A No, an offence under this section can only be committed on a road.

B Yes, a bridleway is a road for the purposes of s. 192(1) of the Act.

C Yes, an offence under this section can be committed on a road or public place.

D No, the location is irrelevant; an offence is committed under this section when a person causes anything to be *on* a road in circumstances that would lead to danger.

Question 7.18

SEXTON was crossing a footbridge directly above a motorway near his house and thought it would be fun to drop stones onto cars that were passing underneath. SEXTON dropped several stones which missed the vehicles travelling under the bridge; however, as a result of several complaints, Constable AYERS had attended the location and caught SEXTON on the bridge.

Considering the offence under s. 22A of the Road Traffic Act 1988 (causing danger to other road users), which of the following statements is correct?

A To prove this offence, the prosecution would have to show that SEXTON intended to cause a danger to the road users.

B To prove this offence, the prosecution would have to show that SEXTON intended to cause damage to one or more of the vehicles.

C To prove this offence, the prosecution would only have to show that SEXTON intended to drop the stones on the vehicles.

D To prove this offence, the prosecution would have to show that SEXTON intended to drop the stones on the vehicles and that it would have been obvious to a reasonable person that to do so would be dangerous.

Question 7.19

Constable FLANAGAN attended a road traffic accident on a road, involving two vehicles; a passenger in one of the vehicles had been injured. On arrival, the officer noticed that visibility was very poor due to smoke and the drivers involved alleged that the smoke was a major cause of the accident. Constable FLANAGAN traced the source of the smoke to a field next to the road, owned by MORSE, who was burning waste.

Could MORSE be guilty of an offence under s. 161A(1) of the Highways Act 1980, in these circumstances?

A Yes, provided the fire was lit within 50 feet of the centre of the highway.

B Yes, but only because one of the passengers was injured.

C No, MORSE did not light a fire on or over the highway.

D Yes, regardless of whether a person was injured or whether the fire was lit within 50 feet of the centre of the highway.

Question 7.20

MAGUIRE owns a large flat bed trailer, which he frequently leaves outside his house, which is situated on a hill. MAGUIRE left the trailer outside the house one evening, but forgot to set the braking mechanism. As a consequence, the trailer rolled down-hill, colliding with another vehicle.

Would MAGUIRE commit an offence under s. 22 of the Road Traffic Act 1988 (dangerous vehicles) in these circumstances?

A No, the trailer was not attached to a motor vehicle.

B No, this offence only applies to the condition of a vehicle.

C Yes, the offence is complete in these circumstances.

D No, this offence only applies to stationary vehicles.

Question 7.21

HARRIS was in a multi-storey car park attached to a shopping centre. The car park was operated by a private company, which owned the shopping centre, but was open to the general public at the time. The car park was covered by CCTV and the night security guard saw HARRIS climb onto the bonnet of a car and then run over the roof, jumping off the vehicle from the boot. He did this to several vehicles in the car park. The night security guard called the police and when they arrived, HARRIS was walking away from the car park.

Has HARRIS committed the offence of tampering with vehicles, under s. 25 of the Road Traffic Act 1988, in these circumstances?

A No, because the vehicles were not on a road.

B No, because the car park was not owned by the local authority.

C Yes, because the vehicles were in a public place.

D No, because he did not interfere with the brakes or mechanisms of the vehicles.

Question 7.22

MEYER was walking down a country road, having abandoned his car which had broken down. MEYER heard a slow-moving tractor approaching and saw that it was towing a trailer loaded with hay. MEYER decided to try to hitch a lift and, as the vehicle passed, he jumped onto the back of the trailer without the driver's knowledge. About a mile further down the road, the tractor turned into a field and MEYER jumped off again to continue walking.

Has MEYER committed an offence under s. 26 of the Road Traffic Act 1988, in these circumstances?

A No, this offence may not be committed in relation to mechanically propelled vehicles.

B No, MEYER got onto a trailer and not a mechanically propelled vehicle or a motor vehicle.

C Yes, the offence is complete in these circumstances alone.

D No, this offence is committed when a person holds onto a motor vehicle for the purposes of being drawn.

Question 7.23

DEERE retired from work and went on a touring holiday to Europe for six months. DEERE's teenage son, JEFFREY, was allowed to use the family car while DEERE was away. In the first month, the car was seized from JEFFREY for using it while causing harassment. Several times during the following months, the relevant authority wrote to DEERE, the registered owner, serving notice that the vehicle had been seized. Upon returning from holiday, DEERE discovered that JEFFREY had ignored all correspondence from the authority and that as no reply had been received, the vehicle had been sold at a car auction.

Would DEERE have the right to claim the proceeds from the sale of the vehicle?

A No, the proceeds may be kept by the authority, as DEERE failed to comply with the seizure notice.

B Yes, DEERE can claim the net proceeds from the sale in these circumstances alone.

C No, unless it can be shown that the authority did not take reasonable steps to contact DEERE before the vehicle was sold.

D Yes, provided it can be shown that DEERE was not aware that the vehicle would be driven in such a manner by JEFFREY.

Question 7.24

PEARCE is a designated police community support officer (PCSO) working on a housing estate. He has received a number of complaints from residents about HOGAN riding his motorcycle in a park nearby. Last week, PEARCE stopped HOGAN while he was riding his motorcycle and issued him with a warning under s. 59 of the Police Reform Act 2002, as he had narrowly missed colliding with some children playing football. PEARCE has today received a further complaint about HOGAN, who again rode his motorcycle in the park, nearly injuring a child. PEARCE attended HOGAN's home address and saw the motorcycle on the road outside.

Does PEARCE have the power to seize HOGAN's motorcycle, under s. 59(3)(b) of the Police Reform Act 2002, in these circumstances?

A No, a PCSO's power is restricted to stopping vehicles.

B Yes, he has the power to seize and remove the vehicle in these circumstances.

C Yes, provided he is accompanied by a police officer in uniform.

D No, as the motorcycle is no longer being used.

ANSWERS

Answer 7.1

Answer **C** — Under s. 14(3) of the Road Traffic Act 1988 it is an offence to:

- drive a motor vehicle; or
- ride in a front seat of a motor vehicle; or
- ride in the rear seat of a motor car or passenger car;

in each case without wearing an adult seat belt.

Section 14(3) goes on to say that, notwithstanding any enactment or rule of law, no person other than the person actually committing the contravention is guilty of an offence by reason of the contravention. This means that, irrespective of the general law relating to the aiding and abetting of offences, the driver of a vehicle will not be responsible for a passenger not wearing a seat belt.

However, the position under s. 15 of the 1988 Act is that in respect of children under 14 years of age who are not wearing seat belts, the driver is responsible for the failure to wear a seat belt.

Since her 15-year-old daughter is responsible for her own actions, PRENTON committed no offence in respect of her and answers A, B and D are incorrect.

PRENTON committed the *substantive* offence in respect of herself and her son; therefore, answer A is also incorrect for this reason.

Road Policing, paras 3.7.2, 3.7.2.2

Answer 7.2

Answer **C** — The law governing the wearing of seat belts by children travelling in the front of a car is currently set out in the Motor Vehicles (Wearing of Seat Belts by Children in Front Seats) Regulations 1993 (SI 1993/31), as amended, while the wearing of restraints by children travelling in the rear of a car is currently set out in the Motor Vehicles (Wearing of Seat Belts) Regulations 1993 (SI 1993/176), as amended.

Dealing with the offences and seating positions in the question; as a passenger aged 14 or over, PAUL is liable for his own actions and DECKER commits no offence in relation to his not wearing a seat belt. Answer A is therefore incorrect.

Where a child is between the ages of 3 and 12, and is under 135 cm in height, they must use an appropriate restraint, such as a booster seat or a booster cushion, depending on their height and weight. Since MANDY is aged 10 and under the required height, she should not have been travelling in a car (in the front or rear) whilst wearing an adult seat belt. Because she is under the age of 14, DECKER is responsible for her actions and would commit an offence. Answer B is therefore incorrect.

Finally, a child under the age of three must use their own suitable child restraint—a child safety seat, whether they are sitting in the front or rear of the car. If the child is sitting in the front passenger seat, the air bag must be deactivated and since it was in this case, DECKER commits no offence in respect of DANNY. Answer D is therefore incorrect.

Road Policing, paras 3.7.2, 3.7.2.3

Answer 7.3

Answer **B** — A person may be exempt from wearing a seat belt, provided they have been issued with a medical certificate, signed by a doctor, stating that the wearing of a seat belt by that person is inadvisable on medical grounds. Answer D is incorrect as a separate certificate is required.

If the certificate is to be used in evidence in answer to a charge under s. 14(3) of the Road Traffic Act 1988, the certificate must be produced to a constable *either* on request, *or* within seven days at a police station. Answers A and C are therefore incorrect.

Road Policing, para. 3.7.2.4

Answer 7.4

Answer **D** — Section 14(2)(b)(i) of the Road Traffic Act 1988 provides a general exemption in relation to the wearing of seat belts by drivers and the passengers in motor vehicles constructed or adapted for carrying goods while on a journey related to the transport of such goods. However, the exemption only applies to journeys that do not exceed the prescribed distance, which is 50 metres (see reg. 6(1)(b) of the Motor Vehicles (Wearing of Seat Belts) Regulations 1993). This means that neither WEBSTER nor his son could claim the exemption at any time in these circumstances and answers A, B and C are therefore incorrect.

There is no mention of a person's age in s. 14(2)(b)(i); therefore, in theory, WEBSTER's son *could* qualify for the exemption if the journeys were shorter. Answer A is also incorrect for this reason.

Road Policing, para. 3.7.2.4

Answer 7.5

Answer **B** — Section 16(4) of the Road Traffic Act 1988 states:

> A person who drives or rides on a motor cycle in contravention of regulations under this section is guilty of an offence...

The relevant regulations are the Motor Cycles (Protective Helmets) Regulations 1998 (SI 1998/1807) as amended.

The helmet worn must either conform to one of the British Standards specified (in reg. 5) and be marked as such or it must give a similar (or greater) degree of protection as one which meets those standards and be of a type manufactured for motorcyclists (reg. 4(3)(a)). Since MICHAELS's helmet was substantial enough to meet British Standard requirements, it conforms to the Regulations and no offence is committed in respect of it. Answers A, C and D are therefore incorrect.

Regulation 4 requires every person driving or riding on a motor *bicycle* on a road to wear protective headgear (thereby exempting people riding tricycles and quad bikes). Further, 'riding on' in this offence means that pillion passengers must wear helmets but s. 16(1) of the 1988 Act exempts people in side-cars from wearing helmets; answer C is also incorrect for this reason.

If the helmet is unfastened or improperly fastened (e.g. with part of the chinstrap undone) the offence will be complete (reg. 4(3)(b) and (c)). This is why KEANE is the only one that commits the offence.

Finally, s. 16(4) provides that only the person committing the offence of not wearing a helmet shall be liable *unless the person is under* 16. This means that MICHAELS has no liability for KEANE's offence; answer A is also incorrect for this reason.

Road Policing, paras 3.7.3, 3.7.3.1

Answer 7.6

Answer **A** — Section 16(4) of the Road Traffic Act 1988 makes it an offence to ride on a motorcycle without a crash helmet. 'Ride on' includes being a pillion passenger.

If the pillion passenger is under 16, the offence is committed by both the rider and the passenger. If the pillion passenger is 16 or over, he or she alone is responsible.

This is in contrast to seat belt legislation, where young passengers are not responsible for their own actions. As the person in the question was 15, both he and the driver commit the offence. Answers B, C and D are therefore incorrect.

Road Policing, paras 3.7.3, 3.7.3.1

Answer 7.7

Answer **C** — Section 23 of the Road Traffic Act 1988 states:

(1) Not more than one person in addition to the driver may be carried on a motor bicycle.
(2) No person in addition to the driver may be carried on a motor bicycle otherwise than sitting astride the motor cycle and on a proper seat securely fixed to the motor cycle behind the driver's seat.
(3) If a person is carried on a motor cycle in contravention of this section, the driver of the motor cycle is guilty of an offence.

There is no specific requirement for the passenger to face the *front* (under subs. (2))—though this is presumably because it did not occur to the legislators that anyone would be daft enough to face the other way! Answers A, B and D are incorrect for this reason.

Under this section it is the *driver* who commits the offence (s. 23(3)), and the passenger can be convicted of aiding and abetting. Therefore, if an offence had been present, answers A and D would have been incorrect for this reason also.

It should be noted that a person travelling as a passenger astride a motorcycle but facing the rear *may* commit an offence of aiding and abetting the driver to drive dangerously, but this is not specifically legislated for.

Road Policing, para. 3.7.3.1

Answer 7.8

Answer **D** — The practice of warning other motorists of the presence of a police speed detection operation can amount to an offence of obstructing a police constable in the execution of their duty (see *DPP* v *Glendinning* [2005] EWHC 2333 (Admin) and *Betts* v *Stevens* [1910] 1 KB 1). Answer C is therefore incorrect.

In such cases, it is critical that it is shown that those warned were either exceeding the speed limit or were likely to do so (answer B is therefore incorrect). However, in the absence of such evidence, merely giving a warning to drivers who were observing the speed limit at the time will not amount to this offence (see *Bastable* v *Little* [1907] 1 KB 59). Answer A is therefore incorrect.

Note that the signal emitted by a hand-held radar speed gun has been deemed *not* to amount to a 'communication' for the purposes of the Wireless Telegraphy Act 1949 and a person intercepting such signals cannot be prosecuted under that legislation (*R* v *Crown Court of Knightsbridge, ex parte Foot* [1999] RTR 21).

Road Policing, paras 3.7.4, 3.7.4.6

Answer 7.9

Answer **A** — Section 85(1) of the Road Traffic Regulation Act 1984 states:

> For the purpose of securing that adequate guidance is given to drivers of motor vehicles as to whether any, and if so what, limit of speed is to be observed on any road, it shall be the duty of the Secretary of State, [in the case of a road for which he is the traffic authority, to] erect and maintain...traffic signs in such positions as may be requisite for that purpose.

The Traffic Signs Regulations and General Directions 2002 (TSRGD) set out the requirements for signs that are used, amongst other things, for speed limits, and the Traffic Signs Manual 2008 (TSM) sets out how the signs approved by the TSRGD are to be used on the roadside.

In *Coombes* v *DPP* [2007] RTR 31 and *DPP* v *Butler* [2010] EWHC 669 (Admin) the courts found that the signs did not conform to the Regulations and therefore the speeding convictions were overturned. Therefore, where a sign fails to conform to the TSRGD and TSM it may be fatal to a case where that sign has been contravened. Answers C and D are incorrect because a case *may* be lost by a failure to follow the Regulations.

However, s. 85 of the Road Traffic Regulation Act 1984 states that traffic signs for indicating speed restrictions must ensure 'adequate guidance is given to drivers of motor vehicles as to whether, and if so what, limit of speed is to be observed on any road'.

Further, in *Peake* v *DPP* [2010] EWHC 286 (Admin) and *Jones* v *DPP* [2011] EWHC 50 (Admin) the courts found that there were 'repeater' signs that provided adequate guidance to motorists and the convictions were ratified despite there being technical faults with some of the signage.

Therefore where such 'adequate guidance' is given, a conviction may stand even where there are technical breaches and answer B is incorrect.

Road Policing, para. 3.7.4.2

Answer 7.10

Answer **C** — The primary responsibility for maintaining highways rests with the highways authority for the relevant area. This includes a general statutory duty to maintain the highway itself (see s. 41 of the Highways Act 1980), which includes a duty, so far as reasonably practicable, to ensure that safe passage along the highway is not endangered by snow or ice (s. 41(1A)).

However, failure by a local authority to erect signs does not amount to a breach of the general statutory duty to maintain highways nor the general duty to promote road safety. As the House of Lords has put it, 'drivers have to take care for themselves and drive at a safe speed irrespective of whether or not there was a warning sign; they were not entitled to suppose that the need for care on their journeys would be highlighted so as to protect them from their own negligence' (*Gorringe* v *Calderdale MBC* [2004] UKHL 15).

Answers A, B and D are therefore incorrect.

Road Policing, paras 3.7.4.2, 3.8.2

Answer 7.11

Answer **B** — Section 88 of the Road Traffic Regulation Act 1984 provides for both maximum and minimum temporary speed limits to be imposed on certain roads.

Traffic authorities may impose temporary speed *restrictions* in connection with roadworks or similar operations near to the road which present a danger to the public or serious damage to the highway (see ss. 14 to 16 of the 1984 Act). These restrictions cannot generally exceed 18 months without approval from the Secretary of State.

As speed *restrictions* rather than speed limits, offences under this heading do not require notices of intended prosecution (*Platten* v *Gowing* [1983] Crim LR 184). Answers A and C are incorrect.

Answer D is incorrect as an NIP *would* normally be required for a speeding offence committed on a restricted road (or a motorway).

Note that when prosecuting for speed restrictions in these circumstances, corroboration is also not required.

Road Policing, para. 3.7.4.3

Answer 7.12

Answer **A** — Section 87(1) of the Road Traffic Regulation Act 1984 provides that speed limits will not apply to vehicles being used for fire and rescue authority, ambulance or police purposes, if the observance of that provision would be likely to hinder the use of the vehicle for the purpose for which it is being used on that occasion.

Section 87(2)(b) provides an exemption to members of the National Crime Agency (NCA), when the vehicle is being used for training purposes. However, s. 87(2)(b) is specific in that it only applies to members of the NCA. The exemption therefore does not apply to people serving in the Fire and Rescue Service when being trained, regardless of any previous training they have received, or how far they drive above the speed limit. Answers B, C and D are therefore incorrect.

Road Policing, para. 3.7.4.5

Answer 7.13

Answer **B** — When a prosecution takes place under s. 89(2) of the Road Traffic Regulation Act 1984 (exceeding a speed *limit*), a person may not be convicted solely on the evidence of one person for exceeding the speed limit. In other words, corroboration is required (unless the offence took place on a motorway). Corroboration is required when the offence takes place on a restricted road. Answer D is therefore incorrect.

Corroboration is normally provided by specialist speed measuring equipment in a police vehicle (such as *Vascar*); however, two police officers may provide sufficient evidence in a case of speeding, but the court will decide how much weight to give to such evidence. It is important to show that the officers saw the vehicle at exactly the same time (*Brighty* v *Pearson* [1938] 4 All ER 127). Answers A and C are incorrect for this reason.

Road Policing, para. 3.7.4.6

Answer 7.14

Answer **A** — Section 89(2) of the Road Traffic Regulation Act 1984 requires that a person prosecuted for driving a motor vehicle at a speed exceeding the limit shall not be convicted solely on the evidence of one witness to the effect that, in his or her opinion, the defendant was exceeding the speed limit. However, corroboration *may* be provided by the equipment in a police vehicle such as LTI 20/20 or Provida or similar speed measuring equipment (see *Nicholas* v *Penny* [1950] 2 KB 466). Answer C is therefore incorrect.

While it may be preferable, it is not necessary in all cases to prove the accuracy of the equipment being used (see *Darby* v *DPP* [1995] RTR 294). Answer B is therefore incorrect.

In *Connell* v *DPP* [2011] EWHC 158 (Admin), the opinion of the police officer was supported by reference to the reading on a Police Pilot device even though the device is an unapproved prescribed device. The magistrates' court allowed the police officer's evidence to be admitted and the Administrative Court upheld the magistrates' court ruling. Answer D is therefore incorrect.

Note that the requirements for corroboration do not apply to general speeding offences on motorways.

Road Policing, para. 3.7.4.6

Answer 7.15

Answer **D** — The Smoke-free (Private Vehicles) Regulations 2015 (SI 2015/286) amended the Smoke-free (Exemptions and Vehicles) Regulations 2007 (SI 2007/765), which designated all road vehicles as smoke-free places when a person under 18 is present in the vehicle.

Regulation 11(1A) of the Smoke-free (Exemptions and Vehicles) Regulations 2007 states:

> A vehicle that is not smoke-free by virtue of paragraph (1), or any part of such a vehicle, is smoke-free if—
> (a) it is enclosed,
> (b) there is more than one person present in the vehicle, and
> (c) a person under the age of 18 is present in the vehicle.

Since the offence is committed when the child is under 18, answers A, B and C are incorrect.

Road Policing, para. 3.7.9

Answer 7.16

Answer **C** — The Smoke-free (Private Vehicles) Regulations 2015 (SI 2015/286) amended the Smoke-free (Exemptions and Vehicles) Regulations 2007 (SI 2007/765), which designated all road vehicles as smoke-free places when a person under 18 is present in the vehicle.

Regulation 11(1A) of the Smoke-free (Exemptions and Vehicles) Regulations 2007 states:

> A vehicle that is not smoke-free by virtue of paragraph (1), or any part of such a vehicle, is smoke-free if—
> (a) it is enclosed,
> (b) there is more than one person present in the vehicle, and
> (c) a person under the age of 18 is present in the vehicle.

Since there were children under 18 present in the vehicle, it was not smoke-free according to the regulations and the law applies:

- to any private vehicle that is enclosed wholly or partly by a roof;
- when people have the windows or sunroof open, or the air conditioning on; and
- *when someone sits smoking in the open doorway of a vehicle.*

Answer D is therefore incorrect.

There is no requirement for the vehicle to be driven on the road before the offence is complete; the requirement is for a vehicle to be smoke-free if it is being used on a road (which includes being parked at the side of a road) and answer B is incorrect.

The regs are designed to protect children from someone who is actually smoking; therefore, only the passenger commits the offence in these circumstances and answer A is incorrect (although it remains to be seen whether a person may be convicted of aiding and abetting this offence).

Road Policing, para. 3.7.9

Answer 7.17

Answer **A** — Under s. 22A(1) of the Road Traffic Act 1988, a person is guilty of an offence if he intentionally and without lawful authority or reasonable cause:

(a) causes anything to be *on or over* a road, or
(b) interferes with a motor vehicle, trailer or cycle, or
(c) interferes (directly or indirectly) with traffic equipment,
   in such circumstances that it would be obvious to a reasonable person that to do so would be dangerous.

Answer D is incorrect, because the offence may be committed by placing something over the road, such as the rope referred to in this question.

However, while the section refers to activities which are committed on a 'road', a 'road' for the purposes of this offence does not include a footpath (or bridleway) (s. 22A(5)), neither does it include public places. Answers B and C are therefore incorrect.

Road Policing, para. 3.7.5

Answer 7.18

Answer **D** — Under s. 22A(1) of the Road Traffic Act 1988, a person is guilty of an offence if he intentionally and without lawful authority or reasonable cause:

(a) causes anything to be on or over a road, or
(b) interferes with a motor vehicle, trailer or cycle, or
(c) interferes (directly or indirectly) with traffic equipment,
   in such circumstances that it would be obvious to a reasonable person that to do so would be dangerous.

This offence requires a defendant to act both intentionally and without lawful authority. The intention in s. 22A only applies to the causing or interfering described— such as an *intention* to drop stones on vehicles as opposed to an accidental act. There is no need to show that the defendant intended to create danger (or in this case cause damage). Answers A and B are therefore incorrect.

Once you have proved that the actions were intended (and not accidental), you would then need to show that it would have been obvious to a reasonable person that to act in that way would be dangerous. Answer C is therefore incorrect.

Road Policing, para. 3.7.5

Answer 7.19

Answer **D** — Section 161A(1) of the Highways Act 1980 states that if a person:

(a) lights a fire on any land not forming part of a highway which consists of or comprises a carriageway; or
(b) directs or permits a fire to be lit on any such land,
     and in consequence a user of any highway which consists of or comprises a carriageway is injured, interrupted or endangered by, or by smoke from, that fire or any other fire caused by that fire, that person is guilty of an offence ...

There is a separate offence under s. 161(2)(a) of the Act of lighting a fire on or over the highway; however, the offence may also be complete if the fire is lit on land adjacent to the highway and answer C is incorrect.

Under s. 161(2)(b), a person is guilty if he/she discharges any firearm or firework within 50 feet (15.24 metres) of the centre of such a highway; however, there are no such restrictions under s. 161A(1), which deals more with the impact of the fire, rather than the location; answer A is therefore incorrect.

Finally, this offence may be committed when users of the highway are interrupted or endangered by the smoke/fire, as well as when people are injured and answer B is incorrect.

Road Policing, para. 3.7.5.1

Answer 7.20

Answer **A** — An offence may be committed under s. 22 of the Road Traffic Act 1988 if a person in charge of a vehicle causes or permits the vehicle or a trailer drawn by it to remain at rest on a road in such a position or in such condition or in such circumstances as to involve a danger of injury to other persons using the road. This suggests that although the offence applies to both motor vehicles and trailers, the trailer must be attached to the vehicle at the time of the offence. Answer C is therefore incorrect.

This offence involves presenting a danger of injury to other road users by the position, condition or circumstances of the vehicle/trailer. Answer B is therefore incorrect.

The danger presented by the condition or circumstances of the vehicle is not confined to occasions when it is stationary, but will also apply to a vehicle/trailer which presents a danger by moving (such as where a driver fails to set the handbrake (*Maguire* v *Crouch* [1941] 1 KB 108)). Answer D is therefore incorrect.

Road Policing, para. 3.7.6

Answer 7.21

Answer **B** — An offence is committed under s. 25 of the Road Traffic Act 1988 when a person gets onto a vehicle, or tampers with the brake or mechanism of a vehicle. Since the offence may be committed in either of these circumstances, answer D is incorrect. Offences under this section may only be committed either on a road or in a car park owned by a local authority. The offence may not be committed in any public place; therefore, answer C is incorrect. Since the offence is not restricted to vehicles parked on a road, answer A is also incorrect.

Road Policing, para. 3.7.7

Answer 7.22

Answer **C** — Section 26 of the Road Traffic Act 1988 states:

(1) If, for the purpose of being carried, a person without lawful authority or reasonable cause takes or retains hold of, or gets on to a motor vehicle or trailer while in motion on a road he is guilty of an offence.
(2) If, for the purpose of being drawn, a person takes or retains hold of a motor vehicle or trailer while in motion on a road he is guilty of an offence.

The offence may be committed by a person who gets onto a motor vehicle *or* trailer while in motion on a road; therefore, answers A and B are incorrect.

It can be committed in several ways (without lawful authority or reasonable cause), including simply getting onto the motor vehicle or trailer. Answer D is therefore incorrect.

Road Policing, para. 3.7.7

Answer 7.23

Answer **B** — The arrangements for the removal, retention, release and disposal of vehicles are contained in the Police (Retention and Disposal of Motor Vehicles)

Regulations 2002 (SI 2002/3049). They cover the seizure, retention and disposal of vehicles under s. 59 of the Police Reform Act 2002.

The Regulations provide that seizure notices must be served on the owner of a vehicle and where the authority is unable to serve a notice on the owner, or the person fails to remove the vehicle from its custody, it must take further steps to identify the owner. Where the person appearing to be the owner fails to comply with a seizure notice, or where the authority has not been able, having taken all reasonable steps, to give the seizure notice to a person, the relevant authority can (subject to specific time limits) dispose of the vehicle (see reg. 7).

Under reg. 8, if the vehicle is sold, the owner can claim the net proceeds (i.e. minus the storage fees) provided the claim is made within a year. It is immaterial that the owner failed to comply with the seizure notice (answer A is therefore incorrect). There is no requirement for the owner to show that the authority has failed to comply with the regulations before making such a claim, or to demonstrate that he or she was not aware of the use of the vehicle which resulted in it being seized. Answers C and D are therefore incorrect.

Road Policing, para. 3.7.8

Answer 7.24

Answer **B** — To exercise one of the powers under s. 59(3) of the Act, a constable in uniform must have reasonable grounds for believing that a motor vehicle is being used on any occasion in a manner which contravenes s. 3 or s. 34 of the Road Traffic Act 1988 (careless/inconsiderate driving and prohibition of off-road driving), and is causing/likely to cause alarm, distress or annoyance to members of the public (s. 59(1)). Under s. 59(2) of the Act, a constable may also exercise a power under s. 59(3) if he or she has reasonable grounds for believing a motor vehicle *has been* used in the circumstances outlined. Answer D is therefore incorrect.

The powers listed under s. 59(3) enable a constable in uniform to stop motor vehicles in contravention of s. 59(1) or (2), to seize and remove motor vehicles, enter any premises (except a dwelling) and use reasonable force if necessary. A vehicle may only be seized if a warning has previously been issued to the user of the vehicle that it will be seized if the use continues or is repeated and it appears to the officer that the use *has* continued or been repeated after the warning. The power to stop, seize and remove vehicles can be conferred on a PCSO, but he or she may not enter premises unless accompanied and supervised by a constable in uniform. Answers A and C are therefore incorrect.

Road Policing, para. 3.7.8

8 | Legislation Affecting the Use of Highways

STUDY PREPARATION

The areas covered by this chapter are wide and varied, ranging from the disposal of abandoned vehicles to powers to seize and retain vehicles under the Police Reform Act 2002.

Many of the police powers covered are particularly useful in practical situations and therefore will be of interest to those who train and test police officers.

QUESTIONS

Question 8.1

DELACRUZ owns a fruit and vegetable shop in the High Street and has been in dispute with SHIELDS who owns a shop across the road, which sells similar goods. DELACRUZ parked a trailer in the lane adjacent to SHIELDS's shop, knowing that it would disrupt deliveries that SHIELDS was expecting. SHIELDS contacted the police and Constable LIU attended the incident. After consulting with both parties, Constable LIU asked for the trailer to be removed as it was causing an obstruction; however, DELACRUZ refused to move it.

Considering the offence of causing an obstruction, under reg. 103 of the Road Vehicles (Construction and Use) Regulations 1986, which of the following statements is correct?

A DELACRUZ is not guilty of this offence; it is only committed by a person who causes an obstruction with a motor vehicle on a road.

B DELACRUZ is guilty of this offence, which may be committed by a person who wilfully obstructs the road with a motor vehicle or trailer.

C DELACRUZ is guilty of causing an unnecessary obstruction of the road and by his refusal to move the trailer, he could also be guilty of obstructing a police officer under s. 89(2) of the Police Act 1996.

D DELACRUZ is guilty of causing an unnecessary obstruction of the road with the trailer, but he could not be guilty of obstructing a police officer under s. 89(2) of the Police Act 1996.

Question 8.2

TOGHILL owns a restaurant, which is managed by STEAD, who placed several tables and chairs on the wide pavement outside the restaurant to attract customers in the summer. STEAD was reported for causing an unnecessary obstruction, and when the case appeared before the magistrates was ordered to remove the obstruction. STEAD refused to do so because of the extra revenue the tables and chairs attracted.

As the owner of the restaurant, could TOGHILL be held liable for the further offence of failing to remove an obstruction, under s. 137ZA of the Highways Act 1980?

A Yes, but only if TOGHILL either consented to the continued obstruction, assisted in it or was neglectful.

B Yes, TOGHILL has absolute liability, as the owner of the restaurant.

C No, only the manager is liable for the obstruction itself and for failing to remove it.

D Yes, but only if TOGHILL either consented to the obstruction, or was neglectful.

Question 8.3

A committee has been formed by a group of local shop owners, who are concerned with incidents of violence that have occurred regularly over the past three months. The shops are located in a pedestrianised area. Access for shop workers is restricted to a lane at the rear of the premises and recently four employees have been the victims of robberies, while walking to their cars in the early evening. The committee invited officers from the local authority and the police to a meeting, to discuss blocking off the lane with alleygates, to protect their employees.

The Highways Act 1980 allows for highways to be stopped up or diverted where it is expedient to do so. Could such an order be granted in these circumstances?

A No, this power is restricted to areas adjacent to educational premises.

B Yes, the highway authority can make this decision, provided it has consulted with the police authority for the area.

C No, this power is restricted to residential areas, or areas adjacent to educational premises.

D Yes, and the highway authority can make this decision without consultation.

Question 8.4

AHMED used a 3.5 tonne van to deliver furniture. AHMED was delivering to a house situated in a street which had a grass verge in the centre of the road dividing two carriageways. There were no parking spaces outside the delivery address; therefore, AHMED parked the vehicle on the grass verge until a space became available.

Has AHMED committed an offence contrary to s. 19 of the Road Traffic Act 1988 (parking commercial vehicles on verges)?

A No, because of the vehicle's weight.

B Yes, as the vehicle was parked on land in the centre of the road.

C Yes, provided the vehicle was causing a danger.

D No, as the vehicle was not parked on a verge at the side of a road.

Question 8.5

KWASHI applied for a disabled badge to be issued under the Chronically Sick and Disabled Persons Act 1970, due to a confirmed disability. KWASHI had not previously been issued with such a badge. However, following checks, the local authority discovered that KWASHI had been issued with two fixed penalty notices in the previous six months, for parking on double yellow lines.

Would the local authority be entitled to refuse to issue KWASHI with a badge because of the parking offences?

A No, the offences did not relate to the misuse of a disabled badge.

B Yes, the offences were committed in the 12 months prior to the application being made.

C No, KWASHI only committed two relevant offences prior to the application being made.

D Yes, KWASHI committed at least one relevant offence prior to the application being made.

Question 8.6

QUINN went shopping on a Sunday afternoon and, to avoid paying car park charges, she parked her car in a private car park of a business premises. There was no barrier at the car park entrance, although there was a sign stating that the car park was private property. QUINN thought it would be okay to park there, believing that no one would be in work on a Sunday. When QUINN returned to her car, she found that another vehicle had been parked directly in front of hers, blocking her car in completely. QUINN tried knocking at the door of the premises and could see lights on inside; however, she was made to wait there for over an hour until the owner of the vehicle, TRENT, came outside.

Would TRENT commit an offence in these circumstances, under s. 54 of the Protection of Freedoms Act 2012 (immobilising vehicles)?

A Yes, TRENT has restricted the movement of QUINN's vehicle.

B No, TRENT may claim a lawful authority for his actions, because QUINN has parked unlawfully on private property.

C No, TRENT has not restricted the movement of the vehicle by attaching an immobilising device to it.

D Yes, provided TRENT has prevented or inhibited the removal of the vehicle for monetary gain or the equivalent.

Question 8.7

DOUGLAS lived near some woodland, which was accessible from the road. One day, he drove to the woodland in his van and abandoned a settee and two chairs in a clearing in the woods.

Has DOUGLAS committed an offence under the Refuse Disposal (Amenity) Act 1978 (disposing of property on land)?

A No, the offence relates to abandoning a motor vehicle only.

B Yes, he has committed an offence in these circumstances.

C No, he has not abandoned anything on a highway or land forming part of a highway.

D No, the offence relates to abandoning a motor vehicle or part of a motor vehicle only.

Question 8.8

Section 3(1) of the Refuse Disposal (Amenity) Act 1978 imposes a duty on local authorities to remove motor vehicles that have been abandoned in their area, in certain circumstances. Before it can remove a vehicle under this section, a local authority must affix a notice to the vehicle advising the owner of its intention.

What is the period of notice that must be given by the local authority in England, to the owner of a vehicle which appears to have been abandoned and ought to be destroyed?

A Seven days.

B 28 days.

C 24 hours.

D 21 days.

Question 8.9

FAULKNER owns a distribution warehouse situated near a Premiership football ground. The warehouse receives deliveries seven days a week and at all hours of the day. FAULKNER is frustrated because every time the football club plays at home, ROSE parks a van in the warehouse car park (which is private property) to sell burgers. This causes disruption at the warehouse because ROSE's van causes an obstruction to drivers attempting to make deliveries. FAULKNER has approached ROSE several times to ask him to leave the premises; however, ROSE makes a significant profit on these occasions and has refused to do so. One Saturday afternoon, FAULKNER called the police to deal with the problem and Constable HANSEN attended. FAULKNER asked Constable HANSEN to remove ROSE's vehicle from the premises.

Did Constable HANSEN have the power to remove ROSE's vehicle, as requested by FAULKNER?

A Yes, provided ROSE's vehicle was causing an unnecessary obstruction.

B No, it is unlikely that ROSE's vehicle created a danger.

C Yes, provided ROSE's vehicle was causing a major obstruction.

D No, Constable HANSEN did not have the power to remove a vehicle which was not on a road or other public place.

Question 8.10

PETERS owned a trials motorcycle, which was not intended for use on roads. Near PETERS's house is an area of common land and he took his motorcycle there one day. PETERS had just started up his motorcycle and had ridden onto the land, approximately 10 yards from the road, when he was stopped by Constable MENDEZ.

Has PETERS committed an offence of driving on land other than a road, in these circumstances?

A No, as he was not driving a motor vehicle.
B Yes, as he has driven on common land other than a road.
C No, he has driven within 15 yards of the road.
D Yes, as he has driven on common land within 15 yards of the road.

Question 8.11

One evening, an accident occurred when a motorcyclist ran into a builder's skip, which has been left on a poorly lit stretch of road. Constable BLAKE attended the accident and decided that the skip should be moved. The officer discovered that MANNING had hired the skip from CORNFIELD. There was a telephone number in chalk on the side of the skip, which turned out to be CORNFIELD's office number, but the office was closed. CORNFIELD was finally contacted the next day and the skip was removed. There was council permission for the skip to be on the road.

Would CORNFIELD be liable for an offence as a result of the difficulty in contacting him?

A No, there were sufficient details on the skip for CORNFIELD to be identified.
B Yes, his name, address and a 24-hour availability phone number should have been marked on the skip, or left with the person who had hired the skip.
C No, as long as a telephone number is marked on the skip, CORNFIELD has complied with the law.
D Yes, CORNFIELD's name, together with either his address or phone number, should be indelibly marked on the skip.

Question 8.12

KAHL was approaching a zebra crossing on his motorcycle when GIBBONEY stepped on to the crossing at the last moment. KAHL did not see GIBBONEY and drove over the crossing, nearly hitting him. GIBBONEY took down the registration number of KAHL's motorcycle.

In relation to KAHL's failure to stop at the pedestrian crossing, which of the following statements is true?

A He is guilty of driving without due care and attention in these circumstances alone, which is an absolute offence.
B He is guilty of failing to stop at the crossing and driving without due care and attention.

C He is guilty of failing to stop at the crossing in these circumstances alone, which is an absolute offence.

D He is guilty of driving without due care and attention in these circumstances alone.

Question 8.13

TROTT was conducting a school crossing patrol outside a school at 7.50 am. BOYCE was riding on the road on his pedal cycle, when TROTT stood in the road to allow some people to cross. As none of the people were school children, BOYCE did not stop his cycle. TROTT was wearing her uniform and exhibiting her sign at the time of the incident.

Has BOYCE committed an offence in these circumstances?

A No, because of the time of day.

B Yes, an offence has been committed.

C No, because the people crossing were not children.

D No, because he was not driving a motor vehicle.

Question 8.14

The Fire and Rescue Service have been called to a large fire at a warehouse premises. Their entrance is blocked by a motor vehicle that is locked, but has the engine running.

What action may the fire and rescue personnel take to move the vehicle?

A They may enter the vehicle if possible, but may not use force to enter the vehicle unless the owner would have consented had they known the circumstances.

B They may enter the vehicle using force if necessary, but they may not drive it without the owner's consent.

C They may enter the vehicle using force if necessary and actually drive the vehicle without the owner's consent.

D They may enter the vehicle using force if necessary and actually drive the vehicle without the owner's consent and have it statutorily removed.

ANSWERS

Answer 8.1

Answer **C** — Regulation 103 of the Road Vehicles (Construction and Use) Regulations 1986 states that no person in charge of a motor vehicle or trailer shall cause or permit the vehicle to stand on a road so as to cause any unnecessary obstruction of the road. These Regulations apply equally to motor vehicles and trailers and answer A is incorrect.

There are two other statutory obstruction offences, under the Highways Act 1980 and the Town Police Clauses Act 1847. Under both of these Acts, a person must have *wilfully* obstructed the highway, or a public footpath or other public thoroughfare; however, under the 1986 Regulations, a person must simply have caused an *unnecessary* obstruction; therefore, answer B is incorrect.

A refusal to move a vehicle that is obstructing the highway when requested by a police officer *can* amount to an 'obstruction' of the officer under s. 89(2) of the Police Act 1996 (see *Gelberg* v *Miller* [1961] 1 WLR 153). Answer D is therefore incorrect.

Road Policing, para. 3.8.2

Answer 8.2

Answer **A** — An offence of obstruction is committed under s. 137 of the Highways Act 1980, if a person without lawful authority or excuse, in any way wilfully obstructs the free passage along a highway. If a person convicted of this offence fails to remove an obstruction, the magistrates' court can make an order requiring them to do so. Failing to comply with such an order is a further criminal offence under s. 137ZA of the Act.

As a result of the Highways (Obstruction by Body Corporate) Act 2004, a director, manager or other officer of a company can be guilty of either of these offences (answer C is therefore incorrect). In order for such a person to be guilty of the offence, it must be proved that the offence was committed with the consent or connivance of the officer, or that it was attributable to their neglect. Answer D is incorrect as the offence may also be committed if the manager assisted (or connived) in causing the obstruction. Answer B is incorrect, as the offence is not one of absolute liability in respect of an officer of the company.

Road Policing, para. 3.8.2

Answer 8.3

Answer **B** — Local highway authorities are empowered to make a stopping up order, under s. 118B, or a diversion order, under s. 119B, of the Highways Act 1980. The power allows the highway authority to either stop up or divert the relevant highway, where they are satisfied that premises adjoining or adjacent to the highway are affected by high levels of crime and that the existence of the highway is facilitating the persistent commission of criminal offences.

If the relevant highway crosses school land, an order can be made if it is expedient for the purposes of protecting the pupils or staff from violence or threats of violence, or from harassment, alarm or distress arising from unlawful activity. However, the power is not restricted to residential areas, or areas adjacent to educational premises. Answers A and C are therefore incorrect.

Neither a stopping up order nor a diversion order can be made until the highway authority has consulted the police authority for the area in which the highway lies. Answer D is therefore incorrect.

Road Policing, para. 3.8.2.1

Answer 8.4

Answer **A** — Under s. 19 of the Road Traffic Act 1988, an offence is committed by a heavy commercial vehicle which is parked wholly or in part on the verge of a road, or any land situated between two carriageways that is not a footway, or on a footway. Answer D is incorrect as the offence may be committed in the middle of the road also.

Answer B is incorrect as the vehicle was not a heavy commercial vehicle, i.e. one which exceeded 7.5 tonnes.

There is no requirement to prove that any danger was caused by the vehicle's presence. Answer C is therefore incorrect.

Road Policing, para. 3.8.3.1

Answer 8.5

Answer **A** — Under reg. 8 of the Disabled Persons (Badges for Motor Vehicles) (England) Regulations 2000 (SI 2000/682), a local authority may require the return of a badge and may refuse to issue such a badge if the person concerned has held and subsequently misused it in a way which has led to a relevant conviction. Regulation 8 was amended by the Disabled Persons (Badges for Motor Vehicles) (England)

(Amendment) (No. 2) Regulations 2011 (SI 2011/2675), reg. 2(6)(a), which substituted 'at least three relevant convictions' with 'a relevant conviction'.

However, the power to require the return of a badge, or refuse to issue one, applies if the person concerned *has held and subsequently misused* it in a way which has led to a relevant conviction. The number of parking offences committed, or when they were committed, is irrelevant when the person has *not* previously held a badge. KWASHI has not misused a disabled badge, and is therefore not bound by this legislation.

Answers B, C and D are therefore incorrect.

Road Policing, para. 3.8.3.3

Answer 8.6

Answer **A** — Under s. 54(1) of the Protection of Freedoms Act 2012, a person commits an offence who, without lawful authority:

(a) immobilises a motor vehicle by the attachment to the vehicle, or a part of it, of an immobilising device, or

(b) moves, or restricts the movement of, such a vehicle by any means,

intending to prevent or inhibit the removal of the vehicle by a person otherwise entitled to remove it.

It is a criminal offence to immobilise a motor vehicle; the offence can be committed by attaching an immobilising device (typically a wheel clamp) to the vehicle or to a part of the vehicle, or by moving it (e.g. by towing away) or by restricting the movement of a vehicle, which could be, for example, by using another vehicle to prevent it being driven away. Answer C is therefore incorrect.

The intent required for this offence is to 'prevent or inhibit the removal of the vehicle by a person otherwise entitled to remove it' (i.e. the owner); there is no requirement to prove that the person did so for monetary gain or otherwise and for that reason answer D is incorrect.

'Lawful authority' is restricted to bodies exercising a statutory authority in specified circumstances, such as the police, the DVLA, local authorities or the Driver and Vehicle Standards Agency (DVSA), all of whom can clamp vehicles to enforce their respective lawful powers. This does not include a private individual acting in such a manner, regardless of whether the other party is trespassing; in fact, the Act was created to *prevent* such actions and in these circumstances, the affected party is expected to pursue parking on private property through civil remedies. Answer B is therefore incorrect.

Note that the Removal and Disposal of Vehicles Regulations 1986 have been amended to allow police officers to remove vehicles from a road, place or 'other land', which effectively provides a power to remove a vehicle from private property which is parked in a way which creates a danger or major obstruction. This does not create a duty for the police to act, but allows them to use their discretion in any given situation to determine the appropriate action to take.

Road Policing, para. 3.8.3.5

Answer 8.7

Answer **B** — An offence may be committed under s. 2 of the Refuse Disposal (Amenity) Act 1978 either by abandoning a motor vehicle or anything which formed part of a motor vehicle (s. 2(1)(a)), or by abandoning anything other than a motor vehicle (s. 2(1)(b)). Answers A and D are therefore incorrect.

The offence is complete when property, as referred to previously, is abandoned either on any land forming part of the highway, or on any land in the open air. Presumably this would include private property, if it is in the open air. Answer C is therefore incorrect.

Road Policing, para. 3.8.4

Answer 8.8

Answer **C** — Section 3(1) of the Refuse Disposal (Amenity) Act 1978 states that where it appears to a local authority that a motor vehicle in their area is abandoned without lawful authority on any land in the open air or on any other land forming part of a highway, it shall be the duty of the authority, subject to the following provisions of this section, to remove the vehicle. Before it can remove a vehicle under this section, a local authority must follow the requirements of the Act and of the Removal and Disposal of Vehicles Regulations (SI 1986/183) in relation to affixing of notices advising the owner (of both the vehicle, and the land if occupied) of its intention.

In order to combat the growing problem of abandoned cars, the notice period required to be given by a local authority in relation to a vehicle which appears to have been abandoned and ought to be destroyed is 24 hours (see reg. 10). Answers A, B and D are therefore incorrect.

Note also that if the local authority has taken possession of a vehicle which is in such good condition that it ought *not* to be destroyed, the owner will have seven days in which to remove it (see reg. 14).

Road Policing, para. 3.8.4.1

Answer 8.9

Answer **C** — The Removal and Disposal of Vehicles Regulations 1986 allow for the removal of vehicles that are either causing a danger or obstruction. These Regulations were amended to allow police officers to remove vehicles from a road, place or other land, which effectively provides a power to remove a vehicle from private property (answer D is therefore incorrect). The inclusion of the phrase 'or other land' came as a consequence of the ban on clamping and towing and provides the police with an appropriate mechanism to allow the removal of vehicles obstructing or preventing a landowner's use of their land.

This extension to the Regulations does not create a duty for the police to act—it allows the police to use their discretion in any given situation to determine the appropriate action to take. However, the police should only use this power where a vehicle is considered to be parked in a way which creates a danger or a major obstruction (SI 2012/2277). Answers A and B are therefore incorrect.

Road Policing, para. 3.8.4.2

Answer 8.10

Answer **B** — Under s. 34 of the Road Traffic Act 1988, a person commits an offence who drives a *mechanically propelled vehicle* on any common land, moorland or land of any other description, not being part of a road. The offence is not restricted to motor vehicles. Answer A is therefore incorrect.

As soon as the person drives on the land, he or she commits the offence. Answer D is therefore incorrect.

A defence is provided for a person who has driven onto the land within 15 yards of the road in order to park the vehicle. There is no general defence of driving within 15 yards of the road only. Answer C is therefore incorrect.

Road Policing, paras 3.8.5, 3.8.5.1

Answer 8.11

Answer **D** — Section 139(1) of the Highways Act 1980 states that a builder's skip shall not be deposited on a highway without the permission of the highway authority for the highway. There are several other regulations as to the *manner* in which the skip should be deposited, to make it visible and ensure the safety of other road users (such as lighting and marking the skip with fluorescent material).

Section 139(4)(b) requires that the skip is clearly and indelibly marked with the owner's name and with his or her telephone number or address.

Since this is the only acceptable way in which the skip should be marked to identify the owner, answers A, B and C are incorrect.

Road Policing, para. 3.8.6

Answer 8.12

Answer **C** — The failure by a driver to stop at a crossing in contravention of the Regulations made under the Road Traffic Regulation Act 1984 is an absolute offence. There is no need to show any particular state of mind by the driver. Further, the failure by a driver to observe the crossing Regulations will not in itself provide sufficient proof that a person has driven without due care and attention (*Gibbons* v *Kahl* [1956] 1 QB 59). Further proof would be required, although such evidence may be presented as part of a case.

Consequently, answers A, B and D are incorrect.

Road Policing, para. 3.8.7.5

Answer 8.13

Answer **B** — Section 28 of the Road Traffic Regulation Act 1984 has been amended by the Transport Act 2000. There are no longer restrictions as to the time of day that an offence may be committed (formerly the hours were 0800 hrs to 1730 hrs). Answer A is therefore incorrect.

A further effect of the 2000 Act was that school crossing patrols are no longer restricted to stopping vehicles for children to cross. They may stop vehicles to allow anyone to cross safely. Answer C is therefore incorrect.

The offence may be committed by a person who is driving or propelling a vehicle. There is no requirement for a person to be driving a motor vehicle. Answer D is therefore incorrect.

Road Policing, para. 3.8.7.6

Answer 8.14

Answer **C** — Powers in the event of emergency are given to the Fire and Rescue Service by virtue of s. 44(2) of the Fire and Rescue Services Act 2004, which states:

(2) In particular, an employee of a fire and rescue authority who is authorised as mentioned in subsection (1) may under that subsection—
   (a) enter premises or a place, by force if necessary, without the consent of the owner or occupier of the premises or place;
   (b) move or break into a vehicle without the consent of its owner;
   (c) close a highway;
   (d) stop and regulate traffic;
   (e) restrict the access of persons to premises or a place ...

These wide-ranging powers give fire and rescue personnel, who are authorised in writing, the practical authority to deal effectively with emergency situations. They need no consent of the owner of the property they enter (including motor vehicles); therefore answers A and B are incorrect. The power, however, does not extend to statutory removal of vehicles; answer D is therefore incorrect.

Although driving a motor vehicle without the owner's consent is an offence, this power gives the relevant personnel a defence to this and they may move it by driving it.

Road Policing, para. 3.8.8.1

9 Construction and Use

STUDY PREPARATION

The area of construction and use probably typifies what most police officers associate with road traffic legislation.

Seen by many as pedantic 'train spotter' law dealing with minor mechanical issues, construction and use legislation is in reality of some practical significance to patrol officers and the wider remit of road safety.

The level of detail that police officers and examination candidates are expected to know has been greatly reduced over recent years, but there is still quite a lot of factual information to absorb.

Although you could probably fill a book such as this with construction and use questions, you will be relieved to find that only a selection of some more relevant points has been included in this chapter.

QUESTIONS

Question 9.1

Constable HEINZE attended a road traffic accident, where STONELEY's unattended car had rolled down a hill, colliding with another parked vehicle while STONELEY was in a shop. STONELEY told the officer that the handbrake had been applied to the vehicle; however, Constable HEINZE suspected that it was faulty. In order to test the handbrake, the officer pushed STONELEY's vehicle along the road with the handbrake applied for 10 metres, forming the opinion that it was, in fact, defective. Constable HEINZE was not a qualified vehicle examiner.

If STONELEY were to be prosecuted for any offences, would Constable HEINZE's evidence in relation to the handbrake be admissible in court?

A No, the vehicle must be tested either by a qualified police officer trained to examine vehicles, or a qualified Department for Transport examiner.
B No, the vehicle must be tested by a qualified police officer trained to examine vehicles.
C No, the vehicle must be tested by a qualified Department for Transport examiner.
D Yes, the vehicle may be tested by a qualified examiner, but this is not absolutely necessary.

Question 9.2

CANTER was riding a motorcycle on a road and was stopped by Constable PARRY, an authorised vehicle examiner. On measuring the depth of tread on the tyres, Constable PARRY found that the grooves of the tread pattern on both tyres measured 1.1 mm.

Which of the following statements is correct in relation to the tyres on CANTER's vehicle, considering reg. 27 of the Road Vehicles (Construction and Use) Regulations 1986?
A The depth of tread on the tyres was lawful for the type of vehicle CANTER was riding.
B The depth of tread on the tyres was unlawful; for this type of vehicle, the depth of tread should have been at least 1.2 mm.
C The depth of tread on the tyres was unlawful; for this type of vehicle, the depth of tread should have been at least 1.5 mm.
D The depth of tread on the tyres was unlawful; for this type of vehicle, the depth of tread should have been at least 1.6 mm.

Question 9.3

POTTER was driving a car, while towing a trailer along the road. POTTER was stopped by Constable GILLANEY because the two rear tyres of the vehicle were so defective that the metal was in contact with the road, and sparks were flying as the vehicle was travelling along. POTTER was carrying wood in the trailer and his son was sitting on top of the load to stop it from falling off.

Ignoring any other offences that he may have committed, would POTTER be guilty of an offence under reg. 27 of the Road Vehicles (Construction and Use) Regulations 1986 (defective tyres)?

A Yes, if it could be shown there was danger to POTTER's son or that damage might have been caused to the road.

B Yes, if it could be shown there was danger to POTTER's son or that damage had been caused to the road.

C Yes, but only if it could be shown there was danger to other persons using the road, or that damage may have been caused to the road.

D No, this regulation applies only to the danger or damage caused by motor vehicles.

Question 9.4

Constable MYERS was on patrol and came across a vehicle which was parked on the road; two of the vehicle's tyres were deflated. The officer was approached by a person who said that the vehicle belonged to her neighbour and it had been in this condition for about three weeks. Constable MYERS then spoke to the owner of the vehicle, GIBSON, who stated that the tyres had faulty valves and that as soon as he could afford to replace them, he was going to use the vehicle on the road again.

Which of the following statements is correct in relation to the tyres on GIBSON's vehicle, considering reg. 27 of the Road Vehicles (Construction and Use) Regulations 1986?

A The fact that the tyres are deflated does not necessarily mean the offence is committed; they would also have to be examined to see if they are defective.

B The offence is committed in these circumstances because GIBSON intends to use the vehicle on a road in future.

C If the tyres can easily be repaired and inflated, it would mean that they are not defective and GIBSON would not commit the offence.

D The tyres are deflated while it is being used on a road now; GIBSON commits the offence in these circumstances.

Question 9.5

YOUNG was a passenger in a motor vehicle that was travelling along a busy dual carriageway. At this time, he was supervising GLOVER, a learner driver. YOUNG received a text message on his mobile phone from his wife, telling him he had to pick up his children from school. It was not practicable to pull over due to the nature of the road, therefore YOUNG sent a text message to his wife saying that he would do so. YOUNG was not using a hands-free device at the time.

Who, if either, would commit an offence because of YOUNG's use of a mobile phone in these circumstances?

A YOUNG for using the phone and GLOVER for permitting its use.

B Only YOUNG commits the offence in these circumstances.

C Neither, as it was not practicable for GLOVER to stop in the circumstances.

D Neither, as YOUNG did not make a telephone call.

Question 9.6

Constable FLANAGAN attended a road traffic accident on a road involving two vehicles; a vehicle being driven by LARSEN had driven into the rear of the vehicle in front at a red traffic light. The driver of the other vehicle stated that as they were approaching the lights, she saw LARSEN constantly looking down at something in his lap. When questioned, LARSEN admitted that he had hired the vehicle that morning with a portable Sat Nav; however, he had left the holder, designed to mount the device on the dashboard, at home. He stated that he had been taking directions from the Sat Nav while it was on his lap and had lost concentration on the approach to the traffic lights.

Could LARSEN be guilty of an offence under reg. 110(1) of the Vehicles (Construction and Use) Regulations 1986, in these circumstances (use of hand-held phones)?

A No, LARSEN was not holding a mobile phone at the time.

B Yes, LARSEN was holding a hand-held device at the time.

C No, LARSEN was not holding a hand-held device at the time.

D No, while the device LARSEN was using is covered by the regs, he was not 'holding' it at the time.

Question 9.7

PCSO WOOD attended a PACT meeting and received a complaint from several people about the behaviour of NOBLE, a local taxi driver. The residents lived in a small cul-de-sac and complained that NOBLE drove into the close at 6.30 am every Sunday morning to take a neighbour to work. They stated that instead of waiting for the neighbour to come out, or knocking on the door, NOBLE would park outside the house and sound the horn very loudly, an action that disturbed their sleep.

In what way could NOBLE be guilty of an offence under reg. 99 of the Vehicles (Construction and Use) Regulations 1986, in these circumstances (sounding an audible warning instrument)?

A By sounding an audible warning instrument while stationary on a restricted road.

B By sounding an audible warning instrument while stationary on a road and by sounding it during the prohibited hours on a restricted road.

C By sounding an audible warning instrument during the prohibited hours on a restricted road.

D By sounding an audible warning instrument during the prohibited hours on any road.

Question 9.8

PHEALAN was driving a dumper truck along the road from one building site to another. The vehicle, which was driven at a speed slightly over 20 mph, is not intended for use on the road and this was a one-off journey.

Which of the following statements is correct in relation to whether the vehicle should be fitted with an audible warning instrument, under the Road Vehicles (Construction and Use) Regulations 1986?

A Because the vehicle was used on a road, and has a maximum speed of more than 20 mph, it should be fitted with an audible warning instrument.

B The vehicle is exempt from the requirement, regardless of its use on the road, because it has a maximum speed below 25 mph.

C The vehicle is exempt from the requirement, regardless of its maximum speed, because it is not a motor vehicle.

D Any mechanically propelled vehicle used on a road must be fitted with an audible warning instrument, unless it is an agricultural vehicle.

Question 9.9

GIBBS was driving a seven-seater people carrier on the way to the beach with his family. All of the seats were full; the front passenger and middle seats were occupied by children, while the two seats at the rear of the vehicle were occupied by adults, both of whom were the holders of full driving licences. GIBBS parked at the side of the road momentarily, to call into a shop to buy some snacks, leaving the engine running and the parking brake set.

Regulation 107 of the Road Vehicles (Construction and Use) Regulations 1986 outlines the offence of 'quitting'. Has this offence been committed in these circumstances?

A No, the vehicle was attended by GIBBS, who was only absent momentarily.

B No, the vehicle was attended as there were two full licence holders present.

C Yes, although there were full licence holders in the vehicle, they were not in a position to intervene should anything have happened.

D No, GIBBS set the parking brake before leaving the vehicle and has complied with the requirements of this Regulation.

Question 9.10

GRAY was driving a motor vehicle on a road, taking garden rubbish to a local tip. GRAY was towing an open trailer, which was also full of garden rubbish and GRAY's 10-year-old son, HARRY, was along for the trip. There was insufficient room in the car for HARRY and GRAY sat him on the trailer, telling him to hold onto a metal bar. GRAY drove slowly to the tip, and they arrived without any incident.

Would GRAY commit an offence under s. 40A of the Road Traffic Act 1988 (dangerous use of a vehicle) in these circumstances?

A No, HARRY was sitting on a trailer; the offence applies to motor vehicles only.

B No, HARRY did not encounter any danger during the journey.

C Yes, the offence applies to motor vehicles and trailers.

D Yes, the offence applies to any vehicle.

Question 9.11

WHEELER was driving a motor vehicle along a dual carriageway during the hours of darkness with a defective headlamp. WHEELER was stopped by Constable SHARMER.

Regulation 23 of the Road Vehicles Lighting Regulations 1989 requires relevant lamps to be clean and in good working order. Which of the following statements is correct as to whether WHEELER could claim a defence to this offence?

A The only defence available to WHEELER is that she had no reason to believe that the defect had occurred.

B WHEELER would have a defence if she could show that the defect had only happened during the journey.

C WHEELER would have a defence if she could show that the defect had only happened during the journey, or that arrangements had been made to rectify it with all reasonable expedition.

D WHEELER would have no defence to this offence in these circumstances.

Question 9.12

DOMINGUEZ was driving his car on a road through a built-up area at 1 pm, when he was stopped by Constable HIND. The officer examined DOMINGUEZ's car and discovered that the rear nearside light was defective.

What general exemption, under the Road Vehicles Lighting Regulations 1989, may DOMINGUEZ claim, to avoid prosecution for the defective light?

A None, as the exemption applies to headlamps only.

B That the defect occurred during the journey, or arrangements have been made to rectify it as soon as possible.

C That the defect occurred during the journey.

D That the defect has only recently occurred, and arrangements have been made to rectify it.

Question 9.13

Constable HANLON, an authorised vehicle examiner, has been working with the Driver and Vehicle Standards Agency (DVSA) in relation to a garage owned by BREARLY. The garage is authorised as an MOT testing station, but is suspected of passing vehicles for their MOT tests, when they should have failed according to the testing standards. Constable HANLON is considering whether or not they could organise for a vehicle with defective brakes to be tested by BREARLY to see whether or not staff at the garage would pass it.

Which of the following statements is correct, in relation to Constable HANLON's idea to conduct such a test?

A A vehicle may be driven to and from the garage by either a vehicle examiner from the DVSA, or an authorised police vehicle examiner.

B Such a vehicle may not be driven to and from the garage, by either a vehicle examiner from the DVSA or an authorised police vehicle examiner.

C A vehicle may only be driven to and from the garage by a vehicle examiner from the DVSA.

D A vehicle may only be driven to and from the garage by an authorised police vehicle examiner.

Question 9.14

Information has been received that a local MOT testing station managed by DIXON is issuing test certificates to vehicles that have defects and which should have actually failed their tests. Consideration is being given to taking a vehicle with a defect to the garage, to see if the fault is identified.

Under what circumstances could the test take place, according to the Road Vehicles (Construction and Use) (Amendment) (No. 4) Regulations 2005 (SI 2005/3165)?

A Such a test may only take place with prior written authorisation from the Secretary of State.

B Such a test may only take place if it is reasonably believed that the defect will not cause a danger of injury to anyone.

C Such a test may only take place if the vehicle has failed a test at another authorised MOT testing station.

D Such a test may only take place if it is reasonably believed that DIXON's conduct may cause a danger of injury to any person.

Question 9.15

SETHI took her car to JEROME's garage as the test certificate was due for renewal. When SETHI returned for her vehicle, JEROME told her that her car had passed, but repairs had been necessary to the brakes and steering. SETHI paid JEROME £200, but as she was driving home, the steering felt unsteady. She took the car to another garage, where she was told that it was unroadworthy and required further repairs.

Would JEROME have committed an offence under s. 75 of the Road Traffic Act 1988 (supplying an unroadworthy vehicle), in these circumstances?

A No, as JEROME did not sell the vehicle to SETHI.

B Yes, the offence is complete in these circumstances.

C No, as SETHI is the owner of the vehicle, JEROME could not supply it to her.

D No, because SETHI had to pay JEROME for the repairs.

Question 9.16

CRAIG realised that the test certificate on his car had expired. His friend, WALSH, owned a garage and was authorised to issue MOT certificates. CRAIG drove his car to WALSH's garage, where it failed the MOT test. CRAIG made arrangements to return the car the next day for work to be carried out, in order to pass the test.

Has CRAIG committed an offence in relation to the vehicle in these circumstances, by driving it either to or from the garage?

A Yes, on his way there only, as he had not arranged a test for the vehicle in advance.

B Yes, on his way there and on his way home, as he had not arranged to test the vehicle in advance.

C No, as he was taking the vehicle to be tested, and returning it after it had been refused a certificate.

D Yes, on his way there only; he is exempt in relation to the return journey, as the vehicle had been refused a test certificate.

Question 9.17

Constable TAIT was dealing with a fail to stop road traffic accident, involving injury to a pedestrian on a zebra crossing. The offending vehicle was a medium-sized goods vehicle, which the officer discovered belonged to BARR. Through enquiries, Constable TAIT also discovered that BARR had failed to stop because he was concerned that the vehicle's brakes were defective and, on examination, the vehicle may be taken off the road, which would affect his livelihood. Constable TAIT found the vehicle outside BARR's home address and contacted the Commercial Vehicle Unit to have it examined. There was no one available at the time and the officer was advised by the Unit to instruct BARR to take it to the examination centre, which was about three miles away.

Considering the power under s. 68 of the Road Traffic Act 1988, could Constable TAIT instruct BARR to do this?

A Yes, Constable TAIT may direct the vehicle to be taken to the examination centre in these circumstances.

B No, the examination centre is too far away to be able to use this power.

C No, only an authorised vehicle examiner can make such a request.

D No, there is no power to direct stationary vehicles in such a manner; this power applies to vehicles that have been stopped during an inspection.

Question 9.18

Constable KELLEHER, an authorised vehicle examiner, attended the scene of a road traffic accident, where GRANT had injured a child crossing the road. Witnesses told the officer that GRANT had stopped for a short while, and made a telephone call. GRANT was overheard shouting into the phone, 'I told you the brakes on this car were dangerous'. GRANT left the scene before the police arrived. Within five hours of the accident, Constable KELLEHER traced the vehicle to GRANT's home address. The vehicle was parked on the driveway and the officer wished to inspect the brakes. GRANT was not at home.

Under what circumstances could Constable KELLEHER examine the vehicle?

A There is no power to examine the vehicle without GRANT's permission.

B Constable KELLEHER may examine the vehicle without permission, because GRANT was involved in a road traffic accident involving injury.

C Constable KELLEHER may examine the vehicle without permission if GRANT is served with a notice, outlining the intention, within 48 hours of the accident.

D Constable KELLEHER may examine the vehicle without permission if the test takes place within 24 hours of the accident.

Question 9.19

Constable LAWRENCE was dealing with a road traffic accident involving a vehicle owned by KIM. The officer suspected that the vehicle's brakes were defective, because of comments made by KIM at the scene. KIM's vehicle was towed away from the scene by a friend and was being stored in the friend's garage. Constable LAWRENCE was an authorised vehicle examiner and attended the garage to test the brakes a few hours after the accident.

Would Constable LAWRENCE have the power to inspect the vehicle on premises, under reg. 74 of the Road Vehicles (Construction and Use) Regulations 1986?

A Yes, provided KIM consents to the examination.

B Yes, and she may enter by force if necessary.

C Yes, and she may enter by force if necessary if the garage owner is not present.

D Yes, provided the owner of the garage consents to the examination.

ANSWERS

Answer 9.1

Answer **D** — Regulations 15–18 of the Road Vehicles (Construction and Use) Regulations 1986 (SI 1986/1078) set out the requirements as to braking systems on vehicles, together with those for their maintenance. It is not absolutely necessary for the person testing the braking system of a vehicle to be a 'qualified examiner'—see *Stoneley* v *Richardson* [1973] RTR 229. In this case, a constable testified to being able to push the defendant's car along with the handbrake applied, and the evidence was accepted by the court. Since the officer was able to conduct this test, answers A, B and C are incorrect.

Road Policing, para. 3.9.3.1

Answer 9.2

Answer **A** — Generally, the requirement under reg. 27(1)(g) of the Road Vehicles (Construction and Use) Regulations 1986 is that the grooves of the tread pattern of a tyre must have a depth of at least 1 mm throughout a continuous band measuring at least three-quarters of the breadth of the tread and round the entire outer circumference of the tyre.

In the case of:

- passenger vehicles *other than motorcycles* constructed or adapted to carry no more than eight seated passengers in addition to the driver,
- goods vehicles with a maximum gross weight not exceeding 3,500 kg,
- light trailers

(first used on or after 3 January 1933 in each case), the depth of tread requirement is increased to 1.6 mm throughout a continuous band across the central three-quarters section of the tyre and around the entire circumference (see the Road Vehicles (Construction and Use) (Amendment) (No. 4) Regulations 1990 (SI 1990/1981)).

Therefore, a tyre on a motorcycle must have a depth of at least *1 mm* throughout a continuous band measuring at least three-quarters of the breadth of the tread and round the entire outer circumference of the tyre. Answers B, C and D are therefore incorrect.

Road Policing, para. 3.9.3.3

Answer 9.3

Answer **A** — Regulation 27 of the Road Vehicles (Construction and Use) Regulations 1986 sets out a number of specific defects that will make tyres unlawful. Under reg. 27(1)(h), an offence is committed where the tyre is not maintained in such condition as to be fit for the use to which the vehicle or trailer is being put or has a defect which might in any way cause damage to the surface of the road or damage to persons on or in the vehicle or to other persons using the road. Since this regulation does not require actual damage to have been caused, answer B is incorrect. There is no requirement to show that other road users were endangered, or that people in or on the offending vehicle may have been placed in danger, therefore answer C is incorrect. Finally, the regulation applies either to vehicles or trailers—there is no mention of 'motor vehicles'; therefore, answer D is incorrect.

Road Policing, para. 3.9.3.3

Answer 9.4

Answer **D** — Regulation 27 of the Road Vehicles (Construction and Use) Regulations 1986 sets out a number of specific defects that will make tyres unlawful. Under reg. 27(1)(b), a tyre will be unlawful if it is not so inflated as to make it fit for the use to which the motor vehicle or trailer is being put.

Under s. 41A(b) of the Road Traffic Act 1988, a person who uses on a road a motor vehicle or trailer which does not comply with such a requirement, or causes or permits a motor vehicle or trailer to be so used, is guilty of an offence. Answers A and C are incorrect; it is irrelevant whether or not the tyres can easily be repaired and inflated.

To avoid the defect at reg. 27(1)(b), the tyre must be inflated so as to make it fit for the use to which the vehicle is being put at the material time; it does not have to be so inflated as to make it fit for some future use, however probable that use might be (*Connor* v *Graham* [1981] RTR 291). Answer B is therefore incorrect.

Road Policing, paras 3.9.3.3, 3.9.3.4

Answer 9.5

Answer **B** — The unlawful use of hand-held mobile telephones while driving a motor vehicle on a road is prosecuted under s. 42 of the Road Traffic Act 1988. The three general offences are:

- driving a motor vehicle while using a hand-held mobile telephone;
- causing or permitting another person to drive a motor vehicle while using a hand-held mobile telephone; and
- using a hand-held mobile telephone while supervising a learner driver who is driving a motor vehicle on a road.

To commit the offence of 'permitting', you have to show the offender was permitting a person to use the hand-held device when *driving*. Since YOUNG was not driving the vehicle, GLOVER cannot be guilty of this offence and therefore answer A is incorrect.

The offence will be committed under *any* of the three subsections if the hand-held device is used either to make a telephone call *or* to *perform any other interactive communication function by transmitting and receiving data*, which will include sending a text message, fax, email or picture. Answer D is therefore incorrect.

Lastly, there is a specific defence to this offence, if the driver (or supervisor) can show that he or she was using the hand-held device to make an emergency call to the police, fire, ambulance or other emergency services, that he or she was acting in response to a genuine emergency *and* that it was impracticable to cease driving (or for the provisional licence holder to cease driving). All three of these circumstances must apply before the defence can be considered. Since YOUNG's text message was not an emergency, it is immaterial that it was not practicable to stop, and he would have no defence. Answer C is therefore incorrect.

Road Policing, para. 3.9.3.6

Answer 9.6

Answer **B** — Regulation 110(1) of the Vehicles (Construction and Use) Regulations 1986 states that no person shall drive a motor vehicle on a road if he is using:

(a) a hand-held mobile telephone; or
(b) a hand-held device of a kind specified in paragraph (4).

The offence is not restricted to mobile telephones, therefore answer A is incorrect.

The 'device' is defined in reg. 110(4) as a device, other than a two-way radio, which performs an interactive communication function by transmitting and receiving data. 'Interactive communication function' includes the sending and receiving of oral or written messages, faxes, still or moving images and access to the internet (reg. 110(6)(c)). Therefore, it covers text messages and photographs sent or received by mobile phones. It could also cover a Sat Nav device, which is capable of receiving oral and written messages and still or moving images. Answer C is therefore incorrect.

A hand-held device is something that 'is or must be held at some point during the course of making or receiving a call or performing any other interactive communication function'. 'Cradling' a phone or device by wedging the phone between the ear and shoulder—or anywhere else—constitutes 'holding' a phone. This would almost certainly apply when a person is 'holding' something in their lap while driving and receiving data and answer D is incorrect.

Road Policing, para. 3.9.3.6

Answer 9.7

Answer **B** — Regulation 99 of the Vehicles (Construction and Use) Regulations 1986 creates two general provisions regarding the use of an audible warning instrument.

First, an offence is committed by sounding an audible warning instrument while the vehicle is stationary on *any* road (except to warn of danger).

Second, an offence is committed by sounding an audible warning instrument between 11.30 pm and 7 am on a *restricted* road.

NOBLE commits both offences in these circumstances, therefore, answers A, C and D are incorrect.

Road Policing, para. 3.9.3.7

Answer 9.8

Answer **C** — Regulations 37 and 99 regulate the fitting and use of audible warning instruments. Every *motor vehicle* which has a maximum speed of more than 20 mph shall be fitted with a horn, not being a reversing alarm or a two-tone horn. The dumper truck is not a motor vehicle; therefore, regardless of its maximum speed, it will not require an audible warning instrument. Answers A and D are therefore incorrect.

The Regulations do indeed apply to agricultural motor vehicles and these will require audible warning instruments if they are being driven at a speed of more than 20 mph. However, answer D is incorrect because the regulations only apply to motor vehicles.

If the dumper truck *was* a motor vehicle, it would require an audible warning instrument because it has a maximum speed *above* 20 mph; therefore, answer B is incorrect.

Road Policing, para. 3.9.3.7

Answer 9.9

Answer **C** — Regulation 107 of the Road Vehicles (Construction and Use) Regulations 1986 prohibits the leaving of a motor vehicle unattended on a road unless the engine has been stopped and the parking brake set; both must be done (*Butterworth v Shorthouse* [1956] Crim LR 341); therefore, answer D is incorrect. Leaving the vehicle with the engine running and/or setting the parking brake amounts to an offence and, to avoid prosecution, it must be shown that the vehicle was left 'attended'.

Any person left 'attending' the vehicle must be someone who is licensed to drive it *and in a position to intervene*, otherwise reg. 107 is breached. The driver of the vehicle in these circumstances cannot claim to be in a position to intervene, by being absent from the vehicle completely. Likewise, it would be impossible for the two full licence holders sitting in the rear of the vehicle to intervene if, for example, one of the children in the front of the vehicle unset the parking brake. This element is not satisfied in these circumstances and answers A and B are incorrect.

Road Policing, para. 3.9.3.8

Answer 9.10

Answer **C** — Section 40A of the Road Traffic Act 1988 creates an offence of:

- using, causing or permitting another to use on a road,
- a motor vehicle or trailer
- which, for whatever reason, involves a danger of injury to any person.

First, the offence applies to motor vehicles and trailers only; therefore, answers A and D are incorrect.

Second, the offence may be committed when the use of the vehicle involves a danger of injury to any person. In *Gray* v *DPP* [1999] RTR 339, the court held that a potential for injury would suffice to prove the offence. In this case, a 7-year-old boy was seen to be travelling in the open back of an uncovered jeep without any fitted restraints. The boy was steadying himself by holding on to the vehicle's roll-bars. The court held that, even though he had travelled in that way without incident many times in the past and that his father, the driver, was generally a responsible parent, the objective test as to the potential for injury meant that the offence had been committed. Answer B is therefore incorrect.

Road Policing, para. 3.9.3.12

Answer 9.11

Answer **D** — Regulation 23 of the Road Vehicles Lighting Regulations 1989 makes it an offence to use, or to cause or permit to be used, a vehicle on a road unless the relevant lamps and reflectors (including some optional ones) are clean and in good working order. Offences of contravening the lighting regulations are charged under s. 41 of the Road Traffic Act 1988.

The general exception to reg. 23 is if the vehicle is being used during daytime hours and the defect only happened during the journey or if arrangements have been made to rectify it with all reasonable expedition (reg. 23(3)). Since WHEELER was using the vehicle during the hours of darkness, this defence is not available to her—also, the defence is specific and not realising the defect had occurred would not be covered. Answers A, B and C are therefore incorrect.

Note that there is a separate offence under reg. 25 to use, or cause or permit to be used, a vehicle with obligatory headlamps on a road unless they are kept lit during the hours of darkness and in seriously reduced visibility. There is an exception to this requirement which applies to vehicles on 'restricted' roads per s. 81 of the Road Traffic Regulation Act 1984 where the street lights are on—but again, this would not provide a defence for WHEELER.

Road Policing, paras 3.9.4.3, 3.9.4.6

Answer 9.12

Answer **B** — It is an offence under reg. 23 of the Road Vehicles Lighting Regulations 1989 (SI 1989/1796) to use, cause or permit to be used a vehicle on a road unless the relevant lamps are clean and in good working order.

There is, however, an exemption under reg. 23(3): if the vehicle is being used during daytime hours and the defect only happened during the journey, or if arrangements have been made to rectify it with all reasonable expedition. Answers C and D are therefore incorrect.

The exemption applies to all relevant lamps, not just headlamps. Answer A is therefore incorrect.

Road Policing, para. 3.9.4.6

Answer 9.13

Answer **B** — The Road Vehicles (Construction and Use) (Amendment) (No. 4) Regulations 2005 and the Road Vehicles Lighting (Amendment) (No. 2) Regulations 2005 provide exemptions for vehicles used by Driver and Vehicle Standards Agency (DVSA) examiners from having to comply with certain requirements of the Road Vehicles (Construction and Use) Regulations 1989 and the Road Vehicles Lighting Regulations 1989.

The exemptions allow DVSA examiners, posing as members of the public, to drive a vehicle with specific, recorded defects, to and from an MOT testing station, to ensure that the MOT tester applies the correct testing standards when conducting an MOT test.

Since the exemption applies to DVSA examiners, answers A and D are incorrect. However, in order to qualify for the exemptions, the examiner must:

- be authorised in writing by the Secretary of State to drive the defective vehicle; and
- reasonably believe that the defects will not cause a danger of injury to anyone while being so used.

This means that only minor defects may be present on the vehicles, such as horns or washers not working, or rear seat belts missing, as opposed to major defects, such as those to the brakes, steering or tyres of the vehicle. Since a vehicle examiner would not be entitled to drive a motor vehicle on a road with defective brakes: answers A, C and D are also incorrect for this reason.

Road Policing, para. 3.9.5

Answer 9.14

Answer **B** — The Road Vehicles (Construction and Use) (Amendment) (No. 4) Regulations 2005 and the Road Vehicles Lighting (Amendment) (No. 2) Regulations 2005 allow Driver and Vehicle Standards Agency (DVSA) examiners to pose as members of the public and to drive a vehicle with specific, recorded defects, to and from an MOT testing station, in order to ensure that the MOT tester applies the correct testing standards when conducting an MOT test. In order to qualify for the exemptions, the examiner must:

- be authorised in writing by the Secretary of State to drive the defective vehicle *and*
- reasonably believe that the defects will not cause a danger of injury to anyone while being so used.

The risk assessment of whether the defects will cause a danger of injury to anyone relate to when the vehicle is being used to drive to and from the test—it does not relate to the conduct of the testing station; therefore, answer D is incorrect. While the vehicle examiner must be authorised in writing by the Secretary of State to drive the defective vehicle, there is no requirement to seek authorisation for each test (answer A is therefore incorrect). Neither is there a requirement to test the vehicle at another authorised MOT testing station prior to it being used and therefore answer C is incorrect.

Road Policing, para. 3.9.5

Answer 9.15

Answer **B** — It has been held that where a garage returned a vehicle to an owner, after stating that it had been repaired and had passed its MOT, when in fact it was unroadworthy, the garage committed the offence of supplying an unroadworthy vehicle (*Devon County Council* v *DB Cars* [2001] EWHC Admin 521). In this case, the court held that 'supplying' involved a transfer of physical control of an item from one person to another (answer C is therefore incorrect). It is both immaterial that the owner had to pay for the repairs, and that the owner did not buy the vehicle from the offender, therefore answers A and D are incorrect.

Road Policing, para. 3.9.5

Answer 9.16

Answer **B** — There are exemptions to s. 47 of the Road Traffic Act 1988 (using a motor vehicle on a road without a test certificate), where a person is taking a vehicle to or from a testing station. However, a driver may only claim exemption if he or she is driving to or from a pre-arranged test. The key is whether the test was pre-arranged, and in this case it was not. Answer C is therefore incorrect.

Although they are worded differently, answers A and D are incorrect for the same reason. There is a further exemption for vehicles which have been refused test certificates. However, this exemption applies only when the vehicle is being driven, by prior arrangement, or brought from the relevant place where the work is being carried out. This exemption allows garage proprietors, who are not registered to supply test certificates, to take vehicles to and from testing stations, and again does not apply in these circumstances.

The last exemption, which again does not apply to the given facts, is where a vehicle is being towed to be broken up, following the refusal of a test certificate.

Road Policing, para. 3.9.5

Answer 9.17

Answer **A** — Section 68 of the Road Traffic Act 1988 provides a power for vehicle examiners to inspect goods vehicles, PSVs and some larger passenger-carrying vehicles. It also provides a power for a police officer in uniform to direct such a vehicle to a suitable place of inspection when found on a road, provided that that place of inspection is not more than five miles from the place where the requirement is made. Since Constable TAIT did not have to be an authorised vehicle examiner, and was directing the vehicle to a centre less than five miles away, answers B and C are incorrect.

The power conferred by s. 68 of the Road Traffic Act 1988 can be applied to stationary vehicles and answer D is incorrect.

Road Policing, para. 3.9.5.2

Answer 9.18

Answer **A** — Regulation 74 of the Road Vehicles (Construction and Use) Regulations 1986 provides a power to test and inspect the brakes, silencers, steering gear and tyres of any vehicle on any premises where that vehicle is located. The power applies to police officers in uniform and other authorised vehicle examiners, but may not take place unless:

* the owner of the vehicle consents;
* notice has been given to that owner (either personally or left at his or her address not less than 48 hours before the time of the proposed test/inspection, or sent to him or her by recorded delivery at least 72 hours before the proposed test/inspection); or
* the test or inspection is made within 48 hours of a reportable accident in which the vehicle was involved.

In ordinary circumstances, Constable KELLEHER could conduct an inspection without giving notice to the owner (as the inspection would take place within 48 hours of the accident) and therefore answer C is incorrect.

However, regardless of whether the person was involved in a personal injury road traffic accident, an inspection under this section must take place with the owner's permission. There is no power of entry to conduct such an examination and it was irrelevant, therefore, what time the officer arrived at the house; if the owner was not present to consent, the examination could not take place. Answers B and D are therefore incorrect.

Road Policing, para. 3.9.5.3

Answer 9.19

Answer **A** — The power applies to police officers in uniform and other authorised vehicle examiners (see reg. 74(1)(a)–(f)). Regulation 74 provides no power of entry and stipulates that the person empowered shall produce his or her authorisation if required to do so. Answers B and C are therefore incorrect.

Regulation 74 also provides that no such test or inspection shall be carried out unless the owner of the vehicle consents. There is no mention of the owner of the premises consenting to the examination, therefore answer D is incorrect.

Road Policing, para. 3.9.5.3

10 Driver Licensing

This chapter is only tested in the Sergeants' examination—Inspectors' examination candidates should not study this material.

STUDY PREPARATION

The law relating to driver licensing is of considerable practical significance.

You need to know how the licensing system works in terms of what licence is needed by what driver for what vehicle; you also need to know the relevant police powers in relation to licences and the attendant offences that can be committed.

Of particular importance is the offence of disqualified driving and the provisions that apply to learner drivers and their supervisors.

QUESTIONS

Question 10.1

SCOTT has secured employment with a haulage company to drive large goods vehicles to various locations in the UK. SCOTT has had to re-train after being made redundant and passed his driving test to drive large goods vehicles late, on his thirty-ninth birthday.

When will SCOTT's licence to drive large goods vehicles be due for renewal?

A The licence must be renewed annually.

B The licence must be renewed in five years.

C The licence will last until SCOTT's forty-fifth birthday.

D The licence will last until SCOTT's sixtieth birthday.

Question 10.2

Constable FIELD stopped a 12-seat minibus being driven by ROGERSON on a road. The vehicle belongs to ROGERSON's employer, who uses it to convey staff to and from work late at night and early in the morning, when there is no public transport available. On this occasion ROGERSON had borrowed the bus, with permission, to take fellow employees on a social outing.

Does the vehicle ROGERSON was driving qualify as being a passenger-carrying vehicle (PCV), in these circumstances?

A No, because the minibus had no more than 16 seats, it could not be classed as a PCV.

B Yes, the minibus had seats for more than eight passengers, so it will be classed as a PCV.

C No, because the minibus was not being used for his employer's purpose at the time.

D No, because the minibus was not being used for hire or reward and had less than the specified number of seats.

Question 10.3

HOWLEY has bought a moped and intends signing up for an approved training course and passing a test of competence to ride it on a road.

In relation to the vehicle HOWLEY has bought, which of the following statements is correct, under s. 108(1) of the Road Traffic Act 1988?

A It may be a two-wheeled or three-wheeled vehicle and must have a maximum design speed of no more than 50 kilometres per hour.

B It must be a two-wheeled vehicle and must have a maximum design speed of no more than 50 kilometres per hour.

C It may be a two-wheeled or three-wheeled vehicle and must have a maximum design speed of no more than 45 kilometres per hour.

D It must be a two-wheeled vehicle and must have a maximum design speed of no more than 45 kilometres per hour.

Question 10.4

CASWELL is a provisional licence holder and has recently completed a compulsory basic training course to ride a motorbicycle.

Which of the following is correct in relation to the documentation CASWELL will require to prove the course has been passed?

A CASWELL will be issued with a certificate, which is valid for two years.

B CASWELL's provisional licence will be endorsed as proof that the course has been passed. The endorsement will be removed if a test is not passed within two years.

C CASWELL will be issued with a certificate, which is valid until a test has been passed—there is no time limit.

D CASWELL's provisional licence will be endorsed as proof that the course has been passed. The endorsement will be removed if a test is not passed within one year.

Question 10.5

JACOBS is 15 years old and one day while her parents had gone out for the day in her father's car, she took her mother's car out for a short drive around the estate on her own. JACOBS was stopped by Constable SHARPE, who realised that she was too young to be driving.

Which offence would JACOBS commit in relation to her use of the vehicle?

A Failing to display 'L' plates and driving unaccompanied.

B Driving whilst disqualified by reason of age.

C Driving otherwise than in accordance with a licence.

D Failing to display 'L' plates, driving unaccompanied and driving otherwise than in accordance with a licence.

Question 10.6

COLLIER, aged 25, passed her full driving test 18 months ago and was issued with a test pass certificate at the test centre on the day she passed. COLLIER became very ill just after passing her test and it took some time before she applied to the DVLA for her full driving licence; she eventually received it 12 months after passing her test (six months ago). COLLIER's boyfriend, BAINES, has recently received his provisional driving licence and she would like to take him out driving.

When would COLLIER be qualified to supervise BAINES, in line with reg. 17(1) of the Motor Vehicles (Driving Licences) Regulations 1999?

A In 18 months, which will be three years after she received her test pass certificate.

B In two years six months, which will be three years after she was issued with her full driving licence.

C She is already qualified; it is more than a year since she passed her driving test.

D In six months, which will be two years after she received her test pass certificate.

Question 10.7

POTTER was supervising GREEN, who was learning to drive. As they were travelling along the road, GREEN collided with a parked car. GREEN panicked and drove off after the accident, without stopping.

Does POTTER have a responsibility for GREEN'S actions in these circumstances?

A Yes, but only if he encouraged the actions.

B No, he is only there to supervise GREEN's driving.

C No, he is only there to provide tuition for GREEN.

D Yes, he should have ensured that GREEN remained at the scene.

Question 10.8

FERDINAND was a passenger in a vehicle being driven by AZIZ, a provisional licence holder. The vehicle was fitted with 'L' plates and FERDINAND, a full licence holder, was supervising AZIZ. The vehicle was stopped by Constable THAME, who observed that both FERDINAND and AZIZ smelled strongly of intoxicants.

In these circumstances, could a supervisor be found guilty of an offence under s. 5(1)(b) of the Road Traffic Act 1988 (in charge of a vehicle while over the prescribed limit)?

A No, they could only be guilty of aiding and abetting a driver who was over the prescribed limit.

B Yes, they could be in charge of the vehicle in these circumstances and be guilty of this offence.

C No, as the driver is in control of the vehicle, the supervisor could not also be in charge of it.

D Yes, but only if it could be proved that the driver was also over the prescribed limit.

Question 10.9

KELLEHER is the holder of a provisional driving licence and has passed a driving test to drive motor vehicles on a road. KELLEHER has been issued with a certificate confirming that her test has been passed and is waiting for her full driving licence.

What restrictions, if any, are now placed on KELLEHER if she wishes to drive a motor vehicle on a road?

A KELLEHER will no longer have to display 'L' plates or be accompanied by a qualified driver.

B KELLEHER will no longer have to display 'L' plates; however, she will still have to be accompanied by a qualified driver, until she receives her full driving licence.

C KELLEHER will no longer have to be accompanied by a qualified driver; however, she will still have to display 'L' plates, until she receives her full driving licence.

D KELLEHER will have to continue displaying 'L' plates and be accompanied by a qualified driver, until she receives her full driving licence.

Question 10.10

SWEETMAN has passed a driving test and is classified as a 'new driver', as defined under s. 3 of the Road Traffic (New Drivers) Act 1995. SWEETMAN's driving licence has recently been revoked as a result of accumulating too many penalty points. SWEETMAN was stopped by Constable BELL while driving a motor vehicle on the road. At the time, SWEETMAN was displaying 'L' plates on the vehicle, but was not supervised by a qualified driver.

Is SWEETMAN guilty of an offence in these circumstances?

A Yes, of driving otherwise than in accordance with a licence.

B No; SWEETMAN has passed a driving test and must display 'L' plates, but does not have to be supervised by a qualified driver.

C Yes, of driving while disqualified.

D Yes, of driving when not supervised by a qualified driver.

Question 10.11

BELL passed her driving test a year ago. Before passing her test, BELL had accumulated points on her provisional driving licence. She has recently been issued with an endorsable fixed penalty notice and is likely to accumulate penalty points on her full driving licence.

If the combined total of points that BELL has accumulated exceeds the limit set in s. 2 of the Road Traffic (New Drivers) Act 1995, is BELL likely to have her licence revoked?

A Yes, provided the second set of points was accumulated within two years of the first set of points.

B No, the first set of points was accumulated while BELL was a provisional licence holder.

C Yes, provided the first set of points was accumulated at least two years before BELL passed her driving test.

D Yes, the Secretary of State has no alternative but to revoke BELL's driving licence in these circumstances.

Question 10.12

WILLEMS has been in a long-standing dispute with her neighbour, HEARN, over the parking spaces outside their respective houses. They share a common parking area, which is not a road or public place because the spaces are available only to them. WILLEMS was annoyed that HEARN's visitors constantly parked in her allocated space. One day, after coming home from work, there was a car parked in her space. WILLEMS lost her temper and deliberately drove at the car at speed, causing extensive damage to it. The police were called and, because of the location of the incident, WILLEMS was arrested for causing criminal damage. She pleaded not guilty to the offence, but was found guilty in court.

Would the Crown Prosecution Service (CPS) be entitled to apply for a disqualification period in respect of WILLEMS in these circumstances?

A Yes, the court may order a disqualification period instead of, or in addition to, the criminal damage conviction.

B Yes, the court may order a disqualification period, but this must replace the criminal conviction, to avoid duplicity.

C No, a person may only be disqualified on conviction in these circumstances when the crime involves an injury to another person.

D Yes, the court may order a disqualification period provided the damage caused to the other vehicle amounts to 'serious' damage.

Question 10.13

A gang was involved in cash-in-transit robberies, which resulted in several security guards being seriously assaulted. The gang used stolen vehicles to commit the crimes, which they later abandoned at different locations. CHAPMAN did not take part in the robberies, but was paid to pick up the gang members in various places and take them safely back to their homes. When the police caught the principal offenders they also arrested CHAPMAN, who claimed that he was unaware of the crimes the gang had committed and was simply a driver. Ten people were charged and convicted in Crown Court with conspiracy to commit five robberies, including CHAPMAN. The court accepted that CHAPMAN had played a lesser part than the principal offenders and the Crown Prosecution Service (CPS) anticipated that he would receive a lesser sentence.

Would the CPS be entitled to apply for a disqualification period in respect of CHAPMAN in these circumstances?

A No, CHAPMAN's vehicle was not used in the commission of the robberies themselves.

B Yes, but only if it can be shown that CHAPMAN's vehicle was used to assist the gang to avoid apprehension after the offence.

C Yes, but only if it can be shown that CHAPMAN's vehicle was used to dispose of evidence related to the offence.

D Yes, if it can be shown that CHAPMAN's vehicle was used to assist the gang to avoid apprehension, or to dispose of evidence related to the offence.

Question 10.14

PHELPS is appearing in court and has been convicted of driving a motor vehicle while over the prescribed limit, an offence which carries an obligatory disqualification period. The defence solicitor has made a case that a period of disqualification would have a significant impact on PHELPS's business and family life and has asked the court for leniency.

How should the court deal with such a request, in order to comply with s. 34(1) of the Road Traffic Offenders Act 1988?

A The offence carries an obligatory disqualification; the court has no option but to impose a period of disqualification of no less than 12 months.

B The offence carries an obligatory disqualification; the court has no option but to impose a period of disqualification of no less than six months.

C Although the offence carries an obligatory disqualification, the court could impose a shorter period of disqualification; however, they must disqualify PHELPS.

D Although the offence carries an obligatory disqualification, the court could impose a shorter period of disqualification, or even not disqualify PHELPS at all.

Question 10.15

Constable BUDIANSKI was on mobile patrol in a police vehicle. The officer was stationary at a set of traffic lights and saw a vehicle on the opposite side of the road, waiting for the lights to change. Constable BUDIANSKI recognised GOODE sitting in the driver's seat and knew that he was a disqualified driver. The officer approached the vehicle and arrested GOODE for that offence.

Given that GOODE is actually disqualified from driving, which of the following would be the key considerations as to whether he could be prosecuted, under s. 103 of the Road Traffic Act 1988, in these circumstances?

A There must be evidence to show that the vehicle had been seen in motion in order to prosecute GOODE.

B GOODE could not be prosecuted as he was not seen driving.

C In these circumstances, the prosecution could convince the court that he had stopped driving and intended carrying on when the lights changed.

D Evidence that a person *has* been driving would be insufficient for this offence; the person must be stopped while driving.

Question 10.16

MEARS is due to appear in court, having been charged with an offence of driving while disqualified. However, MEARS intends using the defence that she was not aware that she was disqualified from driving.

Which of the following statements is correct in relation to the proof that is required to prove an offence of driving while disqualified under s. 103 of the Road Traffic Act 1988?

A MEARS will need to show that she was not disqualified, or alternatively that she was not aware of this fact.

B MEARS will need to show that she was not disqualified *and* that she was not aware of this fact.

C The prosecution will need to show that MEARS was disqualified *and* that she was aware of this fact.

D The prosecution will need to show that MEARS was disqualified, but not that she was aware of this fact.

Question 10.17

VERDI was convicted of failing to cooperate with a preliminary breath test and failing to stop for the police. VERDI had attempted to escape from the police, but was eventually stopped. VERDI refused to provide a roadside breath test, but provided a sample later at the station, which proved negative. The court was considering using its discretion to implement a period of disqualification, until VERDI passed an appropriate driving test.

Which of the following statements is correct, in relation to the court's considerations?

A Because the offence involves a discretionary disqualification, VERDI may be made to sit a regular driving test.

B Because the offence involves a discretionary disqualification, VERDI may not be made to re-sit a driving test.

C Because the offence involves a breath test offence, VERDI may be made to sit an extended driving test.

D Regardless of the offence, an extended driving test will always be the appropriate test when the court makes such an order.

Question 10.18

JELF was driving a motor vehicle on a road and was stopped by Constable STACEY. A Police National Computer (PNC) check revealed that JELF had recently been convicted of speeding, and had been disqualified from driving until passing a driving test. JELF was in possession of a provisional driving licence and was accompanied by FERDINAND, a fully qualified driver. The vehicle was not displaying 'L' plates.

Has JELF committed an offence in these circumstances?

A Yes, of failing to display 'L' plates.

B Yes, of driving while disqualified.

C Yes, of driving other than in accordance with a licence.

D No, JELF was accompanied by a fully qualified driver.

Question 10.19

BARKER has been disqualified from driving by the court until she passes her driving test. BARKER is due to attend court in relation to an offence where the prosecution allege that she failed to comply with the terms of a provisional licence holder when driving a motor vehicle on a road. BARKER intends pleading not guilty to the offence and is disputing the fact that she has failed to comply with the conditions of her licence.

Which of the following statements is correct, in relation to the burden of proof for this offence?

A The prosecution must show that BARKER was driving a motor vehicle on a road; BARKER must show she had a provisional licence and that she was driving in accordance with that licence.

B The prosecution must show that BARKER was driving a motor vehicle on a road, that she had a provisional licence and that she was not driving in accordance with that licence.

C BARKER will have to show either that she was not driving a motor vehicle on a road, or that she had a provisional licence and that she was driving in accordance with that licence.

D The prosecution must show that BARKER was driving a motor vehicle on a road and that she had a provisional licence; BARKER must show that she was driving in accordance with that licence.

Question 10.20

SHELFORD was disqualified from driving by the court just over 12 months ago. At the end of the disqualification period, SHELFORD was free to apply for a new full driving licence and did so. However, two weeks after submitting the application, it has still not been sent by the DVLA. SHELFORD has been offered employment as a delivery driver and rather than losing the position, has started the job before receiving the licence from the DVLA. SHELFORD has been stopped by the police while driving a motor vehicle on a road.

What are SHELFORD's liabilities under the Road Traffic Act 1988 in these circumstances?

A SHELFORD is not entitled to drive a motor vehicle on a road until receiving the licence from the DVLA and has committed the offence of disqualified driving.

B SHELFORD is entitled to drive a motor vehicle on a road if the application has been received by the DVLA and may not have committed an offence in these circumstances.

C SHELFORD has applied for a driving licence after a disqualification period has ended and has no liability once the application is submitted.

D SHELFORD is not entitled to drive a motor vehicle on a road until receiving the licence from the DVLA and has committed the offence of driving otherwise than in accordance with a licence.

Question 10.21

HARVEY appeared in court and was convicted of driving a motor vehicle on a motor-way at a speed of 101 mph. The prosecution asked the court to disqualify HARVEY from driving. The defence managed to convince the court that a long period of disqualification would have a significant impact on HARVEY's business and family life. HARVEY was eventually disqualified from driving for a period of a month, having agreed to take part in a community road safety scheme.

Which of the following statements is correct, in relation to HARVEY's driving licence following this disqualification?

A The driving licence will be retained by the DVLA; HARVEY will need to apply for its return when the disqualification period expires.

B The driving licence will be retained by the court; HARVEY will need to apply for its return when the disqualification period expires.

C The driving licence will be returned to HARVEY; it will become valid again the day after the disqualification period expires.

D The driving licence will be returned to HARVEY; it will become valid again if HARVEY makes an application to the DVLA, after the disqualification period expires.

Question 10.22

FLAHERTY and his wife are American nationals who moved to live permanently in this country two months ago. FLAHERTY is 30 years of age and has been the holder of a full American driving permit for ten years, but his wife has not passed a driving test in any country. FLAHERTY's wife would like to learn to drive and pass her driving test in this country.

Under what circumstances could FLAHERTY supervise his wife as she learns to drive?

A FLAHERTY may only supervise his wife when he has passed a driving test in this country.

B Because of his age and relevant driving experience, FLAHERTY is a qualified driver and may supervise his wife automatically.

C FLAHERTY may only supervise his wife when he has applied for a provisional driving licence in this country to accompany his full driving licence.

D FLAHERTY may only supervise his wife when he has passed a driving test in this country and then demonstrated the relevant driving experience in this country.

Question 10.23

LEBLANC is a French national who has taken up work in the UK and has become a resident. LEBLANC has a full driving permit from France and wishes to drive on the roads in this country.

Which of the following statements is correct, in relation to any restrictions or provisions there may be if LEBLANC wishes to drive in the UK?

A LEBLANC must exchange the French driving permit for a GB licence to drive on roads in this country.

B LEBLANC *may* exchange the French driving permit for a GB licence to drive on roads in this country.

C LEBLANC must pass a GB driving test before driving on roads in this country.

D As a driver from an EU Member State, LEBLANC must use the French driving permit as long as he is a resident in the UK.

Question 10.24

DUBOIS is a Canadian national who has moved to live permanently in the UK. DUBOIS has been the holder of a full Canadian driving permit for five years and wishes to drive in this country immediately.

What restrictions are there, if any, to DUBOIS driving on roads in the UK?

A DUBOIS may use the Canadian driving permit to drive on roads, without restrictions, for a period up to one year.

B DUBOIS must apply for a full GB licence to accompany the Canadian driving permit if she wishes to drive on roads.

C DUBOIS may apply for a provisional GB licence to accompany the Canadian driving permit; if she does, she must abide by the provisional licence conditions until she passes a test.

D DUBOIS must apply immediately for a provisional GB licence to accompany the Canadian driving permit, but she need not abide by the provisional licence conditions.

Question 10.25

AMIR was involved in a road accident during the hours of darkness. A witness stated that AMIR had caused the accident by failing to comply with a 'Give Way' sign. AMIR admitted to Constable WARE that he normally wore contact lenses, but had forgotten to wear them that night.

Under what conditions may Constable WARE require AMIR to submit to an eyesight test?

A In daylight conditions, while wearing his contact lenses.

B In darkness, without his contact lenses.

C In darkness, while wearing his contact lenses.

D In daylight conditions, without his contact lenses.

Question 10.26

Constable MORSE attended a road traffic accident in which HAMILTON had failed to give way at a junction and had driven into the path of GIBSON, who was driving on the main road. GIBSON had swerved to avoid HAMILTON and had collided with a parked car. There was no damage to HAMILTON's vehicle and he admitted to Constable MORSE that he had not seen the Give Way markings at the junction. The officer suspected that HAMILTON's eyesight was defective and submitted him to a test, which he failed. HAMILTON did not wear any corrective lenses for his eyesight and Constable MORSE strongly believed he represented a danger to other motorists, especially as HAMILTON's vehicle was undamaged and he had stated that he would continue to drive.

Given that HAMILTON has committed an offence under s. 96(1) of the Road Traffic Act 1988 (driving with defective eyesight), how should Constable MORSE proceed to prevent him from continuing to commit this offence?

A Constable MORSE must confiscate HAMILTON's driving licence and forward it to the DVLA as soon as reasonably practicable.

B Constable MORSE must notify the DVLA in writing as soon as reasonably practicable, allowing the DVLA to revoke HAMILTON's licence as soon as possible.

C Constable MORSE should notify the DVLA electronically, allowing the DVLA to revoke HAMILTON's licence as soon as possible.

D Constable MORSE should notify the DVLA electronically, allowing the DVLA to apply to the court for HAMILTON's licence to be revoked as soon as reasonably practicable.

ANSWERS

Answer 10.1

Answer **C** — Licences will generally last until the holder's seventieth birthday or for three years, whichever is the longer (see s. 99 of the Road Traffic Act 1988). However, the case is different in respect of large goods vehicles and large passenger-carrying vehicle licences. These licences last until a driver's forty-fifth birthday or five years, whichever is the *longer*. If the driver is between 45 and 65, they last for five years or until the holder's sixty-sixth birthday, whichever is the *shorter*.

Therefore, in SCOTT's case, he was 39 when he passed his test to drive large goods vehicles and the *longest* period between passing the test and the requirement for renewal is six years (as opposed to five years) and the licence will expire on his forty-fifth birthday.

Answers A, B and D are therefore incorrect.

Road Policing, para. 3.10.2.1

Answer 10.2

Answer **D** — A passenger-carrying vehicle (PCV) is defined under s. 121 of the Road Traffic Act 1988 as either:

- a vehicle used for carrying passengers
- which is constructed or adapted
- to carry more than 16 passengers (a 'large PCV')

or

- a vehicle used for carrying passengers for hire or reward
- which is constructed or adapted
- to carry more than eight but not more than 16 passengers (a 'small PCV').

A 12-seat minibus *could* be classified as a small PCV, if it was being used for carrying passengers for hire or reward, but it will not always be one simply because it has more than eight seats. Answers A and B are therefore incorrect.

In these circumstances it was not being used for hire or reward. The fact that it was not being used for the employer's purpose at the time is irrelevant and answer C is incorrect.

Road Policing, para. 3.10.2.1

Answer 10.3

Answer **C** — Under s. 108(1) of the Road Traffic Act 1988, a 'moped' is defined as a two-wheeled or three-wheeled vehicle which must have a maximum design speed of no more than 45 kilometres per hour.

Answer C contains the only correct combination, therefore, answers A, B and D are incorrect.

Road Policing, para. 3.10.3.1

Answer 10.4

Answer **A** — When a person completes a compulsory basic training course, he or she is issued with a certificate which is valid for two years, therefore answers B, C and D are incorrect.

Road Policing, para. 3.10.3.1

Answer 10.5

Answer **C** — Under s. 87(1) of the Road Traffic Act 1988:

It is an offence for a person to drive on a road a motor vehicle of any class otherwise than in accordance with a licence authorising him to drive a motor vehicle of that class.

Offences relating to learner drivers apply to persons holding provisional licences. JACOBS is too young to hold any type of licence and the regulations requiring provisional licence holders to display 'L' plates and be accompanied by a qualified driver do not apply to her. As a non-licence holder, JACOBS commits the offence under s. 87(1). Answers A and D are therefore incorrect.

There is no longer an offence of disqualified by reason of age and therefore answer B is incorrect.

Road Policing, paras 3.10.3.3, 3.10.10

Answer 10.6

Answer **A** — When a person has passed both their theory and practical driving tests, they are issued with a test pass certificate at the driving test centre. They then have two years in which to inform the DVLA and exchange their test pass certificate and provisional licence for a full driving licence (otherwise they lose their driving entitlement and will have to take both the theory and practical exams again). They can do this by post, or if they have a photocard driving licence, it may be done electronically at the test centre.

Under reg. 17(1) of the Motor Vehicles (Driving Licences) Regulations 1999, a person is a 'qualified driver' and able to supervise learners if he or she is 21 years of age or over, holds a relevant licence and has the relevant driving experience.

Generally people will have relevant driving experience if they have held the relevant full driving licence for a continuous or aggregate period of not less than *three* years. Answers C and D are therefore incorrect.

This three-year period is calculated from the time they hold a provisional licence and a valid test pass certificate together, entitling them to a full licence for the driving of vehicles of the same class (theoretically, this should be the day they pass their test). Answer B is therefore incorrect.

Road Policing, para. 3.10.3.3

Answer 10.7

Answer **D** — A person supervising a learner driver is required not to provide tuition for the learner, but to 'supervise'. That means doing whatever might reasonably be expected to prevent the learner driver from acting carelessly or endangering others (see *Rubie* v *Faulkner* [1940] 1 All ER 285). Answer C is therefore incorrect.

Supervising requires some positive action on behalf of the supervisor, and these duties extend to ensuring compliance with other legislative requirements, such as remaining at the scene of an accident (*Bentley* v *Mullen* [1986] RTR 7), or remaining sober when doing so (*DPP* v *Janman* [2004] EWHC 101). Answer B is therefore incorrect. There is no need to show encouragement to commit the offence, merely that the supervisor did not act to prevent the actions. Answer A is therefore incorrect.

Road Policing, para. 3.10.4

Answer 10.8

Answer **B** — The situation of a passenger being drunk while supervising a learner driver was considered by the Divisional Court in *DPP* v *Janman* [2004] EWHC 101. There it was held that, in any ordinary case, the person supervising a learner driver was in control of the vehicle and this was the obvious and normal consequence of their role. Therefore, if the supervisor's blood/alcohol level exceeded the prescribed limit, he or she would commit the offence under s. 5(1)(b) of the Road Traffic Act 1988 simply by supervising a learner driver on a road or in a public place.

Additionally, the contingent role of the supervisor, whereby he or she has to be ready to take actual control of the vehicle at any point, means that it is almost impossible for him or her to argue the defence under s. 5(2) of the Act—because that defence requires the defendant to show that there was no likelihood of his or her driving while still over the limit. The whole purpose of supervising a learner is to intervene as and when it becomes necessary and therefore there is every likelihood of the supervisor having to drive during the journey. Answer C is therefore incorrect.

A 'supervisor' can also be convicted of aiding and abetting where the learner driver is over the prescribed limit or unfit through drink or drugs (*Crampton* v *Fish* [1970] Crim LR 235). This is a separate issue from the *Janman* case, which shows that a supervisor could commit *either* offence, depending on the circumstances, and one is not dependent upon the other. Answers A and D are therefore incorrect.

Road Policing, para. 3.10.4

Answer 10.9

Answer **A** — Regulation 16(10) of the Motor Vehicles (Driving Licences) Regulations 1999 (SI 1999/2864) makes provision for the situation where a provisional licence holder has been issued the relevant certificate stating that he or she has passed a driving test but has not yet received his or her full licence.

In such cases, the requirements to display 'L' (or 'D') plates and to be supervised do not apply.

Answers B, C and D are therefore incorrect.

Road Policing, para. 3.10.6.1

Answer 10.10

Answer **D** — If a person is a 'new driver' and has his or her driving licence revoked after accumulating six penalty points (under s. 3 of the Road Traffic (New Drivers) Act 1995), he or she will not be counted as 'disqualified'. He or she will revert to the position of a learner driver and will have to abide by the conditions of the Motor Vehicles (Driving Licences) Regulations 1999, by displaying 'L' plates and being supervised by a qualified driver when driving a motor vehicle on a road. Answer B is therefore incorrect.

If a provisional licence holder fails to observe these conditions, he or she may be prosecuted for an offence under s. 91 of the Road Traffic Offenders Act 1988 for breaching the Regulations (in SWEETMAN's case, reg. 16(2)(a)). He or she will not be guilty of driving otherwise than in accordance with a licence, or driving while disqualified: therefore answers A and C are incorrect.

Road Policing, para. 3.10.7

Answer 10.11

Answer **D** — The Road Traffic (New Drivers) Act 1995 sets out a probationary period of two years, during which a person may have his or her driving licence revoked by the Secretary of State after accumulating six or more penalty points. In *R (On the application of Adebowale)* v *Bradford Crown Court* [2004] EWHC 1741 (Admin), the Divisional Court held that if a driver attracts penalty points on a provisional driving licence, and then receives further points in the first two years of holding a full licence, taking him or her to six or more points in all, the Secretary of State has no alternative but to revoke the licence under the provisions of s. 3 of the Act. Answer B is therefore incorrect.

The Divisional Court's ruling does not state that the points on the full driving licence have to be accumulated within two years of any other points (therefore answer A is incorrect). Additionally, the ruling does not state that the points on the provisional driving licence have to be accumulated at least two years before a person passes their driving test. Answer C is therefore incorrect.

Road Policing, para. 3.10.7

Answer 10.12

Answer **A** — The Powers of Criminal Courts (Sentencing) Act 2000 gives courts the power to disqualify any defendant from holding or obtaining a driving licence when convicting that person of any offence (and not merely those involving injury to another person). Answer C is therefore incorrect. There is no requirement for the incident (or in this case the damage) to be 'serious' and therefore answer D is incorrect.

The disqualification may be made instead of, or in addition to, any other penalty. Answer B is therefore incorrect.

Road Policing, para. 3.10.11

Answer 10.13

Answer **D** — The Powers of Criminal Courts (Sentencing) Act 2000 gives courts the power to disqualify any defendant from holding or obtaining a driving licence when convicting that person of any offence (see s. 146). The disqualification may be made instead of, as well as in addition to, any other penalty and the disqualification can be for any period.

In the case of the Crown Court, if it is satisfied that a motor vehicle was used by the person convicted or by anyone else for the purpose of committing, or facilitating the commission of, the offence in question, the court may order the person convicted to be disqualified (see s. 147).

Facilitating the commission of an offence includes the taking of any steps *after* the offence has been committed for the purpose of disposing of any property to which it relates or of avoiding apprehension or detection (s. 147(6)).

Answers A, B and C are therefore incorrect.

Road Policing, para. 3.10.11

Answer 10.14

Answer **D** — Section 34(1) of the Road Traffic Offenders Act 1988 outlines that where a person is convicted of an offence involving obligatory disqualification the court must order him to be disqualified for such period not less than 12 months (and not six months), therefore answer B is incorrect.

However, if the court sees fit it can, for special reasons, order a defendant to be disqualified for a shorter period, or not to be disqualified at all. In *DPP* v *Bristow* [1998] RTR 100 the Divisional Court stated that the key question justices should ask themselves when assessing if such special reasons existed on which they might decide not to disqualify was this: what would a sober, reasonable and responsible friend of the defendant, present at the time, but himself a non-driver and thus unable to help, have advised in the circumstances, to drive or not to drive? This is an 'objective' test which was affirmed in *Key* v *CPS* [2013] EWHC 245 (Admin). Answers A and C are therefore incorrect.

Road Policing, para. 3.10.11.1

Answer 10.15

Answer **C** — Under s. 103 of the Road Traffic Act 1988, a person is guilty of an offence if, while disqualified for holding or obtaining a licence, he drives a motor vehicle on a road. Generally, the person must be driving to commit the offence, but the courts have allowed some leeway in respect of the evidence that the person has been driving.

Case law has allowed for the meaning of 'driving' to include occasions where a person *has* been driving but has temporarily ceased (see *Shackleton* v *Chief Constable of Lancashire Police* [2001] EWCA Civ 1975, when a police officer saw a disqualified driver 'jogging' away from a car). Answer D is therefore incorrect.

In *Pinner* v *Everett* [1969] 1 WLR 1266, the House of Lords found that each case should be taken on its merits. Their Lordships held that there was no requirement for the vehicle to be in motion (answer A is therefore incorrect) and that the key considerations in assessing each case on its merits were whether the defendant:

- had actually stopped driving or intended carrying on (e.g. at a set of traffic lights);
- was still driving;
- had arrived at his or her destination or intended to continue to a further location;
- had been prevented or dissuaded from driving by someone else.

These cases demonstrate that to require a witness to have actually *seen* the person driving would be too restrictive and that the courts would consider other circumstantial evidence when deliberating whether to convict a defendant of this offence. Answer B is therefore incorrect.

Road Policing, para. 3.10.11.1

Answer 10.16

Answer **D** — The offence under s. 103 of the Road Traffic Act 1988 is one of strict liability. However, the prosecution will still need to prove that the defendant was, in fact, a disqualified driver. As the onus is on the prosecution, answers A and B are incorrect.

However, there is no need for the prosecution to prove that the defendant knew of the disqualification (*Taylor* v *Kenyon* [1952] 2 All ER 726). Answer C is therefore incorrect.

Road Policing, para. 3.10.11.1

Answer 10.17

Answer **A** — Section 36 of the Road Traffic Offenders Act 1988 gives the court the power to disqualify a person from holding or obtaining a licence until the person passes an 'appropriate' test.

If the person is disqualified under the provisions for 'totting up' penalty points or is found guilty of an offence involving obligatory disqualification; the 'appropriate' test is an *extended* test as defined in s. 36(5)(b).

In other cases the 'appropriate' test will be a regular driving test under s. 89(3) of the Road Traffic Act 1988.

Answers B, C and D are therefore incorrect.

Road Policing, para. 3.10.11.2

Answer 10.18

Answer **B** — Where a person has been disqualified by the court until a test is passed, he or she has to comply with the requirements of a provisional licence holder. This will include driving with 'L' plates and being accompanied by a qualified passenger. Answer D is therefore incorrect.

If a person fails to comply with these requirements, he or she commits the offence of disqualified driving under s. 103 of the Road Traffic Act 1988 (*Scott* v *Jelf* [1974] RTR 256). Answers A and C are therefore incorrect.

Road Policing, para. 3.10.11.2

Answer 10.19

Answer **A** — A person disqualified from holding a licence until he or she has passed another driving test is a disqualified person for the purposes of s. 103 of the Road Traffic Act 1988. That person may only drive a motor vehicle on a road if he or she obtains a provisional driving licence and drives in accordance with the terms of that licence (i.e. being accompanied by a qualified passenger and using 'L' plates).

It will fall to the driver to show that, not only did he or she have a provisional driving licence at the time, but that he or she was driving in accordance with the conditions of that licence (see *DPP* v *Barker* [2004] EWHC 2502 (Admin)). Answers B and D are therefore incorrect. The burden is on the prosecution to show that a defendant was the driver of the vehicle at a particular time; it is not down to the defendant to prove the opposite, therefore answer C is incorrect.

Road Policing, para. 3.10.11.2

Answer 10.20

Answer **B** — Once a period of disqualification ends, the person may apply for another licence. On application for another licence the person falls within the category of someone who 'has held and is entitled to obtain' a licence under s. 88 of the Road Traffic Act 1988.

Section 88 provides an exemption to the offence of driving otherwise than in accordance with a licence (s. 87)—the person can begin to drive again as soon as a proper application has been received by the Driver and Vehicle Licensing Agency (DVLA). The exception applies when the application is received by the DVLA and not when the application is submitted (or when it is returned) and therefore answers A, C and D are incorrect.

If a person drives before applying for a new licence, they commit the offence under s. 87 of the Act and answer A is also incorrect for this reason.

Road Policing, para. 3.10.11.3

Answer 10.21

Answer **C** — A person who receives a disqualification period of less than 56 days (called a Short Period Disqualification) will have his driving record updated by the court with details of the disqualification and the licence will be handed back to them. Answers A and B are therefore incorrect.

The licence will become valid again the day after the expiry of the disqualification and they can then drive again *without the need to apply to the DVLA for return of their licence*. Answer D is therefore incorrect.

Road Policing, para. 3.10.11.3

Answer 10.22

Answer **A** — The entitlement of drivers living outside the UK to drive here under the authority of their overseas permits is governed by the Motor Vehicles (International Circulation) Order 1975 (SI 1975/1208). If such drivers hold a domestic or Convention driving permit issued abroad or a British Forces driving licence, they may drive the vehicles covered by those authorities in Great Britain for one year (Art. 2). Regulation 80 of the Motor Vehicles (Driving Licences) Regulations 1999 makes similar provisions in relation to people who become resident in the UK. That permit allows the holder to take a driving test in that 12-month period. If they do not do so successfully then they will need a GB provisional licence.

However, the permit alone does *not* allow them to supervise learner drivers. Therefore, if FLAHERTY wanted to supervise his wife as she learns to drive in this country, he would have to pass a driving test in this country and abide by the regulations relating to 'qualified drivers' supervising others. Answers B and C are therefore incorrect.

There is no mention of the person having to further qualify once the test is passed by demonstrating the relevant driving experience (three years) in this country. Answer D is therefore incorrect.

Road Policing, para. 3.10.12

Answer 10.23

Answer **B** — The law governing drivers from EU Member States can now be found in the Driving Licences (Community Driving Licence) Regulations 1996 (SI 1996/1974).

Drivers from EU Member States must meet the fitness requirements of British drivers and, provided they are not disqualified, drivers meeting those physical requirements *may* exchange their licence for a part III licence if they have become normally resident in Great Britain (s. 89 of the Road Traffic Act 1988). Answer D is therefore incorrect.

However, it is not compulsory to exchange the driving licence in this manner and answer A is incorrect.

There is no requirement for drivers from EU Member States to pass a GB driving test before driving on roads in this country; therefore, answer C is incorrect.

Road Policing, para. 3.10.12

Answer 10.24

Answer **A** — Regulation 80 of the Motor Vehicles (Driving Licences) Regulations 1999 makes provisions in relation to people who are temporary residents in the UK. The driving permit from their original country allows the holder to drive on roads in the UK for a 12-month period without restrictions. If they wish to drive on the road after this period, they must pass a GB driving test.

A person *may* apply for a provisional GB driving licence during this period, to accompany the driving permit from their home country, but it is not compulsory. Answers B and D are therefore incorrect.

However, if the person does apply for a provisional licence (with a view to taking their test to enable them to drive after the 12-month period has expired) they do not have to abide by the conditions concerning provisional licence holders (e.g. driving whilst supervised and using 'L' plates). Answer C is therefore incorrect.

Road Policing, para. 3.10.12

Answer 10.25

Answer **D** — Under s. 96(1) of the Road Traffic Act 1988, a person commits an offence if he or she drives a motor vehicle on a road while his or her eyesight is such (whether through a defect which cannot be or one which is not for the time being sufficiently corrected) that he or she cannot comply with any requirement as to eyesight pre-scribed under this Part of this Act for the purposes of tests of competence to drive.

Where a constable has reason to suspect that a person may be guilty of driving a motor vehicle on a road with defective eyesight, he or she may require the driver to submit to an eyesight test (s. 96(2)).

The specific requirements as to eyesight are set out at regs 72 and 73 and sch. 8 to the Motor Vehicles (Driving Licences) Regulations 1999 (SI 1999/2864) and include the ability to read characters 79 mm high and 57 mm wide on a registra-tion mark fixed to a motor vehicle from 20.5 metres (or if the registration mark is the new type with narrower characters, 20 metres). Refusing to do so is an offence under s. 96(3).

The driver must be given the eyesight test in good light, while wearing corrective lenses, if they were worn when the person drove the motor vehicle on a road. This means that if the person was not wearing corrective lenses, they must take the test without them. Answers A and C are therefore incorrect. Even if the offence took place in darkness, the driver must take the test in good light. Answers B and C are incorrect for this reason.

Road Policing, para. 3.10.13.3

Answer 10.26

Answer **C** — The agreement with the DVLA allows for the fast-tracking of a revoca-tion of a licence from a motorist who fails a roadside eye test. Under the agreement, a licence can be revoked in a matter of hours rather than days. The system enables the police to notify the DVLA electronically with details of eyesight test failures, allowing a notice of revocation of the licence to be issued to motorists within hours (the police are able to contact the DVLA between 8 am and 9 pm). Previously, the police notified the DVLA in writing or by fax, which in some cases meant that the revocation could take up to four days. Answer B is therefore incorrect.

A motorist who commits the offence under s. 96(1) will have their licence revoked and it will not be returned until a driver can demonstrate that their eyesight meets the required standard; however, this process belongs to the DVLA and not the courts. Answer D is therefore incorrect.

This agreement does not provide the police with a power to confiscate a driving licence (therefore answer A is incorrect). In the circumstances outlined, it is suggested that the officer could use his or her powers to impose bail conditions (under s. 30A of PACE) if the circumstances merit immediate action. This could include requiring the person not to drive and if the person broke the condition, they could be taken to court to reconsider the question of bail.

Road Policing, para. 3.10.13.3

11 Fixed Penalty System

This chapter is only tested in the Sergeants' examination—Inspectors' examination candidates should not study this material.

STUDY PREPARATION

The fixed penalty notice (FPN) system is pretty straightforward. Understand the principles behind it and you will realise that the system is simply designed to speed up the administration of some common offences which won't result in disqualification.

The Road Safety Act 2006 allows for financial deposits to be taken from drivers in certain circumstances, where an offence has been committed which may be dealt with by an FPN. The 2006 Act also extends the power to issue an FPN and demand the production of a driving licence to authorised vehicle examiners.

QUESTIONS

Question 11.1

Where a fixed penalty offence has been committed, s. 52(3)(a) of the Road Traffic Offenders Act 1988 allows for a procedure other than prosecution to be followed during a specified period, known as the 'suspended enforcement period'.

Which of the following statements is correct in relation to the length of this period?

A The suspended enforcement period will be at least 14 days.

B The suspended enforcement period will be at least 21 days, unless otherwise specified.

C The suspended enforcement period will be at least 21 days.
D The suspended enforcement period will be at least 28 days.

Question 11.2

Together with colleagues from the Driver and Vehicle Standards Agency (DVSA), Constable PARKER was conducting road checks aimed at examining drivers' hours. They stopped MURPHY, a UK national, who was driving a large passenger-carrying vehicle (PCV). MURPHY was on the way to a ferry to take his passengers to France for a ten-day tour. On examining the vehicle's tachograph, Constable PARKER noticed that MURPHY had exceeded his driver's working hours. The officer intended issuing MURPHY with a fixed penalty notice for the offence.

Would Constable PARKER be entitled to require a deposit for the fixed penalty notice, under s. 90A of the Road Traffic Offenders Act 1988, in these circumstances?

A Yes, because MURPHY has indicated that he will be leaving the UK for a period longer than seven days.
B No, this power is only available in relation to drivers who are not citizens of the UK.
C No, because MURPHY has not indicated that he will be leaving the UK for a period longer than 28 days.
D Yes, but only if Constable PARKER is satisfied that MURPHY could not be found at an address in the UK.

Question 11.3

VELAZQUEZ, a Spanish national, was issued with a fixed penalty notice for an offence committed whilst driving in the UK. Because VELAZQUEZ told the officer that he was returning to Spain, he was made to provide a financial deposit relating to the notice. VELAZQUEZ has now written to the issuing force stating that he was unhappy with the process and has asked for a refund of the deposit.

Are there any circumstances in which a deposit such as this may be subsequently refunded to a driver?

A No, paying a deposit amounts to accepting liability for the offence; VELAZQUEZ should have made it clear at the time that he wanted to contest the charge.
B Yes, if VELAZQUEZ contests the notice, the deposit may be refunded to him and proceedings may be commenced for the offence.

C Yes, only if VELAZQUEZ contests the notice and the court finds in his favour, the deposit will be returned.

D Yes, if VELAZQUEZ contests the notice and the court finds in his favour, or if the case is not heard within 12 months, the deposit will be returned.

Question 11.4

FISHER works for the Driver and Vehicle Standards Agency (DVSA) and has stopped BUSCH, a German national, during a road check. BUSCH was driving a heavy goods vehicle and FISHER detected that he was committing an offence under s. 64(2) of the Road Traffic Act 1988, of using a goods vehicle with an unauthorised weight. FISHER intended issuing the driver with a fixed penalty notice for the offence. BUSCH was on the way to the ferry port and was leaving the UK within the next 24 hours and FISHER was not satisfied that he could be found if the penalty was not paid. FISHER asked the driver for a financial deposit relating to the notice; however, BUSCH stated that he did not have enough money to pay a deposit.

In relation to the fixed penalty notice, what powers does FISHER have to remove the vehicle to another place, using powers under s. 90A of the Road Traffic Offenders Act 1988?

A FISHER may not remove the vehicle; this power is only given to a constable.

B FISHER may detain the vehicle at the scene until a deposit is paid, but there are no powers to remove a vehicle under this section.

C FISHER may remove the vehicle if the deposit is not paid immediately.

D FISHER may remove the vehicle if the deposit is not paid, but must allow a reasonable time for BUSCH to pay the deposit before removing it.

Question 11.5

MALLOY has borrowed a car from his friend CASEY. Whilst driving the vehicle on the road, MALLOY was stopped by the police and issued with an endorsable fixed penalty notice (FPN) for a defective exhaust. CASEY was aware of the defect to the vehicle.

Are there any circumstances in which CASEY could be issued with an endorsable FPN for permitting the use of the vehicle on a road with a defective exhaust?

A Yes, an endorsable FPN may be issued to a person who is using, causing or permitting the use of a motor vehicle on a road.

B No, an endorsable FPN may only be issued to a person who is using or causing the use of a motor vehicle on a road.

C No, an endorsable FPN may only be issued to a person who is using a motor vehicle on a road.

D No, an endorsable FPN may only be issued to a person who is driving a motor vehicle on a road.

Question 11.6

Constable MARLEY stopped PHELPS for driving a vehicle on a road with a defective exhaust. The officer intended issuing PHELPS with an endorsable fixed penalty notice for the offence. PHELPS was not in possession of a driving licence at the time and was required by Constable MARLEY to produce it, together with the notice, at a police station. The vehicle that PHELPS was driving at the time of the offence belonged to SWINTON.

Who, according to s. 54 of the Road Traffic Offenders Act 1988, is entitled to produce the driving licence and fixed penalty notice at the police station?

A They must be produced by PHELPS.

B They may be produced by anyone, provided they are the holder of a full driving licence.

C They may be produced by anyone.

D They may be produced by PHELPS or SWINTON.

Question 11.7

Detective Constable SALISBURY was in plain clothes driving an unmarked police vehicle at night along a one-way street. The officer almost collided with a vehicle being driven towards her by WARD. The officer managed to stop the vehicle and spoke to WARD, who admitted that he had driven through a No Entry sign at the start of the street, to take a short cut. WARD confirmed that he was a full licence holder, and that the licence had eight penalty points on it.

Given that this offence involves an obligatory endorsement, is Detective Constable SALISBURY precluded from issuing HOPKINS with a fixed penalty notice in these circumstances?

A No, because the number of penalty points on the driving licence will not exceed 11.

B No, as the number of penalty points on the driving licence will not exceed 12.

C Yes, as the number of penalty points on the driving licence will reach 11.

D Yes, because the officer is not in uniform.

Question 11.8

Constable FOSTER is in uniform and working on a joint exercise with SCOTT, a vehicle examiner from the Driver and Vehicle Standards Agency (DVSA). They are stopping and examining motor vehicles for safety purposes and BOZMAN has been stopped as part of the exercise. SCOTT has discovered that BOZMAN's vehicle has a defective tyre. BOZMAN is not in possession of a driving licence at this time.

Which of the following statements is correct, in relation to whether SCOTT was able to issue a fixed penalty notice for the offence?

A SCOTT has the power to issue a notice, because she is accompanied by a police constable in uniform.

B SCOTT does not have the power to issue a notice, because BOZMAN is not in possession of a driving licence.

C SCOTT has the power to issue a notice, provided the number of points for this offence would not render BOZMAN liable to disqualification.

D SCOTT has the power to issue a notice in these circumstances alone, provided she produces her authority to do so.

Question 11.9

PRUITT was stopped while driving a van, as part of a joint operation by the police and the Driver and Vehicle Standards Agency (DVSA). It was discovered that the van had a defective tyre and PRUITT was issued with a fixed penalty notice for the offence by LAM, a qualified vehicle examiner for DVSA. PRUITT was not in possession of a driving licence at the time the notice was issued.

Which of the following is correct, in relation to the production of a driving licence by PRUITT, in order to comply with the fixed penalty notice procedures?

A PRUITT must produce the driving licence in person at a police station within seven days.

B PRUITT must produce the driving licence to a place specified in the notice, by post or in person, within 14 days.

C PRUITT must produce the driving licence to a place specified in the notice, in person, within 21 days.

D PRUITT must produce the driving licence to a place specified in the notice, by post within 28 days.

Question 11.10

SCHIFFER is an Austrian national who is a temporary resident in the UK and is using an Austrian permit as a driving licence in this country. SCHIFFER has received a conditional offer of a fixed penalty notice for activating a speed camera.

Which of the following statements is correct, as to whether or not the DVLA will be able to allocate SCHIFFER with penalty points for this offence?

A SCHIFFER will not receive penalty points on the Austrian driving licence; the DVLA will only be able to create a computer record of the offence.

B SCHIFFER will receive penalty points on the Austrian driving licence for this offence.

C The DVLA may not allocate penalty points on a foreign driving licence; they will have to notify Austrian officials who will deal with the matter as they would for a driver convicted in that country.

D The DVLA may not allocate penalty points on a foreign driving licence; they will have to issue SCHIFFER with a provisional licence with the points on it.

Question 11.11

KELNER has been charged with an offence of removing a fixed penalty notice, which had been fixed to a vehicle outside the premises where she worked. KELNER is pleading not guilty to the offence.

What defence, if any, might be available to KELNER to this offence, contrary to s. 62(2) of the Road Traffic Offenders Act 1988?

A There is no defence to this particular offence.

B KELNER must show that she removed the fixed penalty notice on behalf of the person who parked the vehicle at the location.

C KELNER must show that she removed the fixed penalty notice on behalf of the owner of the vehicle.

D KELNER must show that she removed the fixed penalty notice on behalf of the driver, the person in charge of the vehicle or the person liable for the offence.

Question 11.12

WALLIS has been issued with a conditional offer of a fixed penalty notice after activating a speed camera.

How long does WALLIS have to make a payment in order to avoid attending court?

A 14 days.

B 21 days.

C 28 days.

D One month.

Question 11.13

LARSEN, having activated a camera at a set of traffic lights after driving through a red light, was sent a conditional offer of a fixed penalty notice through the post. However, being concerned about the potential sanction for the offence, LARSEN did not reply to the offer.

What action is likely to happen now under s. 76(5) of the Road Traffic Offenders Act 1988, as a result of LARSEN's failure to respond to the conditional offer?

A The administrating office will notify the police that the penalty notice has not been paid.

B The administrating office will notify the clerk of the court for the relevant area that the penalty notice has not been paid.

C The administrating office should apply to the clerk of the court for the relevant area to issue a summons to be served on LARSEN.

D The administrating office will issue a notice to LARSEN, which will amount to a summons to appear in court.

ANSWERS

Answer 11.1

Answer **B** — Where a fixed penalty offence has been committed, the system allows for a procedure other than prosecution to be followed during a specified period. This period, known as the 'suspended enforcement period', *is at least 21 days following the date of the fixed penalty notice or such longer period as may be specified in it.*

Answers A, C and D are therefore incorrect.

Road Policing, para. 3.11.2

Answer 11.2

Answer **D** — Under s. 90A of the Road Traffic Offenders Act 1988, where any driver cannot satisfy a police officer or vehicle examiner that he or she can be found in the UK when necessary in connection with fixed penalty notice procedures, a deposit may be taken and the deposit may be used to pay any uncontested fixed penalty notice.

This power is available in relation to *any* driver, whether or not they are a UK citizen—the test is whether or not they can be found after the notice has been issued. Answer B is therefore incorrect.

Similarly, the fact that MURPHY is leaving the UK for a period of time is irrelevant, provided he can be found when he returns. Answers A and C are therefore incorrect.

Road Policing, para. 3.11.2.1

Answer 11.3

Answer **D** — Under s. 90A of the Road Traffic Offenders Act 1988, police officers and vehicle examiners are able to require the payment of a deposit by a person they believe to have committed an offence in relation to a motor vehicle who does not provide a satisfactory address in the UK at which it is likely they can be found. The deposit would be used to pay any uncontested fixed penalty notice (i.e. where the offender accepts liability for the offence). However, drivers will be able to contest the charge in court (including contesting a fixed penalty notice). The payment of the deposit does not amount to an admission of guilt; therefore answer A is incorrect.

On the other hand, if the driver contests the notice and the court decides in his or her favour), the deposit would be refunded with the relevant interest. The deposit will also be returned if the case does not go to court within a year (answer C is therefore incorrect).

If the court decided against the driver, the deposit would be retained to be offset against all, or part, of the fine imposed. The deposit is not, therefore, returned to the driver before the court case; it is only returned if the court considers that the driver did not commit the offence and answer B is incorrect.

Road Policing, para. 3.11.2.1

Answer 11.4

Answer **C** — Under s. 90A of the Road Traffic Offenders Act 1988, where any driver cannot satisfy a police officer *or vehicle examiner* that he or she can be found in the UK when necessary in connection with fixed penalty notice procedures, a deposit may be taken and the deposit may be used to pay any uncontested fixed penalty notice. Answer A is therefore incorrect.

Under s. 90D, if the deposit is not paid immediately, the police officer or vehicle examiner may prohibit the removal of the vehicle, or move it to another specified place. There is no requirement to allow a reasonable time for a person to pay the deposit before removing a vehicle under this section. Answers B and D are therefore incorrect.

Road Policing, para. 3.11.2.1

Answer 11.5

Answer **C** — Section 54(1) of the Road Traffic Offenders Act 1988, states:

> This section applies where in England and Wales on any occasion a constable in uniform, or a vehicle examiner who produces his authority, has reason to believe that a person he finds is committing or has on that occasion committed a fixed penalty offence.

The fixed penalty system is not restricted to issuing notices to drivers; therefore, answer D is incorrect.

Section 51(2) of the 1988 Act, however, provides that an offence specified in the schedule is not a fixed penalty offence if it is committed by causing or permitting a vehicle to be used by another in contravention of any statutory provision, restriction or prohibition. Effectively this means that defendants reported for causing or permitting offences may not enjoy the administrative provisions made under the fixed penalty system and the system is restricted to people who are using a motor vehicle on a road. Answers A and B are therefore incorrect.

Road Policing, para. 3.11.3

Answer 11.6

Answer **A** — Under s. 54(4) of the Road Traffic Offenders Act 1988, where the person does not produce their driving licence for inspection at the scene, he or she will be given a notice stating that if, within seven days after the notice is given, he or she delivers the notice together with his or her licence to a constable or authorised person at the police station specified in the notice, the person will *then* be given a fixed penalty notice in respect of the offence (at the station).

Section 54(4A) of the Act states that the notice and licence must be delivered to the police station *in person*. This is consistent with other sections of the Act, which allow for insurance or MOT certificates to be produced by someone other than the driver, but a driving licence must be delivered in person (see s. 164(8)(a)).

Answers B, C and D are therefore incorrect.

Road Policing, para. 3.11.4.1

Answer 11.7

Answer **D** — A person may be issued with a fixed penalty notice (FPN) if he or she commits an offence to which the procedure applies (in this case, an endorsable offence). If a constable intends issuing such an FPN and the person is not in possession of a driving licence, he or she may be required under s. 54(4) of the Road Traffic Offenders Act 1988 to produce it at a police station within seven days. The safeguard built into the process is that the person at the station will have to examine the driving licence for any penalty points and make the decision at that time whether or not the number of penalty points is likely to reach 12.

A person will be liable for disqualification under the 'totting up' procedure if his or her driving licence shows 12 points or more. Answer B is incorrect as an FPN may not be issued if the points are likely to exceed 11, not 12. Answer C is incorrect, as the process can continue if the number of penalty points on a person's driving licence reaches 11.

However, the constable must be in *uniform* in order to give the fixed penalty notice, which means all the above answers are irrelevant; it also makes answer A (which would otherwise have been correct) incorrect.

Road Policing, para. 3.11.4.1

Answer 11.8

Answer **D** — Section 54(1) and (2) of the Road Traffic Offenders Act 1988 states that where a constable in uniform, *or a vehicle examiner who produces his or her authority*, has reason to believe that a person he or she finds is committing or has on that occasion committed a fixed penalty offence, he or she may give the person a fixed penalty notice in respect of the offence. There is no requirement for the authorised vehicle examiner to be accompanied by a police constable in uniform in order to exercise this power and therefore answer A is incorrect.

If the person is not in possession of a driving licence, the authorised vehicle examiner has the same power to require the person, under s. 54(4), to produce it at a police station (within 14 days as opposed to seven days when issued by a police constable), and therefore answer B is incorrect. This is regardless of how many points are currently on the licence (answer C is therefore incorrect).

Road Policing, para. 3.11.4.1

Answer 11.9

Answer **B** — Under s. 54(4A)(a) of the Road Traffic Offenders Act 1988, if a fixed penalty notice is issued by a constable in uniform, delivery of the driving licence must be made in person, within seven days after the notice is given, to a constable or authorised person at the police station specified in the notice (being a police station chosen by the person concerned).

However, under s. 54(4A)(b), where the notice is given *by a vehicle examiner*, delivery of the driving licence may be made (either by post or in person), within 14 days after the notice is given, to the Secretary of State at the place specified in the notice.

Answers A, C and D are therefore incorrect.

Road Policing, para. 3.11.4.1

Answer 11.10

Answer **B** — Section 54 of the Road Traffic Offenders Act 1988 has been amended to facilitate the endorsement of a driver's record held at the DVLA for unlicensed and foreign drivers. Previously a fixed penalty notice could only be issued to a person who held a licence issued in Great Britain. The new system enables a fixed penalty notice which carries an endorsement to be issued to anyone provided that they are not liable to be disqualified under s. 35 of the Road Traffic Offenders Act 1988.

Answers A, C and D are therefore incorrect.

Road Policing, para. 3.11.4.1

Answer 11.11

Answer **D** — Section 62(2) of the Road Traffic Offenders Act 1988 states that a person is guilty of an offence if he or she removes or interferes with any notice fixed to a vehicle under this section, unless he or she does so by or under the authority of the *driver or person in charge of the vehicle or the person liable for the fixed penalty offence in question.*

Answers A, B and C are therefore incorrect.

Road Policing, para. 3.11.4.3

Answer 11.12

Answer **C** — Under s. 75(8)(a) of the Road Traffic Offenders Act 1988, the specified period is 28 days and therefore answers A, B and D are incorrect.

Road Policing, para. 3.11.5

Answer 11.13

Answer **A** — If the defendant fails to pay the fixed penalty and, where appropriate, surrender their licence, the police will be notified (s. 76(5) of the Road Traffic Offenders Act 1988). This will allow the agents acting on behalf of the police to decide how to proceed against the defendant. Answers B, C and D are therefore incorrect.

Road Policing, para. 3.11.5

12 Notices of Intended Prosecution

This chapter is only tested in the Sergeants' examination—Inspectors' examination candidates should not study this material.

STUDY PREPARATION

Like much road traffic legislation, the law governing notices of intended prosecution (NIPs) is concerned with procedural detail. Once you know which offences are generally covered by the NIP procedure, you then need to learn the procedure required for proper service to be accepted by the courts and any exceptions provided for.

Understanding the purpose behind NIPs will help you in learning all this important procedural detail.

QUESTIONS

Question 12.1

Constable DURSTOW had been trying to trace PHELPS, whom the officer knew well, having had dealings with him on several occasions. Constable DURSTOW saw PHELPS driving a vehicle dangerously in a housing estate yesterday; the officer is not pursuit trained and lost sight of the vehicle, which was unregistered. Constable DURSTOW tried several addresses yesterday without success, but saw PHELPS walking down the street today and arrested him for the offence. Constable DURSTOW interviewed PHELPS at the station and a decision has been made by the Crown Prosecution Service (CPS) that the defendant should be charged with dangerous driving.

What action should Constable DURSTOW take, to comply with s. 1 of the Road Traffic Offenders Act 1988 (notice of intended prosecution (NIP))?

A Constable DURSTOW should serve a written NIP on PHELPS at the time of charging him.

B Constable DURSTOW should give PHELPS a verbal NIP at the time of charging him.

C Constable DURSTOW should identify PHELPS's address (or last known address) while he is in police detention and arrange for a written NIP to be sent there.

D Constable DURSTOW is not required to serve any type of NIP on PHELPS, as he is being charged with the offence.

Question 12.2

Constable MADDEN was in a police vehicle on her way to a disturbance in progress when she saw a vehicle driving through a 'No Entry' sign. The officer was unable to deal with the matter at the time because of the incident she was attending; however, she managed to note the registration number of the vehicle. Constable MADDEN went on to a period of rest days and leave at the end of her shift and has returned to work today, seven days after seeing the vehicle drive through the 'No Entry' sign. Her sergeant has advised her to send a written notice of intended prosecution (NIP) to the registered keeper's home address.

How should Constable MADDEN proceed, to comply with s. 1 of the Road Traffic Offenders Act 1988?

A The officer is too late to send a written NIP, it should have been sent to the registered keeper within seven days of the offence.

B The officer is not too late to send a written NIP, it should be sent to the registered keeper within ten days of the offence.

C The officer is not too late to send a written NIP, it should be sent to the registered keeper within 14 days of the offence.

D The officer is not too late to send a written NIP, it should be sent to the registered keeper within 21 days of the offence.

Question 12.3

Constable SHAH attended a call at a local primary school. Witnesses identified ASHLEY, a young person whom the officer knew lived locally. ASHLEY had been in a car doing handbrake turns on the road outside the school and had nearly collided with several pedestrians; the vehicle had driven off at speed onto the main road. After taking details at the scene and due to a busy shift, Constable SHAH eventually managed to attend ASHLEY's home address some eight hours after the incident. The officer reported ASHLEY for the offence of dangerous driving.

Considering the requirement to serve a notice of intended prosecution (NIP) for certain offences, which of the following statements is correct?

A Constable SHAH was required to give ASHLEY a verbal NIP at the time of reporting him for the offence.

B A verbal NIP should normally be given at the time of the offence; however, if this opportunity is lost, it may be given in writing.

C A verbal NIP should only be given at the time of the offence; because this opportunity was lost, there is no requirement to give ASHLEY an NIP.

D Constable SHAH was required to give ASHLEY a written NIP at the time of reporting him for the offence.

Question 12.4

Constable SILVA was conducting road checks with colleagues from the Driver and Vehicle Standards Agency (DVSA); the officer was paired with POTTER, a member of that agency. They were in high visibility clothing at the road check site, which was marked out with signs and cones, meant to funnel drivers into a safe area to be stopped. Constable SILVA tried to stop a van being driven by BARNETT; however, he panicked and drove straight past the officer, colliding with a number of traffic cones, before coming to a halt. Constable SILVA and POTTER spoke to BARNETT and examined the van. They found no offences, and there was no damage to the traffic cones; however, they considered reporting BARNETT for careless driving.

Given that a notice of intended prosecution (NIP) is required in these circumstances, which of the following statements is correct?

A The NIP may only be given by Constable SILVA.

B The NIP may be given by either Constable SILVA or POTTER.

C The NIP may be given by either person, because POTTER is accompanied by a police officer.

D The NIP may only be given by Constable SILVA; POTTER is only entitled to give such a notice when the offence relates to a defect to a vehicle.

Question 12.5

Constable PELLERITO had been attempting to trace CONLEY to deal with him for a driving offence. The officer called at CONLEY's address, but his mother stated he was not there very often and suggested Constable PELLERITO called at a local garage, where CONLEY worked. Three days after the alleged incident took place, Constable PELLERITO attended the premises in possession of a written notice of intended prosecution (NIP), intending to serve it on CONLEY.

Which of the following statements is correct, in relation to Constable PELLERITO's intention to serve a written NIP on CONLEY in these circumstances?

A Constable PELLERITO could serve a verbal NIP on CONLEY in these circumstances; there is no requirement for it to be in writing.

B Constable PELLERITO is correct in serving a written NIP personally on CONLEY in these circumstances.

C Constable PELLERITO should have sent a written NIP to the last known residential premises frequented by CONLEY; there is no facility to serve a written notice personally.

D Constable PELLERITO should have sent a written NIP to an address known to be frequented by CONLEY, such as the garage premises; there is no facility to serve a written notice personally.

Question 12.6

Constable NEWTON attended an accident where CONRAD, who was riding a pedal cycle on the pavement, had knocked over a child. The child did not suffer serious injuries and Constable NEWTON decided to report CONRAD for the offence of careless or inconsiderate cycling.

Should Constable NEWTON serve CONRAD a verbal notice of intended prosecution (NIP), in these circumstances?

A No, NIPs are not required where an offence has been committed involving a pedal cycle.

B No, but an NIP would have been required if CONRAD had been reported for dangerous cycling.

C Yes, an NIP is required as the accident involved a pedal cycle and not a motor vehicle.

D No, NIPs are generally required when a person has been reported for this offence, but there is no requirement to serve one in these circumstances.

Question 12.7

Constable PITTMAN stopped a vehicle being driven by BOONE, and following an examination of the vehicle, the officer saw that the van had a defective tyre. The officer was considering prosecuting BOONE for the offence.

Would Constable PITTMAN be required to give BOONE a notice of intended prosecution (NIP) in these circumstances?

A Yes, because BOONE has committed an endorsable offence, an NIP is required.

B Yes, an NIP is required for any offence committed under the Road Traffic Act 1988.

C No, an NIP is not required for this particular offence.

D Yes, because BOONE has committed a moving traffic offence, an NIP is required.

Question 12.8

CLAYTON was in detention for an offence of causing death by dangerous driving and was charged with this offence on the advice of the out-of-hours Crown Prosecutor. However, a month later, after reviewing the evidence, the CPS decided that the evidence connecting CLAYTON with the death of the victim was not strong and recommended an alternative charge be put to the defendant of dangerous driving. CLAYTON was not served with a notice of intended prosecution (NIP) when charged with the original offence.

Which of the following is correct in relation to the service of an NIP for the alternative offence of dangerous driving, in these circumstances?

A A verbal NIP should now be served on CLAYTON for this offence, otherwise the prosecution will fail.

B There is no requirement to serve an NIP on CLAYTON, and the prosecution may proceed.

C A written NIP should now be served on CLAYTON for this offence, otherwise the prosecution will fail.

D An NIP may not be served on CLAYTON because of time limits, and the prosecution may fail as a result of failing to serve one sooner.

Question 12.9

The police had been dealing with incidents of dangerous driving late at night on an industrial estate. The area was closed off to the public at 6 pm by a barrier at the entrance, but somehow young people had found an alternative way in and regularly raced their cars around the estate. Constable MAYNARD attended one evening and, on arrival, witnessed a collision between two vehicles which were racing together. An ambulance had to be called to the scene because one of the drivers was seriously injured. Constable MAYNARD spoke to the uninjured driver and was considering how to deal with the matter.

If it was decided that a prosecution was suitable in this incident, which of the following statements is correct as to whether a notice of intended prosecution (NIP) would be required under s. 1 of the Road Traffic Offenders Act 1988?

A Even though they were in a private place, 'accident' under this Act is broader than the term used under s. 170 of the Road Traffic Act 1988; an NIP is required.

B The drivers have been involved in an 'accident' as defined in this Act; therefore an NIP is not required.

C The drivers have not been involved in an 'accident' as defined in this Act because the incident did not occur on a road; therefore an NIP is not required.

D The drivers have not been involved in an 'accident' as defined in this Act because the incident did not occur on a road or public place; therefore an NIP is not required.

Question 12.10

Constable FERDINAND was dealing with a road traffic accident in which a vehicle registered to KNOX struck a motorcycle, causing injury to the rider. The offending vehicle drove off without stopping. KNOX had moved address and was not traced until three weeks after the accident. Constable FERDINAND interviewed KNOX, who admitted being the driver at the time of the accident. There was evidence of careless driving and the officer sought advice as to whether KNOX could still be prosecuted for careless driving, given that a notice of intended prosecution (NIP) was not served within 14 days.

Which of the following statements is correct, in relation to the service of an NIP, under s. 1 of the Road Traffic Offenders Act 1988?

A An NIP is not required because KNOX's conduct contributed to the failure to serve it in time.

B A prosecution for careless driving may still proceed, providing an NIP is sent, as soon as reasonably practicable, to KNOX's last known address, or current address if it is known.

C An NIP is not required in these circumstances, KNOX failed to stop at the scene of a road traffic accident.

D An NIP is not required in these circumstances, because the offence arose at the time of a road traffic accident.

Question 12.11

LEWINSKI was driving his motor vehicle along a main road, approaching a set of traffic lights at a junction. Due to a lack of concentration, LEWINSKI drove through a red light and collided with a heavy goods vehicle. LEWINSKI suffered severe head injuries as a result of the accident and was taken to hospital, where he remained for several weeks. Because of his injuries, LEWINSKI was not able to recall being involved in the accident. The officer in the case is contemplating whether or not a notice of intended prosecution (NIP) should be served on LEWINSKI, for driving through the red light.

Would the officer be correct in serving an NIP because of the serious injuries, in these circumstances?

A Yes, as LEWINSKI was severely injured as a result of the accident.

B No, an NIP is never required when the driver has been involved in an accident.

C It is immaterial whether he was injured or not, because the accident was not of a minor nature.

D Yes, an NIP is always required when the driver is injured as a result of an accident.

Question 12.12

GODDARD has been summonsed to court for an offence of careless driving.

What evidential proof will be required by the court that GODDARD has been served with a notice of intended prosecution (NIP), under s. 1(1) of the Road Traffic Offenders Act 1988?

A The prosecution must show that the requirements of s. 1(1) of the 1988 Act have been complied with through oral testimony.

B The prosecution must show that the requirements of s. 1(1) of the 1988 Act have been complied with through documentary evidence.

C The court will always assume that the requirements of s. 1(1) of the 1988 Act have been complied with.

D The court will always assume that the requirements of s. 1(1) of the 1988 Act have been complied with until the contrary is proved.

Question 12.13

Constable HAMILTON has been attempting to serve a notice of intended prosecution (NIP) on KUBICA, whom the officer witnessed driving dangerously. Constable HAMILTON attended KUBICA's home address, but was told that the suspect was staying in France for six weeks. Constable HAMILTON returned to KUBICA's home address the following day and served a written NIP on the suspect's father.

Has an NIP been served correctly in these circumstances?

A Yes, the NIP has been served in these circumstances.

B No, the NIP should only be served on the person who was believed to be the driver.

C No, Constable HAMILTON was aware that KUBICA would not be at the address to receive the NIP.

D No, Constable HAMILTON should have arranged for a written NIP to be sent to KUBICA's home address by recorded delivery.

Question 12.14

COSTAS is facing prosecution for an offence of dangerous driving, contrary to s. 2 of the Road Traffic Act 1988. COSTAS is pleading not guilty, citing a technical reason: that the notice of intended prosecution (NIP) was not served correctly. COSTAS admits to having received a written NIP by post, but claims not to have received it within the required timescales. The prosecution will claim that the NIP was sent by registered post within the required timescales.

Which of the following statements is correct, in relation to a driver being properly warned of a prosecution, under s. 1 of the Road Traffic Offenders Act 1988?

A There is a presumption that if an NIP was sent by registered post or recorded delivery, it was served within 14 days.

B There is a presumption that if an NIP was sent by registered post or recorded delivery, it was served within two days.

C There is a presumption that if an NIP was sent by registered post or recorded delivery, it was served within five days.

D There is a presumption that if an NIP was sent by registered post or recorded delivery, it was served within seven days.

Question 12.15

HARDING is appearing in court for a speeding offence. HARDING is pleading not guilty, claiming that a notice of intended prosecution (NIP) was never served on him with the details of the offence, in accordance with s. 1 of the Road Traffic Offenders Act 1988. It has been established that an NIP was sent to HARDING, by second class post.

Which of the following statements is correct in relation to whether HARDING was correctly served with an NIP?

A The NIP was sent to HARDING by second class post; therefore it was not served correctly.

B The NIP was sent to HARDING by second class post; it must be sent by first class post on every occasion, therefore, it was not served correctly.

C The NIP has been correctly served on HARDING; any postal service may be used to serve such a notice.

D The NIP was sent to HARDING by second class post; it must be sent either by registered post or recorded delivery on every occasion; therefore it was not served correctly.

ANSWERS

Answer 12.1

Answer **D** — Under s. 1 of the Road Traffic Offenders Act 1988, before certain offences can be prosecuted the defendant must have *either* been:

- warned of the possibility of prosecution at the time of the offence; or
- served with a summons (or charged) within 14 days of the offence; or
- a notice of intended prosecution (NIP) must have been sent to the registered keeper within 14 days of the offence.

Therefore, as PHELPS is being charged with the offence, the provisions of s. 1 do not apply and an NIP is not required.

Answers A, B and C are therefore incorrect.

Road Policing, para. 3.12.1

Answer 12.2

Answer **C** — Under s. 1 of the Road Traffic Offenders Act 1988, before certain offences can be prosecuted, the defendant must have either been:

- warned of the possibility of prosecution at the time of the offence, or
- served with a summons (or charged) within 14 days of the offence, or
- a notice of intended prosecution (NIP) must have been sent to the registered keeper within 14 days of the offence.

Therefore, even if a verbal NIP is not given at the time, the officer can recover the situation provided a notice is sent to the registered keeper within 14 days of the offence (answers B and D are incorrect). Answer A is incorrect because a written NIP can still be sent.

Road Policing, para. 3.12.1

Answer 12.3

Answer **B** — Under s. 1 of the Road Traffic Offenders Act 1988, before certain offences can be prosecuted:

- the defendant must have been warned of the possibility of that prosecution at the time of the offence (s. 1(1)(a)); or

- the defendant must have been served with a summons (or charged) within 14 days of the offence (s. 1(1)(b)); or
- a notice setting out the possibility of that prosecution must have been sent to the driver or registered keeper of the vehicle within 14 days of the offence (s. 1(1)(c)).

The verbal notice of intended prosecution (NIP) must be given *at the time of the offence* and not at the time of reporting the person for the offence and answer A is incorrect.

If this opportunity is lost, the officer must consider alternatives to warning the person of the prospect of an impending prosecution in writing. Since there are alternatives and the defendant must be served with an NIP for this offence, answer C is incorrect.

Under s. 1, a written NIP *or* a summons should be sent to the offender's known address within 14 days of the offence. This is the course Constable SHAH should have taken and answer D is incorrect.

Road Policing, para. 3.12.1

Answer 12.4

Answer **A** — Under s. 1 of the Road Traffic Offenders Act 1988, before certain offences can be prosecuted, the defendant must have either been:

- warned of the possibility of prosecution at the time of the offence, or
- served with a summons (or charged) within 14 days of the offence, or
- a notice of intended prosecution (NIP) must have been sent to the registered keeper within 14 days of the offence.

If the person giving it is not empowered to make a decision whether or not to prosecute (such as a vehicle examiner employed by the vehicle inspectorate), the warning or notice will not be deemed to have been served (*Swan* v *Vehicle Inspectorate* [1997] RTR 187). Therefore, POTTER is not entitled to give an NIP and answers B, C and D are incorrect.

Road Policing, para. 3.12.1

Answer 12.5

Answer **B** — Under s. 1(1A) of the Road Traffic Offenders Act 1988, a notice required by this section to be served on any person may be served on that person:

(a) by delivering it to him;

(b) by addressing it to him and leaving it at his last known address; or

(c) by sending it by registered post, recorded delivery service or first class post addressed to him at his last known address.

A written notice *may* be served personally, provided the defendant fully understands what is said to them—in fact, if neither the defendant nor the registered keeper have a fixed abode, reasonable efforts must be made to serve the notice of intended prosecution (NIP) personally. Answers C and D are therefore incorrect. Also, nothing in s. 1 requires an NIP to be served at a residential premises and answer C is also incorrect for this reason.

Finally, for a verbal NIP to be given, the defendant must have been warned of the possibility of that prosecution *at the time of the offence* (s. 1(1)(a)). Answer A is therefore incorrect.

Road Policing, paras 3.12.1, 3.12.4

Answer 12.6

Answer **D** — There is a list of offences which require a notice of intended prosecution (NIP) contained in sch. 1 to the Road Traffic Offenders Act 1988 and these include dangerous, careless or inconsiderate cycling. Answer A is therefore incorrect.

Section 2(1) of the Road Traffic Offenders Act 1988 lists the exemption from the requirement to serve an NIP, namely, the requirement to serve an NIP does not apply in relation to an offence if, at the time, or immediately afterwards and owing to the presence of the *vehicle* concerned on a road, an accident occurred. The exemption is not restricted to motor vehicles, which means that since CONRAD was involved in an accident while riding a vehicle on a road, an NIP would not be required (even if the offence reported was dangerous cycling). Answers B and C are incorrect for this reason.

Road Policing, paras 3.12.2, 3.12.3

Answer 12.7

Answer **C** — The offences which require an NIP are listed in sch. 1 to the Road Traffic Offenders Act 1988 and include:

- Dangerous, careless or inconsiderate driving.
- Dangerous, careless or inconsiderate cycling.
- Failing to comply with traffic signs and directions.

- Leaving a vehicle in a dangerous position.
- Speeding offences under ss. 16 and 17 of the Road Traffic Regulation Act 1984.

The list of offences in sch. 1 is exhaustive; other offences, even if similar in nature to those in the list, will not be covered by the requirements of s. 1(1) (*Sulston* v *Hammond* [1970] 1 WLR 1164).

Answers A, B and D are therefore incorrect.

Road Policing, para. 3.12.2

Answer 12.8

Answer **B** — Under s. 1(1) of the Road Traffic Offenders Act 1988, before an offence to which the section applies can be prosecuted, the defendant must have been warned of the possibility of that prosecution at the time of the offence. If this is not done, he or she must be notified by way of summons (or charge) within 14 days, or a notice setting out the possibility of that prosecution must have been sent to the driver or registered keeper of the vehicle within 14 days of the offence. Section 1(1) does not allow for notices of intended prosecution (NIPs) to be served outside these timescales; therefore, answers A and C are incorrect.

Section 2(4) of the Act outlines that a failure to observe the requirements of s. 1(1) will not necessarily bar an alternative conviction, where the original offence prosecuted was not one requiring an NIP, but where the alternative offence *would* ordinarily require such a notice. Section 24 contains a list of such alternatives, which includes an alternative charge of dangerous driving, where the defendant was originally charged with causing death by dangerous driving. Therefore, although the CPS decision in this particular case fell outside the normal 14 days' time limit for serving an NIP, the prosecution may still proceed on the grounds that the defendant has been charged in the alternative. Answer D is therefore incorrect.

Road Policing, paras 3.12.2, 3.12.3

Answer 12.9

Answer **C** — Under s. 1 of the Road Traffic Offenders Act 1988, before certain offences can be prosecuted the defendant must have been warned of the possibility of that prosecution by being given a notice of intended prosecution (NIP). However, s. 2(1) of the Road Traffic Offenders Act 1988 states that the requirement to serve an NIP does not apply in relation to an offence if:

- at the time or
- immediately afterwards and
- owing to the presence of the vehicle concerned
- on a road
- an accident occurred.

Each of these features must be present to remove the need for an NIP to be served or a warning given.

'Accident' *is* broader than the expression used under s. 170 of the Road Traffic Act 1988; however, although such 'reportable' accidents extend to public places as well as roads, the exemption under s. 2(1) is limited to an accident that occurs on a *road* at the time or immediately after the offence.

Since the incident occurred in a private place, an NIP is not appropriate in these circumstances and answers A, B and D are incorrect.

Road Policing, para. 3.12.3

Answer 12.10

Answer **D** — Section 2(1) of the Road Traffic Offenders Act 1988 states that a notice of intended prosecution (NIP) does not need to be served if at the time or immediately afterwards, and owing to the presence of the motor vehicle concerned on a road, an accident occurred. This means that an NIP was not required in these circumstances, regardless of the defendant's actions after the accident. Answers A, B and C are therefore incorrect.

Road Policing, para. 3.12.3

Answer 12.11

Answer **C** — Generally, a notice of intended prosecution (NIP) is *not* required if at the time of the offence, or immediately afterwards, an accident occurred owing to the presence of a motor vehicle on a road (s. 2(1) of the Road Traffic Offenders Act 1988). However, there is an exception to this rule. Where the driver of a motor vehicle is unaware that an accident has taken place because it is so minor, there *will* be a need to serve an NIP (*Bentley* v *Dickinson* [1983] RTR 356). Answer B is incorrect as the exception shows that sometimes an NIP may be required following an accident.

When the accident is so severe that the driver of the vehicle is unable to recall it, an NIP is *not* required (*DPP* v *Pidhajeckyj* [1991] RTR 136). Answer A is incorrect because of the ruling in this case. Answer D is incorrect as there is nothing in the Act stating that an NIP is required every time a driver is injured in an accident.

Answer C is *correct* because it is *not* relevant whether the driver was injured, as the accident was not of a minor nature (and *Bentley* does not apply), and therefore it falls within the scope of s. 2(1).

Road Policing, para. 3.12.3

Answer 12.12

Answer **D** — Section 1 of the Road Traffic Offenders Act 1988 relates to the notice or warning in relation to notices of intended prosecution (NIP).

Subsection (3) of this section relates to a presumption in relation to NIPs, in that:

(3) The requirement of subsection (1) above shall in every case be deemed to have been complied with unless and until the contrary is proved.

The effect of s. 1(3), therefore, is to place the burden of proving failure to comply with the section on the defence on a balance of probabilities. Answer C is therefore incorrect. The prosecution have no such evidential burden. Answers A and B are therefore incorrect.

Road Policing, para. 3.12.4

Answer 12.13

Answer **A** — Section 1 of the Road Traffic Offenders Act 1988 states:

(1A) A notice required by this section to be served on any person may be served on that person—
(a) by delivering it to him;
(b) by addressing it to him and leaving it at his last known address; or
(c) by sending it by registered post, recorded delivery service or first class post addressed to him at his last known address.

In the case of *Hosier* v *Goodall* [1962] 2 QB 401, a notice of intended prosecution (NIP) served on the defendant's spouse or partner was sufficient. Answer B is therefore incorrect.

In the case of *Phipps* v *McCormick* [1972] Crim LR 540, it was found that if the defendant is not at his or her home address, for instance because he or she is in hospital or on holiday, service to his or her last known address will suffice, even if the police are aware of that fact. Answer C is therefore incorrect.

Under s. 1(1A), any method of service of an NIP will suffice, therefore, provided the NIP has been served correctly, the method of service is unimportant. Answer D is therefore incorrect.

Road Policing, para. 3.12.4

Answer 12.14

Answer **B** — Under s. 1 of the Road Traffic Offenders Act 1988, before certain offences can be prosecuted, the defendant must have either been:

- warned of the possibility of prosecution at the time of the offence, *or*
- served with a summons (or charged) within 14 days of the offence, *or*
- a notice of intended prosecution (NIP) must have been sent to the registered keeper within 14 days of the offence.

If the driver is not warned of the possibility of prosecution at the time of the offence, then a notice must be sent to the registered keeper of the vehicle, in writing, within 14 days of the offence.

Section 1(1A)(c) of the Road Traffic Offenders Act 1988 states that a notice required by this section to be served on any person may be served on that person:

> by sending it by registered post, recorded delivery service or first class post addressed to him at his last known address.

Generally, proof is required that the NIP was sent to the registered keeper of the vehicle within 14 days of the offence; however, there is an irrebuttable presumption that if an NIP is sent by registered post or recorded delivery then it has been served within *two* days.

Answers A, C and D are therefore incorrect.

Road Policing, para. 3.12.4

Answer 12.15

Answer **A** — Under s. 1 of the Road Traffic Offenders Act 1988, before certain offences can be prosecuted, the defendant must have either been:

- warned of the possibility of prosecution at the time of the offence, *or*
- served with a summons (or charged) within 14 days of the offence, *or*
- a notice of intended prosecution (NIP) must have been sent to the registered keeper within 14 days of the offence.

If the driver is not warned of the possibility of prosecution at the time of the offence, then a notice must be sent to the registered keeper of the vehicle, in writing, within 14 days of the offence. Section 1(1A)(c) of the Road Traffic Offenders Act 1988 states that a notice required by this section to be served on any person may be served on that person:

> by sending it by registered post, recorded delivery service or first class post addressed to him at his last known address.

Since the NIP can be sent by any of these methods, answers B and D are incorrect.

However, such a notice may be sent to the person by registered post, recorded delivery service or first class post addressed to him or her at his or her last known address. This means that an NIP will *not* be correctly served if it is sent by second class post (answer C is therefore incorrect).

Note that there is a rebuttable presumption that service by first class post would not suffice, if the defence can give evidence that the notice was received after the 14-day period (*Gidden v Chief Constable of Humberside* [2009] EWHC 2924 (Admin)).

Road Policing, para. 3.12.4

13 | Forgery and Falsification of Documents

This chapter is only tested in the Sergeants' examination—Inspectors' examination candidates should not study this material.

STUDY PREPARATION

The end of the road—or at least for road policing!

There are relatively few offences involving forgery and falsification, although as much road traffic law—and its enforcement—relies upon records, these offences are more relevant than they may at first appear. The following deals with occasions where a defendant has, or uses, false documentation.

QUESTIONS

Question 13.1

MERCER is appearing in Crown Court, having been charged with forging certificates of insurance, which it is alleged he was trying to sell in a pub. MERCER has pleaded not guilty to the offence.

Which of the following statements is correct in relation to the required intent to prove an offence under s. 173(1) of the Road Traffic Act 1988?

A It must be proved that MERCER intended to make a gain for himself, or expose another person to a loss.

B It need only be proved that MERCER intended to make a gain for himself.

C It need only be proved that MERCER intended to deceive someone else.

D Because MERCER is alleged to have made the documents (as opposed to simply being in possession of them) this is an absolute offence and there is no requirement to prove intent.

Question 13.2

HOLLAND thinks he has discovered a method of producing a copy of a driving licence and has persuaded NIXON to lend him a recently issued licence to try out the forging software. NIXON knew what HOLLAND's intention was. HOLLAND produced a couple of examples but the forgeries were so poor that he gave up because they would not deceive anyone.

Has either of them committed an offence of forgery of a document within the meaning of s. 173 of the Road Traffic Act 1988?

A Yes, but only NIXON for lending the document to HOLLAND, because the forgery was unsuccessful.

B No, the document produced by HOLLAND did not closely resemble a document or other thing to which this section applies.

C Yes, NIXON for lending the document to HOLLAND and HOLLAND for forging a document.

D No, neither has altered a document or other thing to which this section applies.

Question 13.3

Constable HAMAN stopped NORTH whilst driving a motor vehicle on a road. A Police National Computer (PNC) check revealed that the vehicle's insurance had expired 24 hours previously. NORTH stated he had renewed the insurance by telephone the previous day and was waiting for the certificate to arrive. Constable HAMAN issued NORTH with an HORT/1 for the production of his certificate. NORTH had not actually renewed his insurance and when he arrived home, he made a fake certificate by scanning the expired document, changing the dates and then printing off a copy. However, NORTH lost his nerve and did not produce the fake document at the police station.

At which point, if any, could an offence be proved against NORTH, under s. 173 of the Road Traffic Act 1988 (forgery of documents)?

A When he made a false statement relating to the insurance to Constable HAMAN.

B When he scanned the insurance document into the computer.

C When he actually made the fake insurance document.

D He did not commit this offence, because he did not actually alter the original document.

Question 13.4

STANGER runs an international road haulage company and has recently married. He wishes to start another business in his wife's name and applies for an international road haulage permit for her. His wife has a recent conviction for drink-driving, although she is currently not disqualified. STANGER is unaware of this, as his wife does not wish him to know, and he claims on the application form that neither he nor his wife have any previous convictions. As a result, a permit is issued, when it may not have been had the conviction been declared.

Has an offence of making a false statement to obtain the grant of an international road haulage permit been committed?

A   Yes, as a false statement has been made; STANGER's wife knows it to be false and it is an application on her behalf.

B   Yes, as STANGER has gained an advantage by not declaring the conviction in that a permit was issued that may not have been.

C   No, because STANGER had no intention of deceiving the issuers of the permit when he made the declaration.

D   No, because STANGER did not knowingly make a false statement as he was unaware of the conviction.

Question 13.5

FRANCIS is the transport manager of a haulage company. Before going on holiday, FRANCIS was aware that five of the company's vehicles were due to be submitted for goods vehicle tests while he was away. When FRANCIS returned, all five had been tested and issued with certificates. When FRANCIS examined the certificates, he suspected that they were forgeries. FRANCIS turned a blind eye, knowing the company was in financial difficulty. He provided one of the certificates to a driver, which was then produced to the police.

Under what circumstances could an offence be proved against FRANCIS, under s. 174(2) of the Road Traffic Act 1988 (producing documents which are false)?

A   If it can be shown FRANCIS either knew the certificate was false, or was reckless as to whether or not it was.

B   If it can be shown FRANCIS either knew the certificate was false, or was reckless as to whether or not it was and that someone gained by the transaction, though not necessarily him.

C   If it can be shown FRANCIS knew the certificate was false.

D If it can be shown FRANCIS knew the certificate was false and that someone gained by the transaction, though not necessarily him.

Question 13.6

ROSS was involved in a road traffic accident, during which she knocked a pedestrian over. There was no damage to her vehicle; however, the police dealt with the incident and issued ROSS with an HORT/1. When she got home, ROSS realised that her test certificate had expired the day before. Knowing she could be prosecuted, ROSS contacted her friend, CRUTCHER, who ran a testing station, and asked him to put her car through an MOT and to backdate her test certificate. CRUTCHER agreed to do so and ROSS was issued with a test certificate backdated to the day before.

Has CRUTCHER committed an offence under s. 175 of the Road Traffic Act 1988 (issuing false documents), in these circumstances?

A No, the offence under this section applies to documents that have been altered; it would be necessary to prosecute CRUTCHER for conspiracy instead.

B Yes, provided it can be proved that CRUTCHER knew why ROSS had made this request.

C Yes, provided it can be proved that CRUTCHER either knew why ROSS had made this request, or was reckless as to why she had done so.

D Yes, CRUTCHER could be prosecuted, because he issued a false document, whether he knew ROSS's intentions or not.

Question 13.7

While on mobile patrol, Constable FRENCH stopped a large goods vehicle being driven by PARSONS. Constable FRENCH was not an authorised vehicle examiner, but had recently been studying to go on a traffic officer's course and decided to examine the vehicle. The officer noticed that the plate attached to the vehicle authorising its 'plated' weight had been interfered with in that the characters and words had been scratched out. Constable FRENCH suspected that the plate had been fraudulently altered.

What powers would Constable FRENCH have in respect of the vehicle and the plate attached to it, under s. 176 of the Road Traffic Act 1988?

A Constable FRENCH may seize the vehicle to which the plate is attached until it has been examined.

B None, Constable FRENCH will have to call an authorised vehicle examiner, who may detach the plate from the vehicle.

C Constable FRENCH may detach the plate, and cause it to be examined by an authorised vehicle examiner.

D None, the power under this section relates to seizing documents and a plate is not a document.

Question 13.8

MARTIN and STOUT own car showrooms next to each other. Often, they park cars on the road while moving other vehicles around in the showrooms. Occasionally, when doing this, both MARTIN and STOUT have been reported for keeping vehicles on the road without an excise licence. To try to avoid being booked again, they now park vehicles outside with trade plates fitted. One day, all of STOUT's trade plates were being used on other vehicles, therefore MARTIN lent him several sets of trade plates to park some vehicles on the road.

Which of the following statements is correct in relation to either MARTIN's or STOUT's liability for an offence, of forgery, under s. 44(1) of the Vehicle Excise and Registration Act 1994?

A Both persons could be guilty of this offence provided it can be shown that they intended to deceive someone.

B Both persons could be guilty of this offence in these circumstances alone; there is no requirement to show intent on either person's behalf.

C Both persons could be guilty of this offence, provided it can be shown that they intended to cause economic loss.

D Only STOUT could be guilty of the offence; s. 44(1) does not cover circumstances of lending anything to another person.

Question 13.9

NOLAN works in the admin department of a haulage company and is responsible for filing tacograph records submitted by the drivers. NOLAN is aware that drivers frequently alter their drivers' hours because they make regular jokes about it, but she shares the common view that it is done in the best interests of the company in respect of profit margins. NOLAN is not directly involved in changing any records, but is aware of what is happening and is prepared to produce the false records on behalf of the company should an inspection take place.

Section 38 of the Goods Vehicles (Licensing of Operators) Act 1995 deals with offences of forgery or alteration of documents relating to goods vehicle operators. Would NOLAN be liable for such an offence in these circumstances?

A No, while documents have been forged or altered, they have not been used to deceive any person at this stage.
B Yes, NOLAN is in possession of documents that have been forged or altered and are calculated to deceive.
C No, NOLAN is not in possession of documents or other things that are covered by this Act, even though they have been forged or altered.
D No, the documents NOLAN possessed were altered by another person.

Question 13.10

GARDNER parked in a pay-and-display car park and went shopping, paying for three hours' parking. After an hour, GARDNER decided to go home and returned to the car park. As GARDNER was leaving, LASSITER parked in the vacant space. GARDNER stopped and gave LASSITER the pay-and-display parking ticket, which was still valid for another hour. LASSITER displayed the ticket on the car windscreen and went shopping.

Has either GARDNER or LASSITER committed an offence contrary to s. 115 of the Road Traffic Regulation Act 1984 (misuse of parking documents) in these circumstances?

A Only LASSITER could be guilty of the offence, provided it can be proved that the owner of the car park suffered some economic loss.
B No, this is a civil matter between the owner of the car park and LASSITER, who has not paid to park in the car park.
C Yes, both persons could be guilty of this offence; it can be proved that they intended to deceive someone.
D Yes, both persons could be guilty of this offence in these circumstances alone; there is no requirement to show intent on either person's behalf.

ANSWERS

Answer 13.1

Answer **C** — Under s. 173(1) of the Road Traffic Act 1988, a person who, with intent to deceive:

(a) forges, alters or uses a document or other thing to which this section applies, or
(b) lends to, or allows to be used by, any other person a document or other thing to which this section applies, or
(c) makes or has in his possession any document or other thing so closely resembling a document or other thing to which this section applies as to be calculated to deceive,
is guilty of an offence.

This is a crime of 'specific intent', that being that the defendant simply intended to 'deceive' another person, as opposed to an intent to make a gain for themselves or expose another person to a loss (which is terminology from the Fraud Act 2006). Answers A and B are therefore incorrect.

The required intent is the same whichever subsection the defendant is charged under; therefore answer D is incorrect.

Road Policing, para. 3.13.2.1

Answer 13.2

Answer **C** — Under s. 173 of the Road Traffic Act 1988:

(1) A person who, with intent to deceive—
    (a) forges, alters or uses a document or other thing to which this section applies, or
    (b) lends to, or allows to be used by, any other person a document or other thing to which this section applies, or
    (c) makes or has in his possession any document or other thing so closely resembling a document or other thing to which this section applies as to be calculated to deceive,
    is guilty of an offence.

'Forges' for this purpose means *making* a false document or other thing in order that it may be used as genuine (s. 173(3)). Therefore, although the document produced by HOLLAND was not a success (or closely resembling a document) he *has* made a false document to which this section applies, which is sufficient to commit the offence regardless of whether or not he altered anything.

NIXON does commit the offence, but so does HOLLAND.
Answers A, B and D are therefore incorrect.

Road Policing, para. 3.13.2.1

Answer 13.3

Answer **C** — Under s. 173(1) of the Road Traffic Act 1988, a person who, with intent
to deceive:

(a) forges, alters or uses a document or other thing to which this section applies, or
(b) lends to, or allows to be used by, any other person a document or other thing to which
   this section applies, or
(c) makes or has in his possession any document or other thing so closely resembling a
   document or other thing to which this section applies as to be calculated to deceive,
is guilty of an offence.

The person does not have to actually alter the document to commit the offence; the
fact that NORTH made or had in his possession any document or other thing so
closely resembling a document or other thing to which the section applies, as to be
calculated to deceive, would amount to an offence and in this scenario, it would be
when the document was printed off (or made). Answers B and D are therefore
incorrect.

Finally, there is a separate offence under s. 174 of knowingly making a false statement for the purpose of obtaining the grant of a licence, or of preventing the grant
of any such licence, or of procuring the imposition of a condition or limitation in
relation to any such licence; however, this offence is not applicable when simply
making a false statement to a police officer who has asked a driver to produce a document; therefore, answer A is incorrect.

Road Policing, paras 3.13.2.1, 3.13.2.2

Answer 13.4

Answer **D** — There is a specific offence under s. 174(1)(e) of the Road Traffic Act 1988,
of knowingly making a false statement for the purpose of obtaining the grant of an
international road haulage permit.

However, such an offence must be committed knowingly whether the application
is for the applicant himself or another person. Knowingly is very different from
intent, and this offence requires no intent; answer C is therefore incorrect. Without
the 'knowingly' the offence is not complete, even though STANGER's wife knew

about the conviction (although this may negate the legality of the actual permit); answers A and B are therefore incorrect.

Road Policing, para. 3.13.2.2

Answer 13.5

Answer **A** — Under s. 174(2) of the Road Traffic Act 1988:

A person who, in supplying information or producing documents for the purposes either of sections 53 to 60 and 63 of this Act or of regulations made under sections 49 to 51, 61, 62 and 66(3) of this Act—
(a) makes a statement which he knows to be false in a material particular or recklessly makes a statement which is false in a material particular, or
(b) produces, provides, sends or otherwise makes use of a document which he knows to be false in a material particular or recklessly produces, provides, sends or otherwise makes use of a document which is false in a material particular,
is guilty of an offence.

FRANCIS's actions are covered by s. 174(2)(b), in that he provided a false goods vehicle test certificate, which was required to be produced under s. 53 of the Act. Section 174(2)(b) is clear that the offence can be committed by a person who produces, provides etc. any document which he or she either knows to be false in a material particular or is reckless as to this fact. Answers C and D are therefore incorrect.

There is no need to show that the person actually gained anything, or brought about the desired consequences (see *Jones* v *Meatyard* [1939] 1 All ER 140). Answers B and D are incorrect for this reason.

Road Policing, para. 3.13.2.2

Answer 13.6

Answer **D** — Section 175 of the Road Traffic Act 1988 states that if a person issues:

(a) any such document as referred to in section 174(5)(a) or (b) of this Act, or
(b) a test certificate or certificate of conformity
and the document or certificate so issued is to his knowledge false in a material particular, he/she is guilty of an offence.

The offence under this section is complete when the document is issued falsely— there is only a requirement to show that the person issuing the documents *knew that they were false* (see *Ocean Accident etc. Co.* v *Cole* (1932) 96 JP 191). There is no requirement to show that the defendant knew what the documents would be used for (or was reckless as to their use). Answers B and C are therefore incorrect.

Test certificates bearing a false stamp *or ones which have been backdated* are 'false in a material particular' (see *Murphy* v *Griffiths* [1967] 1 WLR 333). Answer A is incorrect for that reason.

Road Policing, para. 3.13.2.3

Answer 13.7

Answer **B** — Section 176(4) of the Road Traffic Act 1988 provides a power to seize either a document or a plate from a vehicle where the constable reasonably believes that an offence under s. 173 (forgery or falsification) has occurred. Since the power also applies to plates on a vehicle, answer D is incorrect. However, the officer removing the plate must be an examiner appointed under s. 66A of the Act. Since Constable FRENCH is not an authorised vehicle examiner, one must be called to the scene to detach the plate and therefore answer C is incorrect. The power under this section relates to seizing documents (or plates) and does not allow the seizure of a vehicle by the officer. Answer A is therefore incorrect.

Road Policing, para. 3.13.2.4

Answer 13.8

Answer **B** — Section 44(1) of the Vehicle Excise and Registration Act 1994 states that a person is guilty of an offence if he or she forges, fraudulently alters, fraudulently uses, *fraudulently lends* or fraudulently allows to be used by another person anything to which subs. (2) applies. Section 44(2) applies to a trade plate (including a replacement trade plate) and since the offence under s. 44(1) does cover the circumstances of lending anything to another person, answer D is incorrect.

Section 44(1) does not require the prosecution to show an intent to deceive on behalf of the person fraudulently using or lending the trade plates. Answer A is therefore incorrect. Similarly, in *R* v *Terry* [1984] AC 374, the court decided that there is no need to prove any intent to cause economic loss (and answer C is therefore incorrect).

Road Policing, para. 3.13.3

Answer 13.9

Answer **C** — Under s. 38(1) of the Goods Vehicles (Licensing of Operators) Act 1995, a person is guilty of an offence if, with intent to deceive, he or she:

(a) forges, alters or uses a document or other thing to which this section applies;
(b) lends to, or allows to be used by, any other person a document or other thing to which this section applies; or
(c) makes or has in his possession any document or other thing so closely resembling a document or other thing to which this section applies as to be calculated to deceive.

The offence may be committed by a person who is simply in possession of a document which is calculated to deceive; therefore, answers A and D are incorrect.

However, s. 38(2) of the Act is specific about the documents to which the section applies (which are similar to those covered in the main offence under s. 173 of the Road Traffic Act 1988), which are:

- any operator's licence;
- any document, plate, mark or other thing by which, in pursuance of regulations, a vehicle is to be identified as being authorised to be used, or as being used, under an operator's licence;
- any document evidencing the authorisation of any person for the purposes of ss. 40 and 41;
- any certificate of qualification under s. 49; and
- any certificate or diploma such as is mentioned in para. 13(1) or (1A) of sch. 3.

Tachographs are not covered; therefore, answer B is incorrect. Note that offences relating to drivers' hours and accurate recording of such are covered by the Transport Act 1968 and the people in this scenario would most likely be liable under this Act.

Road Policing, para. 3.13.3

Answer 13.10

Answer **C** — Section 115(1)(a) of the Road Traffic Regulation Act 1984 states that a person shall be guilty of an offence who, with intent to deceive, uses, or lends to, or allows to be used by, any other person any parking device or apparatus designed to be used in connection with parking devices, *or* any ticket issued by a parking meter, parking device or apparatus designed to be used in connection with parking devices.

It would surprise many people that this is an offence, as it is common practice between people parking in pay-and-display car parks. Many car park owners try to combat such fraud by forcing the customer to input their registration number in the machine, which is then displayed on the ticket. In summary, this is a criminal offence (and not a civil matter), which can be committed by a person who uses or lends to another person, a parking ticket with *intent to deceive* (the deceit being that the ticket was paid for by the person displaying it). Answers B and D are therefore incorrect. There is no requirement in this section to prove that a person intended to cause economic loss, or that economic loss was caused (although this would obviously be useful in any court case if the loser is claiming compensation). Answer A is therefore incorrect.

Road Policing, para. 3.13.3

Question Checklist

The following checklist is designed to help you keep track of your progress when answering the multiple-choice questions. If you fill this in after one attempt at each question, you will be able to check how many you have got right and which questions you need to revisit a second time. Also available online; to download visit www.blackstonespoliceservice.com.

	First attempt Correct (✓)	Second attempt Correct (✓)
1 Definitions and Principles		
1.1		
1.2		
1.3		
1.4		
1.5		
1.6		
1.7		
1.8		
1.9		
1.10		
1.11		
1.12		
1.13		
1.14		
1.15		
1.16		

	First attempt Correct (✓)	Second attempt Correct (✓)
1.17		
1.18		
1.19		
1.20		
1.21		
1.22		
1.23		
1.24		
2 Key Police Powers		
2.1		
2.2		
2.3		
2.4		
2.5		
2.6		
2.7		
2.8		

	First attempt Correct (✔)	Second attempt Correct (✔)
2.9		
2.10		
2.11		
2.12		
2.13		
2.14		

3 Offences Involving Standards of Driving

	First attempt Correct (✔)	Second attempt Correct (✔)
3.1		
3.2		
3.3		
3.4		
3.5		
3.6		
3.7		
3.8		
3.9		
3.10		
3.11		
3.12		
3.13		
3.14		
3.15		
3.16		
3.17		
3.18		

4 Reportable Accidents

	First attempt Correct (✔)	Second attempt Correct (✔)
4.1		
4.2		
4.3		
4.4		

	First attempt Correct (✔)	Second attempt Correct (✔)
4.5		
4.6		
4.7		
4.8		
4.9		
4.10		
4.11		
4.12		
4.13		
4.14		
4.15		

5 Drink, Drugs and Driving

	First attempt Correct (✔)	Second attempt Correct (✔)
5.1		
5.2		
5.3		
5.4		
5.5		
5.6		
5.7		
5.8		
5.9		
5.10		
5.11		
5.12		
5.13		
5.14		
5.15		
5.16		
5.17		
5.18		
5.19		

	First attempt Correct (✓)	Second attempt Correct (✓)
5.20		
5.21		
5.22		
5.23		
5.24		
5.25		
5.26		
5.27		
5.28		
5.29		
5.30		
5.31		
5.32		
5.33		
5.34		
5.35		
5.36		
5.37		

6 Insurance

	First attempt	Second attempt
6.1		
6.2		
6.3		
6.4		
6.5		
6.6		
6.7		
6.8		
6.9		
6.10		

7 Legislation for the Protection of Road Users

7.1		

	First attempt Correct (✓)	Second attempt Correct (✓)
7.2		
7.3		
7.4		
7.5		
7.6		
7.7		
7.8		
7.9		
7.10		
7.11		
7.12		
7.13		
7.14		
7.15		
7.16		
7.17		
7.18		
7.19		
7.20		
7.21		
7.22		
7.23		
7.24		

8 Legislation Affecting the Use of Highways

8.1		
8.2		
8.3		
8.4		
8.5		
8.6		
8.7		

	First attempt Correct (✓)	Second attempt Correct (✓)
8.8		
8.9		
8.10		
8.11		
8.12		
8.13		
8.14		

9 Construction and Use

	First attempt Correct (✓)	Second attempt Correct (✓)
9.1		
9.2		
9.3		
9.4		
9.5		
9.6		
9.7		
9.8		
9.9		
9.10		
9.11		
9.12		
9.13		
9.14		
9.15		
9.16		
9.17		
9.18		
9.19		

10 Driver Licensing

	First attempt Correct (✓)	Second attempt Correct (✓)
10.1		
10.2		
10.3		

	First attempt Correct (✓)	Second attempt Correct (✓)
10.4		
10.5		
10.6		
10.7		
10.8		
10.9		
10.10		
10.11		
10.12		
10.13		
10.14		
10.15		
10.16		
10.17		
10.18		
10.19		
10.20		
10.21		
10.22		
10.23		
10.24		
10.25		
10.26		

11 Fixed Penalty System

	First attempt Correct (✓)	Second attempt Correct (✓)
11.1		
11.2		
11.3		
11.4		
11.5		
11.6		
11.7		

	First attempt Correct (✔)	Second attempt Correct (✔)
11.8		
11.9		
11.10		
11.11		
11.12		
11.13		

12 Notices of Intended Prosecution

12.1		
12.2		
12.3		
12.4		
12.5		
12.6		
12.7		
12.8		
12.9		
12.10		

	First attempt Correct (✔)	Second attempt Correct (✔)
12.11		
12.12		
12.13		
12.14		
12.15		

13 Forgery and Falsification of Documents

13.1		
13.2		
13.3		
13.4		
13.5		
13.6		
13.7		
13.8		
13.9		
13.10		